PERFORATED
FIBER

**The True Story
of Hope and
Perserverance**

M. TRIPLETT | H. TRIPLETT

ISBN: 1492805300
ISBN 13: 9781492805304

Dedications

I dedicate this book to my Grandmother Mabel and my little sister, Serena. Thank you for everything that you did for me. I miss you. I want to especially thank my wife for inspiring me and helping me write this book. I want to thank my brother Haven for filling in the details of my life that no one else would tell me and for assisting me with the reference documentation. I dedicate this book to my friend Douglas Greer, who has gone on to greener pastures. I also want to thank those of you who took the time to read the pre-published manuscript and provided your valuable feedback.

-M. Triplett

I dedicate this book to my wife and soul mate for her loving encouragement and support. I dedicate this book to my children, Haven Jr. and Natoya. You now have some insight into who your father was, who he now is, and who he is trying to become. I hope that we can build upon this knowledge and can develop the relationship that was taken from us so many years ago. I dedicate this book to my brother Maurice for his unwavering courage as we helped each other through the trials and tribulations of our past. His strength has allowed us to embrace our future and reclaim our rightful place in the present. I dedicate this book to all those individuals who have either been a victim or witness of violence. I dedicate this book to those who have been perpetrators of violence and have found the strength and courage to question why. I dedicate this book to everyone who helped me confront and overcome the adversity of my past. Finally, I dedicate this book to my lawyer, John M. Thompson, and his wife, Linda, who represented my case on appeal.

-H. Triplett

Contents

PerForated Fiber

<u>Perforated</u>: *pierced with one or more holes*

<u>Fiber</u>: *the inherent complex of attributes that determine a person's moral and ethical actions and reactions*

Prologue

I could see three figures in front of my house. As I got closer, I noticed it was Butchy, my mom, and my brother Ervin. Butchy was standing on the ground in front of the three porch steps, and my mother and Ervin were on the porch facing him. As I got closer, I could see that my mother and Ervin had a butcher knife, and they were pushing it downward toward Butchy.

The blade was about a foot from his chest as he struggled against my mother and brother's hands to keep it away. When I finally got to the porch I heard my mother say, "Reesie, help us!" so I did. I put my hand on top of theirs and started to push down also. I could feel Butchy's hands trembling, but the knife never moved. We all struggled for about a minute, and the next thing I knew my mother had taken the knife and she and Ervin went back in the house. I stayed outside on the porch after just trying to help murder my own father because I was happy to see him.

I was born into an impoverished environment and grew up around uneducated, dangerous people. By the time I was twenty, I had experienced and witnessed more tragedy than most people do in a lifetime. My father was a drug dealer and drug user. I was an eyewitness to physical abuse in my home. Both of my brothers were involved in violent crimes. There were several deaths in my family. I often lived in environments where we barely had the necessities to survive. These things give you a brief overview of the life I lived as a child, an adolescent, and a young adult. However, you will need to read the entire book if you wish to see each situation through my eyes.

As an adult reflecting on the story of my life, I concluded that the dramatic circumstances of my birth answered the question "Why is this my life?" It had nothing to do with drawing the short straw or that life had dealt me bad cards. This was my *destiny*. As you read the story of my life, you will find that even though my childhood was showered with tragedy, I still feel that I am one of the luckiest people on earth. Through it all, I still emerged physically and mentally healthy and was able to acquire the life skills needed to secure a decent life.

This brings me to the purpose of this memoir. Its primary purpose is to help me reflect on my past so that I can rationalize the perseverance of man. What is it that allows a small percentage of individuals who grow up in a neighborhood like I did escape the guarantee of a life in prison or death? What is it that allows these individuals to escape unscathed with minimal damage from bad environments? These are questions that had puzzled me for years. Until I could write the story of my life in this book, read it, and read it again, I was at a loss. I can answer these questions now on a personal level.

Although a great portion of this book deals with death, neglect, and poverty, it is not meant to be a "dark" book. At the same time, its reality has not been watered down or changed. I did, however, purposely inject humorous thoughts as I narrate the details. This mostly was done to emphasize just how ridiculous some of the events were. My guess is that many of you will end up on an emotional rollercoaster and won't believe what you are reading; however, my story is true to life.

Lessons Pt I

"Teach me and I grow... Teach me and I wither."

She was the most amazing person that I've ever known. Her name was Mabel Morgan, and she was my paternal grandmother. Because of our age difference and adults who did not pass on tradition, I wasn't fortunate enough to learn the story of her life. My grandmother and I were still very close. The time we shared together was vital to my childhood development. My grandmother knew so much—she was both book and street smart. I'm not sure how she learned it all, but I was glad she shared her knowledge with me whenever I was with her. Even the *little* lessons she taught me left a lifelong imprint on my character. She died when I was twenty.

I remember, when I was four, she would drive me down to the Boulevard. The Boulevard was the name of a quarter-mile stretch of Congress Avenue in West Haven, Connecticut. There she would play her lottery numbers. Before we left the house, she would always rub the head and stomach of a little orange Buddha statue that she kept on her mantelpiece for good luck.

On the way, I would always ask her to help me read the billboards. I wanted to understand the street signs. I remember asking her what the sign with the arrow that pointed up to the sky meant. She told me that it meant to drive straight ahead. That wasn't good enough. I needed to know why it was pointing up to the sky. It just didn't make sense. But my grandmother was great. She stuck with it, entertaining me and satisfying my curiosity. She never got upset with me and somehow always helped me understand.

No one else was this patient with me. No one else would take time to teach me things and help me figure things out. This is why she was very special to me. I loved my grandmother.

When we would arrive at the lottery office, a guy named Freddy would always come up to the car and say, "Hi, Ma." Everyone called my grandmother "Ma." I remember that Freddy was always smoking a cigar. When he came to the driver's side of the car, I would smell a combination of sweet-smelling smoke that was cloaked by a blunt tobacco odor. It was a very distinct smell. One that made me go back and forth between "That smells good" and "Ugghh, that stinks." I could recognize that smell anywhere—that smell was Freddy. My grandmother and Freddy would always engage in idle chitchat. Sure enough, he would ask what numbers she was planning to play. My grandmother would always respond like a politician who had just been asked, "What exactly will you change if you win?" She would respond but never answer the question. Even at the age of four I knew why Freddie was asking my grandmother for her numbers; it was because he knew she would hit the number almost twice a month. I guess that little orange Buddha statue actually worked. I tolerated him, but I didn't really like Freddy.

One of the very first lessons my grandmother taught me began with opening the car door. I would try to get out the passenger side of her car by myself. The problem was that the door was heavy and would stick. To open it, I needed to use the force of my whole body. Once the door finally opened, I would fall right out of the car, and most of the time I would hit my face on the sidewalk. Even though it was painful I would shake it off, wouldn't cry, and wouldn't let my grandmother know that it happened. This was how I learned to survive: ignore pain, don't complain, and persevere. One time my grandmother saw me open the door, fall out of the car, and hit the ground face first. She stayed calm, and in a comforting, relaxed voice, she said, "Mojo, when you open the door and you start to fall, throw your hands up in front of you." All she had to do was tell me once, and I got it. The next time I fell out, I found myself in a push-up position with my feet on the car seat. It worked!

Looking back, I now realize that a big reason I am here and alive today is because I followed my grandmother's instructions and learned from her teachings. It was a blessing in disguise that all the other adults in my life, who could have been negative influences, neglected me. My grandmother undoubtedly was one of the most positive influences in my life.

My paternal grandparents, Theodore and Mabel Morgan, had eight children. Most of them used nicknames, and that is how they were known. By age and order of introduction, there was Sonny, Herbie, Jitterbug, Pinky, Chick, Bunny, Butch, and Brenda.

My uncle Sonny was probably the only one of my grandmother's children who showed any potential for success in life. He and his wife had an apartment in New Haven. I was never invited inside. I would later find out the reason. My uncle Sonny did not allow my father in his house because he knew my father sold drugs and did not want to be affiliated in any way with that activity. This included having the son of the drug dealer in his home. The saying "guilt by association" comes to mind. The only person he allowed in his apartment was my grandmother. My uncle Sonny's apartment was built from wood, not brick and mortar like the projects where I lived. I imagined that it was extravagantly furnished and decorated inside. It had two private entrances—front and back—no community hallways, and always looked like it was freshly painted. It had to have been nice in there.

My uncle Herbie loved two things: fishing and women, and not necessarily in that order. By the time Uncle Herbie was twenty-five, he had fathered seven children by six different women. The juggling act Uncle

Herbie must have had to do with his girlfriends would have been a sight to see. I wonder how he managed it. Ten years later, he fathered two more children with his wife, my aunt Leona. As far as fishing was concerned, the only thing I remember was that I would always ask to go with him, and the answer was always "I will take you next time." After hearing this response for the sixth time, I stopped asking.

My uncle Jitterbug was an amputee. He had one leg and used crutches to get around. It seemed like his entire existence was spent eating pizza and small snack packs from the local market store. He always had a small bed of rice with rib tips on top. The only other thing he would do is sit in the front of my grandmother's house when the weather was nice. He would watch kids in the community play and wave hello to people as they returned home from work. I have no idea where he got the nickname "Jitterbug," but my best guess is that during the time when he had both legs he might have been a pretty good dancer. He died when I was sixteen. I'm not sure of the cause.

My aunt Pinky had five children who were fathered by the same man, my uncle Dougie. I don't have many memories of my Aunt Pinky, and I don't know how she got her nickname. All I remember is that she got hooked on drugs later in her life and died when I was seventeen. I never really got to know my uncle Dougie. All I can tell you is that he was crazy as a hoot, as my grandmother used to say. When I was four years old, I remember seeing him cut a man over and over at my grandmother's house. I don't know why he was upset with the man, but I remember that every few seconds his hand made a downward motion and the shirt the man was wearing ended up with another tear. Finally the man took off his shirt. His chest had been sliced to pieces by Dougie's knife. I still remember the look of horror on the man's face. He stood with his arms away from his body while his cuts bled. He began pleading to Dougie for mercy. Finally, someone yelled, "Get that baby out of here!" so I can't tell you how things ended. This was my first exposure to this level of violence. Fortunately, I was too young to be influenced, traumatized, or afraid. But not to worry; I wasn't going to be deprived because this was just the beginning. There was a lot more to come.

My uncle Chick must have studied karate at one time in his life because my older cousins told me that he was the one who taught me how to properly execute a chop and punch. They also told me that I would run around my grandmother's house, assume a karate stance, and challenge everyone to a sparring battle because of his teachings. I remember an amazing tattoo that he had on his bicep. It was a picture of a beautiful naked woman sitting in a wine glass. She was perfectly positioned so that her privacy was maintained. She was hugging herself with her legs crossed and hanging over the rim of the glass. I was fascinated by the creativity of the artist. When my uncle sat still, I would stare at his tattoo for what felt like hours.

I credit Uncle Chick with being the first person to show me how to steal. It happened at the Greyhound bus station when we were waiting for a bus from Springfield to New Haven. He was taking me to my grandmother's house for the summer. He took me into a convenience store, looked around for a while, and then asked me if I wanted anything. I told him that I wanted a small crossword puzzle book that I took off the shelf and handed to him. I'm not sure if he knew I was watching as he held the book so that his hand almost entirely covered it. Then in a slow, nonchalant fashion, he slipped it into his pocket. After seeing this, I said, "Uncle Chick, ain't you gonna pay for that?" Fortunately, no one else heard me as I watched him take his index finger, put it over his lips, and make the "shhhh" sound to let me know that I should be quiet. Shortly after that we left the store, and I had two new things: the crossword puzzle book and a signed diploma from my uncle Chick for completing How to Steal and Not Get Caught, course level 101. My uncle Chick later moved to Worcester (pronounced "Wussta," for those not from the Massachusetts area) and was later murdered in that town when I was nineteen.

My aunt Bunny made me feel like I was her favorite nephew. She would give me a box of Count Chocula™ or Captain Crunch™ cereal every time I visited. I think her decision of exactly which box to give me basically came down to the one that had the least amount of cereal left. Regardless, it was the best gift a poor, hungry kid from the ghetto could get—forget GI Joe and the kung-fu grip. My Aunt Bunny had seven children and relied mostly on state programs to survive. She eventually moved to Massachusetts from New Haven, which was the same thing my mother did. I don't know how that all worked out, but it seems as though they sat down and planned it. We ended up living about two miles away from each other in Springfield. The last time I saw my Aunt Bunny was when I was twenty-one. She asked me to loan her forty dollars, and I never saw her again. I think she moved to Florida.

Butch's real name was Lynwood, and he was my father, a term I use loosely. Butch had a case of psoriasis so bad that the state declared him unable to work. His fall back was selling drugs to make a living. He did this for about ten years, starting with cocaine and ending with crack. He finally got hooked on drugs and contracted AIDS from using dirty needles.

I remember my last visit to see him at Yale-New Haven hospital in the oncology department. He was on his deathbed. I remember how fragile he looked as he pulled the sheets up to just below his face as if he were cold. We greeted each other like acquaintances rather than father and son. Then he looked at me and said, "I have AIDS." I felt nothing when he told me. No sadness, no loss, nothing. I guess the absence of emotion stemmed from the missing father-son relationship that should have been present as I grew from a teen to a young adult. It was clear to me that the love and admiration I once had for him as a child had faded.

I think I stayed about five minutes after he told me about his illness then I said, "Okay, bye" like I would someday see him alive again. But we both knew that wasn't going to happen. He was dying, and I had no plans to make another trip to New Haven to see him unless I was there to pay my final respects. A few months later he died. I was twenty; he was forty-three.

When a loved one dies, at some point during the mourning process, most people flashback to happy memories. They think about times they shared with the person when he or she was alive. I remember trying to do this when I saw my father in his casket. All I could remember were a few scattered childhood memories. At that point, I knew one thing. I would not allow this to occur with my children when I became a dad. I planned from that day to make a full investment in our relationship. I would spend time with them through the phases of their lives. I would be their superhero and life support when they were children. I would be their teacher and pass on wisdom when they became teenagers, and I would be a friend and confidant when they became adults. I would never know what that felt like with my father, but at this point I didn't care and it really didn't matter.

Having no feelings of sadness when I saw my father in a casket only made me realize that we never really formed a bond at all. It felt like I was at a stranger's wake; I had no connection with the person in the front of the room lying in the coffin. I accepted this and decided that I would not stay for the burial. I made one last trip to his casket to say goodbye then I went back home to Massachusetts. I later realized that I only attended the wake out of respect for the person who gave me life; for without Butch, there would have been no me.

My aunt Brenda had long black hair that grew down to the small of her back and was a very pretty woman. Every time she, my uncle Ronnie, and my cousin Ronnie Jr. (nicknamed Little Ronnie) came to my grandmother's, it was a treat. They had to be the best-looking family in Connecticut. I always thought they were a celebrity family because their last name was Pressley just like Elvis's, who was bigger than life at that time. Being a child, I failed to notice that their name was spelled with double "s" and Elvis spelled his last name with only one "s." If I had noticed, I still don't think that would have changed my admiration for them. Later in her life, my aunt Brenda began using cocaine. Her thoughtless decision to do this destroyed her family, robbed her of her beauty, and eventually took her life. She died when I was sixteen.

In case you weren't counting, over a four-year period I attended five funerals among my father, two aunts, and two uncles. It made me think about the Kennedy family and how for a period of time it seemed like their family was constantly plagued by death and tragedy. I guess catastrophe is colorblind and doesn't discriminate by social class.

Kennedys (fifteen-year period)

1984	David Kennedy dies	Drug overdose
1986	Patrick Kennedy	Treated for cocaine addiction
1991	William Kennedy Smith	Acquitted of rape charges
1997	Michael Kennedy dies	Skiing accident

My Family (eight-year period)

1981	Uncle Chick killed	Murdered while sleeping
1985	Aunt Brenda dies	Drug overdose
1985	Uncle Jitterbug dies	Cause unknown
1986	Aunt Pinky dies	Drug overdose
1989	Butchy dies	Drugs/AIDS

The story of my grandmothers' children is tragic. What is worse is the fact that not one of them realized just how lucky they were to have her as their mom. She never judged them and was always there for them when they needed something. She had an open-door policy for her kids. It didn't matter to her that they were adults with no life goals. When they came knocking, there was a bed and a hot meal waiting. I don't think she did them any favors by giving them sanctuary from hard times, but at least no one would ever be able to say that her children were not always her first priority. I would have done anything for a mom like her when I was growing up. I would have appreciated and thrived from her kindness and love instead of taking it for granted like my aunts and uncles.

I looked forward to summer vacation from school. Without fail, my mother would leave me at my grandmother's for the entire summer. I had the best of three worlds there. I could play with my cousins, I wasn't far from my father's apartment, and I did not have to deal with whatever boyfriend my mother was dating at the time.

My grandmother would take care of me and my six cousins for the entire summer. By age and nickname, there was Douglas (Brother), Gwendolyn (Rudy), Kathy, Claire, George (Head), me (Mojo), and Pete. George's nickname was short for "hard head" because he would not do what my grandmother told him to do, so he would always get into trouble. It was the funniest thing to see George get into trouble. When my grandmother would hit him the first time, he would start to cry, but he was faking and she knew it. Then she would hit him again, and he would start laughing, and everyone else would start laughing too. On the third hit she would get him good, and then the real tears would come. In those days, "timeout" had nothing to do with child discipline; it was only a term used to indicate a break in a sporting event. Frankly, my cousins were so unruly that a timeout would have been ineffective and would have amounted to a waste of time.

My grandmother's choice disciplinary tool was the paddle that came from the toy that had a rubber string and ball attached to it. Children would use it to see if they could keep hitting the ball with the paddle. If we did not behave, my grandmother used it to administer discipline the old-fashioned way. You might get hit on the arm, leg, head, or wherever she could get you. I had seen George get hit with the paddle several times. It did not look like he was having fun, so I decided I would behave and do what my grandmother told me. I think I made a good choice.

All of my cousins except for Rudy were white-skinned, but they were all mixed, part white, part black. All of them were my Aunt Pinky and Uncle Dougie's kids. Their white skin color came from my Aunt Pinky's light complexion, which she received from her mother (my grandmother), who was 100-percent Portuguese. Rudy was brown-skinned because my uncle Dougie was black. Brother and Pete both had afros. They were white kids with afros—not the Justin Timberlake afro either; think of the great painter Bob Ross. The rest of them except for Rudy had the typical straight hair most white people have.

I had so much fun with them. One thing we all liked to do was watch the daily television lineup that included "The Mod Squad," "The Dukes of Hazard," "Baretta," "The Six-Million Dollar Man," "The Bionic Woman," and "Starsky and Hutch." We all cheered anytime one of the Duke boys went up a ramp and launched their car ten feet in the air and landed. And we all laughed when something happened to Boss Hogg. It was great to be with all my cousins and with my grandmother. Saturday morning was reserved for Looney Tunes. We would all watch cartoons then go outside and play.

Every summer my grandmother had us all join the local summer camp. It was sponsored by the parks and recreation department and was primarily for low-income families. This was day camp. It started at 8:00 a.m. and ended at 3:00 p.m. There was free lunch, arts and crafts, swimming, and other types of recreation. One of the things everyone liked to do was pile on the merry-go-round and let Henry, one of the camp counselors and also a track runner, push us as fast as he could. We would stay spinning for what seemed to be an hour. Some kids got sick, some just got dizzy, and others would scream, "Let's do it again!"

Camp was great, but it was also the place where I almost met my demise. On swim day, I would stay in the shallow end of the pool along with the rest of the kids who probably didn't know how to swim either. On this particular day I saw my cousin George standing alongside the pool, so I went to ask him if he was going to put on his swim trunks and go swimming. The last thing I remember was him pushing me while saying, "Go get in the pool and go swimming." I had asked him this question at the eight-foot marker, and I found myself slowly sinking to the bottom of the pool, unable to get back to the surface. I remember it was calm and quiet, and darkness began to close in all around me. Suddenly I was pulled to the surface. A girl named Barrie, who lived across the street from my grandmother, had saved me. I started coughing up pool water and began to return to full consciousness. After a minute or two I was fine, but I didn't go back swimming. I didn't say much to anybody for the rest of the day or when we walked back to Grandma's house. I remember all of my cousins talking about what had happened on the way back home. They were worried for George's safety and what would happen to him if I mentioned it to my father. I never did, and no one ever talked about it again.

My father lived about fifteen miles from my grandmother, so I would split my time between both places. My father's apartments were always messy, and it always smelled like something had been burned. The light was usually dim, and the largest television was a thirteen-inch black and white that had an unraveled metal coat hanger for an antenna. The cupboards were usually bare, and the refrigerator usually had a pitcher of ice water and a quart of milk that was always two-thirds gone.

My father's girlfriend's name was Yvonne, and in no uncertain terms she was amazingly ugly. She had to be around thirty, but she looked more like forty-five, and she walked slowly and gingerly as if her entire body was in pain. I noticed that her hands looked permanently swollen. Both of them also had sores that hadn't quite healed in various places. As a matter of fact most of the people who came to visit my father had the same problem with their hands. At the time, I wasn't brave enough to ask what the problem was, so I just didn't stare too long and kept my mouth shut. I later learned that this problem was common among dope addicts.

One time I remember waking up in the backseat of my father's car. Apparently he had just finished giving Yvonne an injection of whatever drug she liked. This caused her to grab two handfuls of my dad's hair (he had one of the biggest afros you can imagine). She pulled his head toward her then pushed it away. She did this about five times before she let go. I thought she was hurting my father, so I said, "Dad, are you okay?" He looked at me, laughed, and said, "Yeah, I'm fine." By the time he told me he was okay, Yvonne had sunk down in the front seat. Her eyes had glazed over, and she looked catatonic. I had no idea what was going on, and, as I said before, I didn't ask.

We lived in the Ashmun street projects in New Haven. In our lovely neighborhood, survival hinged on getting assistance from the state. If you had come to visit me, you might have been inclined to think my neighborhood was going to be a nice place to live. If you came by way of downtown New Haven, you would have crossed the New Haven Green. This was a park centrally located downtown between a bevy of shops and the local shopping mall. Then you would have gone by Yale. Yes, the Ivy League university—Yale! Perhaps you wouldn't have noticed the wrought-iron fence that encompassed the entire school like I noticed. Hopefully, as you walked by the fence you would not have gotten a funny vibe like I did. A vibe that translated to the words, "Stay out! You don't belong in here!"

Once you passed by Yale and took a right on Dixwell Avenue, you might have noticed a drastically diminished quality of life. To the right you might have noticed a quaint brick and mortar housing complex with equal amounts of garbage spread about the entire neighborhood. A good community always shares. You might have noticed the large green steel apartment doors that kept residents safe at night. These doors were so strong, the police needed to use the RAM in order to break the door open. This made it easier for them when they showed up to take you to jail. Now that's a quality door. You might have noticed a few alcoholics with tattered clothes and scruffy beards sitting on the stoop, each of them with a brown paper bag containing a bottle of Wild Irish Rose or Thunderbird. You might have noticed these things. On the left you might have seen a vacant lot that had an old abandoned car that was rusting because it had been there through several rain and snow storms. You might have seen a dented refrigerator that had the freezer door broken off and garbage piled inside.

As you approached my neighborhood paradise, you might have noticed the strong smell of urine that reeked through the hallways. If you came to my apartment on the fifth floor, you were better off taking the stairs. The one elevator in my apartment building moved at a rate of about two minutes per floor. If you cared to look in the corner of the elevator on your ride up, you would see a black, caked-up substance that seemed to grow there like moss. Once you reached my apartment, you might have noticed the dim, flickering lighting in the hallways. You may have noticed that the front doors of each apartment were no more than fifteen feet apart. Space was at a premium. The standard apartment size was around six hundred square feet for a family of three. Hey, that was the best the state could do. Trust me when I tell you that no one complained.

Step inside. Now you might have noticed the Goodwill furniture and smell of burning incense. This was needed to mask the urine scent from outside. You might have noticed the beads that hung down from each archway that divided the rooms. You would probably have noticed a stack of dishes in the sink and smelled the garbage in the trash can. If you had snuck in the kitchen at midnight and quickly turned the light on, you would have noticed the massive infestation of cockroaches. This amenity came with every apartment.

Will anybody be staying for dinner? Tonight we will be having the state-issued canned ham and the great-tasting (it really did taste good) block of cheddar cheese that came in the cardboard box stamped "USDA government cheese." To drink you would have your choice of either Kool Aid made with almost one pound of sugar or a glass of milk. This milk came in a washing-powder-size white box and had the words "powdered milk" written on the front. All you had to do was add water. Ahhhh… Sounds good, don't it? I will reiterate that not one resident complained about the accommodations and food. This was our life. This was survival.

I was too young to remember anything about my brother Haven's dad. But I heard he was killed in a dice game before I was born. I did, however, remember my brother Ervin's dad. His name was Ervin Triplett Sr.

His nickname was Trip, which was short for Triplett. I don't remember him being affectionate to me in any way. I never felt a father-son bond with him. I later found out that the absence of affection that I was sensing from Trip was real. My brother Haven gave me all the details in one of our many phone conversations.

Haven told me that by the time I was four, Trip and my mom were separated. He told me that the reason they separated was directly tied to my birth. I was born a love child! Now it all made sense. Now I knew why I never felt loved by Trip. Now I understood why the first man I recognized as my father had disappeared from my life, shortly before my fourth birthday. Questions that puzzled me for over twenty years now had answers. Tattered memories began to fit together like puzzle pieces, and the snowy picture finally became clear.

I immediately reflected back to the past after our conversation. It was evident to me that my first breath of air intensified the marital problems between my mom and Trip. *I* was the reason two adults who were already part of a struggling, hopeless family split apart.

Before my conversation with Haven, I still wasn't exactly sure who my father was. I felt loved around Butchy, but I was confused about the man named Trip, who lived in the same house as I did. It was only logical that I would identify him as my father. Until Haven cleared up the mystery, I had my own conspiracy theory. I believed that my mother had kept her indiscretions a secret during her pregnancy with me. When I was born, she pawned me off to Trip as his son. I believe that Trip actually thought I was his son for some period of time. I don't know exactly what happened when the drama unfolded and the truth came out. What I do know is that Trip was no longer there, and I started seeing Butchy more often.

My confusion about the identity of my real father continued. My brothers repeatedly told me that Butchy was not my dad. They assured me that Trip was my dad. I didn't believe them. Every time they told me that Trip was my father, I would immediately proclaim that Butchy was my dad. The reality is I don't think they knew who my father was either. I think our mother had told them that Trip was my father at one time, so this is what they believed. I wonder if my mother ever thought about the damage this experience would have on me. Knowing her, I would guess that she never really thought it through. I bet she figured there was no harm done, and all things were still equal. She still had a man in her home, and I still had a dad. It didn't matter if it was Trip or Butchy. People must have been objects in her rudimentary thought process.

Once my conversation with Haven had concluded, I still did not feel 100 percent certain that Butchy was my father. I believed everything that he told me, but I had been confused so long that I still questioned whether I now knew the absolute truth. My doubts all went away when I moved to Arizona and I started seeing small, dry patches on my legs. My first thoughts were that they might be a result of the dry summer heat or the mineral-filled hard water used for taking showers. I decided to go to a dermatologist to find out why they had suddenly appeared. The dermatologist told me that the dry patches were actually mild psoriasis. She also told me that there is no cure and that this skin ailment is genetic. Now I was certain that Butchy had been my father.

This confirmation made me think back to the time when I was a young child and Butchy was still my hero. He and my mother had separated, and he no longer lived with us. This meant that I would now only see him maybe once every three months, and during summer vacations. I recall a period of time when I hadn't seen Butchy for two months. But we did speak to each other on the telephone. In five different phone conversations with him, he said that he was going to come see me. Each time he promised to bring me a pair of sneakers. What a feeling! The sneakers were a nice gesture, but I was more excited about seeing my dad. Four of the five times Butchy said he was coming to see me I waited with anticipation and counted down to the day of his arrival. I remember the feeling of disappointment every time he did not show up. But on the fifth time he showed up! I was so happy to see him that I forgot all about the sneakers he promised to bring. But he had them too. He gave me a box with a new pair of blue and white Pro-Keds. They were the latest, top-of-the-line sneakers that you could get. What a day that was. I think I smiled for a week.

At a time before Trip and my mom separated, I remember him going on a rampage and abusing me, Haven, and Ervin. He blamed us for breaking his audio component set. When he asked us who broke it, we all pleaded innocent. Unsatisfied with our answer, he began yelling at us and sent us to bed. As we were lying in bed, I remember him picking up part of the metal bed frame that was in the room. It was supposed to support the box spring but just never got assembled. Instead, it sat in the corner, and the box spring and mattress were on the floor. I remember him swinging the frame down toward the end of the bed where our feet were. He struck Haven and Ervin on the ankles, but he missed me because my legs were too short. Haven and Ervin screamed in pain, and then my memory fades.

During our discussion, my brother Haven later told me about an argument between Trip and our mom. He ended up right in the middle of their tug of war. Trip and our mom were arguing about something until it became physical. Trip started manhandling our mom. She screamed to Haven, who was seven at the time, to bring her a knife. Haven went to the sink, and all the knives were dirty, so he began washing one off. Our mother yelled, "Haven, hurry up. What's taking so long!" Haven replied, "I'm washing the mustard off." After hearing his response, she angrily yelled, "Bring the damn knife now!"

I guess our mother figured that at the age of seven, Haven was old enough to know that she needed the knife to inflict injury, not to cut through a steak. How he was supposed to have acquired this knowledge at his age, I'm not sure. Haven was just an innocent child being told to participate in the malicious injury of another person. He got yelled at and did everything wrong this time, but he would have more chances to get it right. This was just the beginning. She would continue drafting a blueprint of violence for Haven to follow, up through his adolescent years. This time our mom told Haven to get a knife so that she could use it to hurt someone; as a young adult, Haven would take it upon himself to decide what weapon to get and what to do with it. I am convinced that Haven did not stand a chance of having a normal childhood, from the day my mother lay on the gurney and the doctor said, "Push!"

When some get taught, they grow, while others
wither under the same teaching. I now realize this—
teaching is meaningless if a student has no desire to learn.

"Teach me and I grow... Teach me and I wither"

Lessons Pt II

"Teach me and I gain knowledge... Teach me and I gain nothing."

I t is heartbreaking to watch a loved one go through life and make one bad decision after another, especially when you are powerless to help. It is even worse when your livelihood and survival depend on these decisions. This is the story of my mother's life and my life. I watched my mother consistently select the worse options she had available in life, starting with her choice of men and ending with poor financial decisions that kept her buried in debt. As a firsthand witness who lived through the chaos created by these decisions, I can without a doubt tell you that they played a key role in systematically destroying our family.

Many times I could not understand why certain decisions were made. I found myself trying to answer simple questions like "Is this the life my mother planned for herself? Is she happy with the result?" I can only conclude that the answer was yes. Her destructive behavior had begun long before I was born.

My mother did not have an adequate parental model to learn from as she became an adult. She was surrounded by family members who did not explain the importance of education or care about her safety. From what I know of her father and older brother, I can only imagine the cold household where she was raised. It had to be devoid of love and compassion, full of anger and hate, and absent of happiness and hope. I'm sure it was similar to the home environment that she eventually created for her own family.

I realize that the neglect my mother received as a child was a primary reason our home was built from dysfunctional building blocks. However, I believe my mother owed it to herself and her children to begin the cycle of change. It was her responsibility to find a way to overcome the past and give the next generation a chance at normalcy.

My maternal grandfather, Isaiah Williams, was a quick-tempered, gun-wielding bootlegger. He was also a single-leg amputee. With his limited mobility, he needed someone to help him get through life and sustain his bootleg business. My brother Haven became this person. Haven quickly found out that if you acted up or got out of line, my grandfather would grab his cane or crutches and take a swing at you. Anytime he did this, he would say, "Let me help you get your mind right." If you were so bold to try to retaliate, you might end up looking down the barrel of a .32, which he kept loaded under his pillow. I once saw him pull it out and shoot at a man that he was kicking out of his house.

My grandfather kept several large grocery paper bags along the side of his bed that were shielded from plain view. In those bags was the lifeblood of his existence: Seagram's gin, Mad Dog 20/20, Thunderbird, and Wild Irish Rose. Whatever you needed, he had it. If he didn't have it, he could get it.

Business was best on Sundays because at that time in New Haven, all liquor stores were closed. It was illegal to sell liquor on Sunday under the Connecticut blue laws. My grandfather knew this, so he devised a plan to capitalize on this situation. Every Sunday he would cook up a feast and tell everyone who stopped by for a taste to go in the kitchen to make a plate first. It couldn't get better than that! First he would fill their bellies with his Southern gourmet cooking, and then they would buy a bottle of liquid love and be on their way. My grandfather was a true businessman. He knew that good customer service, good food, and good product established good will and loyalty. Because of this, my grandfather's business was never shut down, and he never had a problem with the police. The only reason he finally closed his doors was because his health declined, and he could no longer continue.

My mother's brother, my Uncle Ike (Isaiah Williams II), was named after my grandfather. I remember that I used to love going to Uncle Ike's house. He actually owned it—a great big house in New Haven. It had three floors. His family lived on two of them, and he had converted one to an apartment that he rented. He had a backyard, a pool table, an air hockey table, and a bar in his basement. My uncle Ike had six kids. In order of birth, they were Derwin, Isaiah III, Rodney, Bridget, Wesley and Raquel; all had nice clothes and their own bedrooms. I'm not sure they realized how lucky they were.

At the time I couldn't figure out why my uncle was living such a plush life and my mother, his sister, seemed to be living a constant struggle. I had an idea after observations that I made when we visited my uncle and cousins. I noticed that the affection my uncle showed for his sister was superficial. It appeared to only occur because they came from the same bloodline. It seemed like my uncle treated my mother as if she were a second-class citizen. It was as if she had done something that was unforgivable—as if she were a failure.

Even at my young age, I could tell that my uncle was the type of guy who looked out only for himself. No one else mattered. As long as he was living well, he was happy. He always tried to get everyone to do things for him and would only reciprocate if there was something in it for him. My guess is that my uncle's self-serving attitude made my mother feel that she did not deserve to be valued, to be loved, or to be treated special. If her own brother treated her this way, why would she have higher expectations of anyone else?

It was evident that my grandfather did not spend time nurturing his daughter to equip her with the tools she would need as an adult. He didn't show her what it meant to be independent or to teach her what to look for in a companion. He did not teach her that self-preservation is a priority over loyalty and love for an abuser. He didn't teach her that she should fight for her children and that they should always be considered first. He did not teach her the basics of creating and raising a family. I know this as a fact because all four of us—my brother Haven, my brother Ervin, me, and my little sister, Serena—all had different fathers. The result of my grandfather's neglect was traumatic for my mother and showed itself in many different forms.

From the time I was in second grade to the time I graduated high school, eight different men lived with us. I wrote "lived with us" because six out of the eight did not have jobs and they were essentially freeloaders. The other two who did have jobs were alcoholics and earned significantly less than my mother. They too were liabilities. It was so bad that most times their salary never made it to the house. On paydays, they went to the bank to cash their checks then they would make a beeline to the liquor store.

Every single one of them, including the man who I identified as my father, physically abused my mother. One of them was illiterate, and three barely graduated high school. Come to think of it, I never saw their diplomas, so I can't be sure they actually did graduate.

Some of the first memories I recall as a child occurred when we lived on 223 Eastern Avenue in Springfield, Massachusetts. I remember that most of the time it was cold in the house in the winter because the basement always flooded and turned out the gas burner. To stay warm throughout the night we would go to bed fully clothed and get under three heavy blankets. I guess the problem was bad plumbing. I also remember that the faucet on the kitchen sink did not work at times—plumbing again. When this happened, Ervin and I would wash dishes in the bathtub. Evidently, our landlord was not that interested in making this cozy paradise any better, so these plumbing issues happened all the time. I think we all got used to it. At least I know I did.

At this time Butchy was living with us. His favorite spot was on the couch, and his favorite pasttime was teasing me. I never thought it was funny, though. Most times I ended up feeling ashamed and embarrassed. His favorite way to tease me would start with us lying on the couch together. Then he would pass gas. It didn't matter who was in the room. It would be those "silent-but-deadly" types that you couldn't hear and smelled horrible. Once the first person smelled it, he would blame it on me. I would always say it wasn't me then start crying. The more I cried, the more he said it was me. I remember him laughing while he was blaming me, and I remember my mother laughing too. I bet they thought they were just poking fun and playing a game with me. But almost forty years later, I remember that embarrassed feeling like it occurred yesterday. That should tell you just how *funny* I thought it was.

Teaching me what I should and should not do was not one of Butchy's strong points. Most times he just confused me with his flawed parenting. There was a time when I was eating with Butchy and Ervin, and they both started calling me a faggot. Butchy would go first then Ervin. I was sure something I was doing wrong caused them to do this, but I couldn't figure it out. With an angry, pissed-off look on his face, Butchy said, "You don't eat with two hands. Only faggots eat that way!" This was his chosen way to teach me a lesson. I guess having my fork in one hand and a piece of bread in the other implied that I was a faggot...wow! How the hell is a six-year-old supposed to figure this out?

I guess the only good side to the "teasing" I received from Butchy was that it didn't happen that frequently. Even though we lived in the same house, he was seldom around. A majority of his time was spent in West Haven, where he would live and freeload off my grandmother, and when he felt like it he would reclaim his place on the couch at my mother's apartment in Springfield.

I'm not sure what happened between my mom and dad to finally make them separate, but at some point I noticed that Butchy was gone, and a new man moved in. His name was James Jackson, but everyone called him J.C. Shortly after J.C. moved in, Butchy visited me at school. I was in the second grade. This was the first and only time my dad visited me in school. I was excited that I was going to see my father. When he stepped into my classroom, the teacher asked me, "Do you know this man?" I remember nodding my head yes as I felt my face flush with embarrassment. Butchy was not a well-kept man. My teacher and the entire class noticed. I heard one of my classmates make a comment that my dad was ugly. It bothered me. For a split second I thought to say something, but I did not want to get into trouble, so I acted like I didn't hear it. My classmate had made the insulting comment because my dad's hair was uncombed and his clothes were old and dirty-looking. He also had a faint smell of body odor. I don't think anyone in the class was close enough to notice it, but I did.

I was six years old, and my dad was still my superhero. I was happy to see him in spite of his flaws. He told the teacher he needed to speak to me outside the class for a moment. She gave permission, and we went outside. He asked me one question: "What is the name of the new guy living with you?" I told him "J.C." Then he said bye and left. That was it.

Later that same day, a few hours after I had been home from school, a brown Riviera sped recklessly by my house. My mom was sitting on the porch, and I was standing in the doorway. I noticed that Butchy was in the passenger seat of the car. He yelled, "I know the name of the guy you live with; it's J.C.!" He said this with happiness and joy in his voice like he knew that knowing J.C's name was going to bother my mother. As soon as I heard the words, I put it all together. His visit to my class was only so he could execute this ridiculous verbal drive-by. I mean really? He came to his six-year-old son's second-grade class and used the fact that he was my father to get this information. It didn't even matter to him that before his visit I had not seen him for six months!

After the car sped by, I remember feeling confused and manipulated. I felt confused because I did not understand why my father felt the need to taunt my mom and make her feel bad. After thinking about it for a while, it made sense. He loved to taunt people and make them feel bad. He had done the exact same thing to me—"You don't eat with two hands. Only faggots eat that way!" I felt manipulated because he was my dad, he knew I trusted him, and he used that to his advantage. I certainly didn't think he would take the information I gave him and use it to hurt my mom. If I would have known that, I would not have given it to him. My mother never figured out how Butchy got the information about J.C. She didn't ask me about it, and I did not take the initiative to tell her. If I had, I'm sure I would have received a whippin'.

After a day or so, it was all water under the bridge. I did not hold this incident against my dad, and all was forgiven. All I thought about now was him stopping by to see me in the near future.

We probably stayed at Eastern Avenue a month or two after J.C. moved in, and then we moved again. Our new place on Florence Street was a bit better. This of course had nothing to do with J.C. because, like my father, he did not have a job and he was a couch dweller. At least my mom was consistent when it came to men. He was on the couch when I left for school, and he was there when I returned home. It didn't take him long to realize that he was a kept man. He also realized that my mother was not going to intervene when he bossed me around. He began to abuse his newfound authority.

He would sit around the house all day watching television and using glasses and plates to eat the lion's share of the scraps we had in the cupboard. I never realized how much energy one could expend turning

TV channels all day. As soon as I would come home from school, he would tell me that I had to do my chores. He especially made sure that I washed the dishes. He pressed me to make sure everything was cleaned up before my mother came home from work. My effort helped him to maintain his spotless image.

I always had a feeling that my brother Ervin never liked me. He seemed to have some deep-seeded hatred for me. I had no idea what I had done to him. Because of this, I never felt like I could look up to or confide in him. Here is how I rationalized Ervin's attitude toward me. I believe Ervin and his dad probably had a good relationship at one time. After I was born, his dad's attitude about everything changed. I remember he no longer cared about anything—his job, keeping a roof over our heads, his son...nothing. That was the beginning of the end. My gift of life was the reason Trip began to doubt that Ervin Jr. was his son. It was my entire fault that my brother lost the closeness he once had with his dad. It was my fault that my brother was no longer nurtured and loved. This circumstance had a traumatic impact on Ervin, but it wasn't the end. What I did not know was that Ervin had also been molested by my Uncle Chick. Haven later explained this to me in a phone conversation. Once I heard the story, I understood why we never had a normal relationship as brothers.

Ervin put me in several dangerous and harmful situations because of the abuse and mistreatment he had endured. There was a time when he and I watched a knife-throwing expert on TV. The man had his assistant stand against a wall, and with pinpoint accuracy, he threw knives above and below her arms, and he also threw a knife just above her head. It was amazing! Ervin evidently thought this act would be easy to imitate and used me as his assistant. He made me stand up against a wood wall at an elementary school down the street from our house. Then he walked about ten feet away from me, and prepared to throw metal-tipped darts in my direction. The first one was way off its mark and ended up stuck in my stomach. I grabbed the dart, doubled over, and started crying. I heard Ervin laughing, and, through my tears, I looked up to see a big smile on his face... The memory fades.

Ervin and I were never close, and now that he was a young teen in middle school we began to split apart even more. This was evident as he began to beat me up on a regular basis when my mother wasn't home. Perhaps it is true that "all big brothers do that." However, I think these circumstances were unique. There was a time when Ervin was upset with me for no reason I could recall. Maybe he just felt like torturing me. He began to punch me in my arm. I tried running away. I couldn't get far because I was inside the house and he could catch me easily. Our single-level apartment had three exits. There were two in the front and one in the back. I ran to each exit to unlock the door to get outside, but I couldn't. As I reached each door, he was right there terrifying me with the threat of a painful punch. Every time I ran to the next exit, he would make sure the door I had just left was locked. I tried several times to get the doors unlocked so I could get outside, but he was too quick. I remember the look that I saw in his eyes as he chased me. It was demented. He didn't care about me at all and wanted to make this experience hell for me.

After I had been subjected to this horror for more than thirty minutes, my brother Haven came home. However, Ervin had rigged all the doors by moving a little mechanical switch below each of the lock mechanisms so that Haven's keys wouldn't work. Haven could hear me screaming and began to knock harder and harder, with no response. My screams for help caused him to kick in the front door. I didn't see him deal with Ervin, but in the end Ervin had calmed down and had a bloody lip.

During this time, Ervin was in middle school, and he was starting to get into trouble a lot. He was getting suspended from school on a regular basis. I remember that periodically a guy named Tyrone would stop by every now and then to see him. I thought they were friends. I later found out that Tyrone was Ervin's juvenile case worker. Ervin must have gotten into some real trouble and was now dealing with the court. They were making a statement by assigning Ervin a case worker. To me, the message was loud and clear. If the case worker failed to rehabilitate Ervin, the next step would be a comfortable stay at a luxurious group home.

Most times when Tyrone stopped by, I was home and would answer the door. It was always the same routine. He would ask me if Ervin was home, and I would always tell him that I hadn't seen him. At the time, it never occurred to me that Ervin was supposed to be home for these regularly scheduled visits. I remember the last time Tyrone stopped by and Ervin was not there. I could see the disappointment in his face. If I could put words to the look, they would be "Your older brother is screwing up, and I can't help him. He is going to end up in a very bad situation."

As I mentioned earlier, Ervin had been exposed to horrific trauma that no child should ever experience. He had been taught to deal with his own problems. This is why he was an emotional wreck. He had no outlet, no one to talk to, no one there to notice his silent cries for help. He was suppressing his feelings, numbing his nerve endings to dull the pain, and harboring anger that would eventually drive him crazy.

It was probably six months since the last time I had seen Butchy. My mother didn't want him to know where we lived, but he found out anyway. It was a little after sun down, and I was on my way home after playing with friends. I could see three figures in front of my house. As I got closer, I noticed it was Butchy, my mom, and my brother Ervin. Butchy

27

was standing on the ground in front of the three porch steps, and my mother and Ervin were on the porch facing him. As I got closer I could see that my mother and Ervin had a butcher knife, and they were pushing it downward toward Butchy.

The blade was about a foot from his chest as he struggled against my mother's and brother's hands to keep it away. When I finally got to the porch, I heard my mother say, "Reesie, help us!" so I did. I put my hand on top of theirs and started to push down also. I could feel Butchy's hands trembling, but the knife never moved. We all struggled for about a minute, and the next thing I knew my mother had taken the knife and she and Ervin went back in the house. I didn't go inside with them because I was happy to see my dad. You would have figured that he would have been mad or upset with me after almost helping to kill him, but he wasn't. The only thing he said to me was, "Now go in the house and ask your mother if she had enough," so I did. When I asked her she didn't respond, so I went back outside, and Butchy said, "What did she say?" and I said, "She didn't say anything," and the memory fades away.

I often wonder what would have happened if my mother, Ervin, and I had been able to overcome Butchy's strength. What if he had slipped and the butcher knife had plunged through his chest? Even today, I visualize the front-page report that would have been printed in the newspaper: "*Woman and Sons Murder Estranged Boyfriend, Father.*" The consequences that would have followed would have been tragic. My mother surely would have gone to jail, and Ervin and I would have become wards of the state. Ervin was eleven; I was eight.

My father wasn't the only man my mother had domestic disputes with; she and J.C. had their fair share as well. I'm not sure what the argument was about, but I remember waking up at around 8:30 p.m., and I saw J.C. and my mother arguing. I watched as J.C.–wearing only his boxer shorts—grabbed a bed lath and struck my mother on the shoulder. For some reason my mother's male companions loved using pieces of bed-frames as weapons. First it was Trip and the bedframe; now it was J.C. and a bed lath. When the lath made contact, I heard the hollow sound that bone makes when it is impacted and doesn't break. I remember hearing my mother scream in pain. Then she ran into the kitchen to get a knife. J.C. only had time to grab the mattress off of the bed as a shield in case my mother tried to stab him…then the memory fades away.

Arguments, violence, and physical abuse between my mother and her boyfriends were common in my household. They never fazed me. The crazy thing was that my mother always stayed in a relationship with these men. It was a sure thing that the day after an argument, my moth-er and her abuser could be found cuddled up on the couch and watch-ing TV. They always appeared to be back in love. I could only think that both of them had short memories. Did they really forget that they were trying to kill each other just hours ago? It was insane to watch. I never forgave any of the men that hit my mom. I hated every one of them. I became angry with my mom because she was letting the abuse continue.

My life was hard enough as I faced adversity every day. I was hoping for a break, but it never came because the following year I was scheduled to attend the same elementary school that Ervin had attended. The name of the school was Elias Brookings (Brookings). I knew that I was going to be prejudged because Ervin had left a path of destruction at the school. Ervin had told me about the havoc he had wreaked on one teacher in particular, Ms. Brown. Even after he left the school, his reign of terror on Ms. Brown continued. I was a witness.

We lived about five hundred feet from Brookings and would usu-ally walk by it to go to the school park. One day Ervin convinced me to skip school to go to the park with him. We usually walked through the empty parking lot in the front of the school. This time we had to use the sidewalk because the parking lot was full of cars as school was in session. When we were halfway past the parking lot, I heard Ervin say, "There goes Ms. Brown's car right there." He went over to the car and grabbed the antenna with both hands and bent it in four different directions. As he deformed the antenna, I remember thinking; *I sure hope he has the right car.* I'm not sure why, but he passionately hated Ms. Brown. As we continued toward the park I heard Ervin say, "That's why I pissed in her shoe...bitch!" I didn't know what to think except that he must have really hated that lady.

When I received my middle-school class schedule for the following year, I realized just how unforgiving life was. My homeroom and spelling classes were going to be taught by—guess who—Ms. Brown! Initially she didn't seem so bad; however, after being in class a few days, my opinion started to change. I noticed that she never smiled and that she did not go out of her way to be kind to any students, like some of my other teachers. I observed her body language and facial expressions as she dealt with her students. I quickly learned it was easy to tell when she was in "no-nonsense" mode. She would let her circular rimmed glasses slide down her nose so that she could look at you with piercing eyes over the top rim. As she did this, she would drop her already husky voice an octave to let you know that "playtime" was over. She never asked, but I could tell by the way she looked at me that she knew that Ervin and I were brothers. She had no idea that I was nothing like Ervin, but I knew I was already marked as the enemy. I tried to keep my nose clean and do my homework, which in this case was extremely easy. I was always the first one in the class to finish the writing assignment.

Ms. Brown and two other teachers ran their classrooms jointly. This is how they determined the appropriate academic level for each student. Ms. Brown taught a basic lesson plan, Mrs. Chartier taught an intermediate lesson plan, and Mrs. Hutchings taught an advanced lesson plan.

Ms. Brown knew that I belonged in Mrs. Chartier's class, but I believe she extended my stay in her class on purpose. She wanted to be there when I finally got out of line. Then she would crush me and get back at Ervin for all the problems he had caused her.

It finally happened. She set me up good. The next day's lesson plan was structured around home economics. We were all going to learn how to cook in Mrs. Chartier's class. Ms. Brown instructed us to bring an oven mitt to class. I had one of those at home, so I brought it in and was looking forward to cooking. Ms. Brown had told us that as soon as we finished our classwork we could take our oven mitts next door to Mrs. Chartier's class to cook.

As always, I was the first one finished, so I stood up with my oven mitt and headed next door. Ms. Brown got in my way and said, "Where are you going?" I said, "Next door to cook." She said, "No, you're not." I said, "I finished my work. You said when we finished our class work that we could go next door to—" As I was finishing my statement, she used her hip to pin me to the blackboard. She grabbed my oven mitt from my hand and sharply said, "Sit down! You're not going anywhere!" I was humiliated and felt like crying, but I didn't. I just sat at my desk and took her medicine, just like I did when my brother Ervin and my dad taunted me. I started thinking that I should go to the principal or tell my mom. I rationalized that these were both bad ideas. I imagined that the principal would not believe me and that I would just get into more trouble. And I imagined that my mother would come to school and start a fight with Ms. Brown. Neither scenario would benefit me, so I just let it go. I never got to cook.

I ended up getting out of Ms. Brown's line of fire by keeping my head down, staying out of trouble, and always finishing my classwork way ahead of all the other students. She had no choice but to finally transfer me to Ms. Chartier's more advanced class. Whew! What a relief! After all these years, I still wonder if she realized that I was nothing like my brother Ervin.

Two years had passed, and our stay at the apartment on Florence Street was over. I don't have proof, but I'm sure we had been evicted because our landlord was always looking for the rent. I would always answer the door when he came by to pick it up. He had a thick Jamaican accent and would always ask me, "Is yar madda dere?" and I would always tell him no, whether she was or not, because that is what she had told me to do.

My mother ended up finding an apartment on Chester Street in a neighborhood that everyone referred to as "down the hill." If you were coming to my neighborhood you would be walking downhill; if you were leaving my neighborhood you would be climbing uphill. We lived directly across the street from a housing project on the second floor of a house. I had made friends with some of the kids who lived in the projects, whose families were just as screwed up as mine. I had also made friends with kids that lived in the "rich" part of the Forest Park area of Springfield. I now know that this was just a section of middle-class families; however, from a quality-of-life viewpoint, they were rich to me. There was a stark contrast between the families of my two sets of friends. The families of my "rich" friends always asked me to stay for dinner and I always learned something new when I visited. In the projects nobody asked me to stay for dinner and I think I actually lost intelligence, being in their presence. I didn't know it at the time, but there was a real problem being around people like that. The damaging effects manifested through all my friends that lived in the projects. It seemed that there was an epidemic disease that spread in the form of violence, diminished hope, and dreams that were bounded by the environment.

Mostly what I learned in that environment is the tougher you were, the more respect, girls, and friends you would have. You were labeled an "outcast," "sucker," or "sellout" if you did not assimilate and choose one of the many available pathways to failure that the ghetto had to offer. Maybe I can lay out the picture more clearly: Smoke weed and have babies before you get out of middle school. Carry a knife and hurt or kill anyone that looks at you the "wrong" way. Drop out of school.

Acquire fashionable clothes and a car without having a job. Go to jail and return to your neighborhood and demand respect. And don't even dream about moving. It is critical that you base decisions about your future on being able to stay in close proximity to "friends" in your neighborhood. This type of thinking was the perfect formula for failure. Anyone with potential who lived in that environment was sure to waste their lives.

I have a theory on why I wasn't sucked into the abyss of failure to find the same fate as others who lived in my environment. I succeeded because my grandmother's words had no competition. No one else taught me the things that she had. She taught me humility, talked to me about the importance of education and taught me how to conduct myself with dignity and respect. Her words and teachings were undisputed, uncontested, and became anchored in my subconscious. She is why I succeeded beyond even my own expectations.

I was also lucky enough to get words of wisdom that reinforced my grandmother's teachings from a black man who lived in one of my neighborhoods. His name was Allan, and he was about six years older than I was. He always wore a dark blue laborer's uniform. I would see him from time to time at the one pizza shop in the neighborhood. He would be there picking up his dinner, and I would be there playing the PAC-MAN™ videogame. This of course was when I could muster a few quarters. For some reason, which I still can't figure out today, Allan took an interest in me. I'm not sure if it was because I was respectful and said hi when I would see him or if it was something else. Every single time he saw me he would ask me two questions: "You doing what you're supposed to do? You staying out of trouble?" Then he would lecture me about staying in school and poof! He was gone. This happened at least ten times while I was in middle school. He always left me thinking—not just thinking about his lecture but about life and possibilities. I started to realize that I was only in my environment because I was born into it, not because I wanted to be there, had to be there, or should be there. This allowed me to dream about a better life and allowed me a brief exodus from my impoverished existence. The imagination is extremely important when you are faced with a real-life struggle for survival.

My favorite book is *Man's Search for Meaning*, written by Viktor Frankel. It analyzes how a man's state of mind and imagination helped him survive a most horrifying circumstance as a World War II Holocaust victim. Frankel used his state of mind and imagination to free himself from the mental anguish that accompanied the physical torture he received from his captors. Frankel's traumatic experience helped me understand that the most powerful tool people can use to free themselves from horrific circumstances is the mind.

Allan's impact on me was invaluable. If I had the chance I would personally thank him for helping me to change the way I thought about life. Today, *I* am Allan. I try to influence at-risk youth in the same manner. I am compelled to give back to young people in need of guidance because I myself benefitted from a stranger's inspiration. How wonderful it would be if there was a world full of Allan's who simply want to make a positive difference in a young person's life.

Many of my friends in the projects had older brothers who were in their twenties that were still living at home. None of them had jobs. None of them were going to college. To me, this seemed normal. In fact, I lived with adults who exemplified this behavior.

I don't remember once hearing about anyone in my neighborhood getting a good job, receiving a promotion at work, or graduating from college. There was never a mention of someone achieving something positive; however, discussions about tragedy and death were rampant. I always knew about the tragic circumstances of many of my friends. Sometimes misfortune occurred by chance. Mostly it occurred as a result of making bad decisions.

Dwayne drowned taking a swim in the local lake. Tony went to prison for accidentally killing his brother Ricardo during a nightclub brawl. Tyrone became a weed head and didn't graduate. Eric figured selling drugs was the pathway to success.

The demise of my friends helped me to understand why it is important to have a solid family structure or influential people in your life. My friends all needed an Allan in their lives. They needed someone who could provide guidance and answer basic questions. I could have easily ended up the same way as my friends if the most powerful influences in my life would not have been there. I was lucky, though. I at least was able to get tidbits of knowledge and information from Allan, my brother Haven, and my grandmother.

I've realized from everything I've been through that neither money nor material possessions determine whether an individual can achieve a rewarding and sustained life. The fundamental behaviors for achieving this includes: learning from life experiences, adhering to lessons learned, practicing good judgment, and following directions. Money and material possessions don't help. Every one of my friends had families that were more financially stable than mine. One would think this financial advantage would have improved their chances to achieve a better life. Apparently it didn't. Many of them ended up in squalor or died prematurely while I was able to earn a bachelor's degree in electrical engineering and build a good life for myself. More evidence to support my claim: Think back to the Kennedys, the epitome of wealth, power, and privilege. Yet members of this famous family had similar fates as the relatively dirt-poor souls in my family.

Speaking of dirt poor, I grew to appreciate basic things in life that most people take for granted. Things like having heat during the winter and supplying the house with groceries. I remember playing in front of Tyrone's house on several occasions when his mother and grandmother would show up with a carload of groceries. It was always the same routine as our playtime was interrupted. His grandmother would call him to help bring the groceries in the house. I would leave and return another time. Tyrone was fortunate because my family had to replenish their cupboards any way they could, even if it meant stealing.

I remember the time when Haven and I were browsing in the Mini Food Basket convenience store and Haven told me he was ready to check out. I noticed that he had a gallon of milk in his hand as we approached the cashier. I remember that exact moment. There were no customers in the store and that it was strangely quiet. Before I knew it, Haven had bolted out of the store. Instantly I figured out he was buying the milk with his five-finger discount. On high alert, I took off past the clerk, who was standing behind one of those counters that had a platform floor. This added height gave him visibility through the entire store so he could watch for shoplifters. That worked out well!

Besides not working this time, it also made it difficult for him to jump over the counter to get me. As I ran past him, I took a quick look in his direction to see if he was going to try to grab me or give chase. He did neither. He just stood there frozen. I expected him to at least yell, "Get back here!" but he didn't. Perhaps everything just happened too fast. As we ran away from the store I heard Haven yell, "Run, Maurice, run!" I made my legs go as fast as they could, but I was unable to keep up with him. Trailing behind, I watched Haven as he ran as fast as he could up a hill that was half a mile long with a grade of about sixty degrees. Unable to scale the hill like he did, I quickly decided to take a different route back to our house. When I finally made it off the main road to a side street, I knew I was safe because I could now hide behind a car or run through a backyard as an escape route. Now that I was safe I started to worry about Haven because I did not want him to get into trouble. I didn't think about it too long though. I knew Haven could take care of himself, plus the joy from thinking about the gallon of milk he had, swamped out my worry. Being involved with situations like this is why I knew that Tyrone indeed, was lucky to have a car pull up in front of his home with a load of groceries.

At different times in my life I've often heard people make absolute statements like "He steals; he is a bad person." My personal life experience made me wise enough to know that this is not always true. Sometimes more thought is needed to understand a person's actions. Perhaps asking, "Why did the person steal? What is he dealing with?" is a good place to start. I think experiences like the Mini Food Basket incident made me think this way. After all, I did not consider myself or my brother Haven bad people, yet we were stealing, and we knew it was wrong. I guess that doesn't matter in the eyes of some people, but so be it. What we did was not for sport; it was for survival.

Tyrone and his brother didn't have to steal like Haven and I did in order to get a decent meal. I remember one time when I went to see if he could come outside and play. He came out of the house holding two pieces of buttered toast. At that moment, I realized just how fortunate he was. I said, "You're lucky; you always have food." He didn't respond. He just chomped away. Then he smiled as if to say, "Yup, you're right." Tyrone was well fed and had nice clothes and a family who supported his education. Yet Tyrone still ended up being a high-school dropout and weed-head. He sealed his own fate when he made the bad decision to follow and adopt the misguided values of his environment. In the south, the ghetto is known as the "Trap" precisely for this reason. Tyrone had gotten caught up in a trap and was unable to escape.

Middle school is a harsh environment where each adolescent is competing to fit in. This wasn't a problem for me because fitting in wasn't a priority for me. It paled in comparison to my grandmother's words of wisdom and what she wanted me to accomplish. Her words silently played over and over in my head on a daily basis: "You never mind about those other kids; you get your work done."

I would never fit in, and I was okay with that which is why I never tried. If I had, I would not have been successful anyway because of my Goodwill clothing and my humble attitude. Being around my grandmother so much had caused me to become a very respectful little boy. This was looked upon as a weakness in my neighborhood. Most times, kids from my neighborhood were aggressive and angry. Some were angry as a defense mechanism to prevent others from even thinking of making fun of them. Others were angry because living in my neighborhood—by definition—meant that you needed to be able to protect yourself. Most of the people from my neighborhood seemed to be pissed at the world for no good reason. The truth was that they had extremely good reasons. Think about it. Your electricity gets turned off every couple of months; you survive on scraps for food, and faithfully run out of oil needed for the furnace to produce heat during the winter. It is no mystery why people dealing with these circumstances would have a bad disposition in general.

I was angry like that at one time, but my grandmother and the Allan's in my life helped to change my attitude. I was now at a point in my life where I just wanted to have fun. I thought everyone should be the best person they could be and treat everyone with decency. Unfortunately middle school changed my view on that. Almost daily I endured verbal attacks and hostility. Most of the verbal attacks against me came from the older little black kids who lived in my neighborhood. Many of them had better clothes and sneakers than I did. They zeroed in on my worn-out hand-me-down sneakers that I would get from my brothers or cousins. Or they would make fun of my "jeepers." These were cheap sneakers that Kmart sold for $4.99. If you didn't have a pair of twenty-dollar Chuck Taylor Converse, you would hear about it. You were out of style, and no one wanted to be your friend.

It got worse. In seventh grade girls started to notice boys, and for some strange reason we started wanting to be around them. Kicking them out of the clubhouse was a thing of the past. I didn't stand a chance of getting the girls to like me wearing jeepers. It just wasn't going to happen. I accepted the fact that I was never going to get a pair of Converse. They were way out of my budget. It was common that most of the kids I knew would already have their second pair of Converse while I was still managing with one pair of jeepers. Unable to afford new footwear, I had to make my jeepers last. Sometimes I would wear the sole down until holes went straight through the bottom. I would easily solve this problem by putting a piece of cardboard inside my sneakers to cover the holes. It would last for days.

I was fortunate that my first year in middle school began when my city first started busing inner-city kids to the rural areas. This was a noble attempt to integrate the school system. Little did I know at the time, but this change would be extremely beneficial to my growth and quality of life. I was now getting exposed to white people and the "white" values and culture. For some reason it was easy for me to establish friendships with the little white kids. I don't quite understand the psychology of it all, but maybe it was because I had cousins who had the same color skin. For whatever reason it was, I am glad I did not get infected by the racism plague that was rampant at the time. If I had, it would have been detrimental to my growth.

Building these new relationships with the white middle-school kids exposed me to all types of different things. Seeing life through their eyes helped me broaden my perspective on life. It seemed like it didn't matter to my white friends or their family members that I was poor. In contrast, the older black kids who lived in my neighborhood seemed to always make it a point to emphasize my misfortune. This is why I would sometimes prefer to walk one mile to the white neighborhood to play with my white "rich" friends. This was my temporary escape from being ridiculed.

I learned new things from being in their households. When they ate dinner, they sat at the kitchen table as a family, and each family member would discuss events from their days. In my house, it was rare that we would sit down at the table as a family and eat dinner. When we did, the room was silent. The focus was on filling your belly.

An experience that I had while visiting one of my white "rich" friends named John gave me a new perspective on being carefree. On one of my visits to his home, John had found some chewing tobacco that belonged to his dad. Without even thinking about the consequences, he decided we should imitate the adults and chew it. We sat in the window of his bedroom and stuffed our mouths full of tobacco. We made sure we pressed it in between our cheek and gum like John had seen his dad do several times. Our gums were on fire! But we just grimaced and started to spit the juice from his bedroom window. What a great experience for me. It was something that I would never have been exposed to if I had not made friends with him. There was something liberating about the whole experience. Maybe it was the fact that John took his dad's tobacco without fear of getting into trouble. Maybe it was the fact that I knew there would be hell to pay if I would have tried the same thing in my house.

There was another time at John's house when his dad planned to make homemade pizza, and the family consensus was that I should stay for dinner. Pretending to be polite, I said, "No, thank you," but in the back of my mind I was hoping they would not accept no for an answer. When they asked me to stay for dinner the second time, I "reluctantly" accepted. While John's dad was making the pizza, John and I watched him flour the dough, flatten it out, press out the bubbles, and throw it in the air. Every time he did, John and I would yell, "Oohhhh!"

I ended up staying past nine that night. When it was time for me to leave, John's dad offered to give me a ride home. I said, "No, thank you." But unlike with declining to stay for dinner, this time I meant it. I would have been embarrassed if they saw where I lived. Besides, I lived in a treacherous, unsafe neighborhood. The code of the street was survival of the fittest, and Darwin never went on vacation. He would just lurk and wait for an opportunistic moment to wreak havoc on an unsuspecting victim. A good-hearted white man driving a shiny black Cadillac in a neighborhood where he does not belong would have certainly qualified. That aside, a ride home was totally unnecessary. I didn't mind walking,

I didn't have a curfew, and it was common for children from my neighborhood to be out way past nine-thirty at night. There was no need for John and his dad to risk the possibility of being assaulted just to give me a ride home. I again let them know that I appreciated the offer then I respectfully declined the ride. But John's dad insisted and would not accept no for an answer.

As we approached my home I kept an eye out for trouble. Ironically my street was empty, and it was unusually quiet that night. I guess even Darwin took a break every now and then. Luck was on my side because my street was already too dark for John and his dad to fully appreciate my humble residence. I slept well that night because I had a full belly from eating pizza, I had been in a healthy family environment, I learned a few new things, and my friend and his dad had safely returned home from my neighborhood.

One of the most important lessons I learned as I was growing up was taught to me by a white football coach. It cost twenty dollars to join the Holy Name Raiders football team, a community team that was made up of all little white boys who were the same age as I was. I had become familiar with the team by seeing them practice at a city park in Forest Park. I somehow found out that in addition to the twenty-dollar registration fee, you needed to have your own cleats and mouthpiece. Everything else was supplied by the coach.

As with the Converse sneakers, I couldn't afford this either, but since tryouts were free I had nothing to lose. I thought it might be fun too. I spent some time trying to rationalize why the coach would even allow a poor little black boy who can't afford the registration fee to try out on a team of all little white boys. I didn't let that stop me from asking, though. Surprisingly he said, "Sure, you can try out." I remember the coach. I will never forget him because he treated me just like he treated the other players. I'm sure the other little boys noticed this too. What was strange was that I never received one insult or felt a funny vibe from anyone on the team. It was like the coach had disciplined his team on racial equality.

I tried out in my street clothes and jeepers because buying a pair of cleats and a pair of gym shorts was out of the question. Tryouts were relatively easy. I did the running drills, pass drills, and calisthenics without a problem. I did so well at the practice that I thought if I did have the money to play, I would probably have been a true talent on the team. For the next tryout session, we were going to practice while we were wearing our football pads and helmets. The coach told me that he would supply the uniform and helmet but that I would need to get my own mouthpiece. I knew I couldn't afford a mouthpiece, so I showed up for practice the next day without one. Uncle Chick, Ervin, and Haven had taught me that when you don't have money to buy what you need—steal it! I decided to steal a mouthpiece from a helmet that was sitting around idle. I figured nobody needed it, no one would miss it, and they wouldn't be able to prove that I took it anyway. I had no idea that a mouthpiece was boiled and custom formed to a unique set of teeth. In the moment it didn't matter. I had my mouthpiece, and I was one step closer to being a Holy Name Raider. I was ready to play.

My theft somehow got back to the coach during practice. When tryouts concluded, this is how I found out: he called everyone into a huddle and told us all—twenty-five little white boys and one little black boy—to get down on one knee. He began to speak about how important it is to take your commitment to the Raiders seriously and lectured about how you should put in a 110-percent effort on the team. Suddenly out of nowhere, he looked directly at me and said, "In the Raiders camp, if you need something you don't take it; you ask for it, and we will help you get it." As abruptly as he started the verbal onslaught that he directed at me, he ended it and went right back into his speech about how you need to be at practice every day and how you need to read your playbook, and that was it. Practice was over, and we were dismissed. His words shook me. They spun me like a whirlwind. I was not used to this type of discipline. There was no belt, no whippin', and it was almost like my crime was all forgiven. I was stunned.

I had shown very poor character that day. I figured that a group of the little white boys would try to chase me down and give me a good pounding – it was the least that I deserved. But it never happened. I was left to take my two-mile walk home and think about where I went wrong. I was too embarrassed to return to the next practice, so I gave up my dream of playing on the team.

I gained a new perspective that day. I thank and credit the coach and the team for opening my eyes to a new world. They helped to dispel the idea of racism everywhere and helped me realize that each individual should be judged by his or her character alone.

When some get taught, they acquire wisdom from the teacher, when others are taught by the same teacher, the wisdom is rejected. I now realize this—the students who benefit from teaching are those who seek to embrace knowledge.

"Teach me and I gain knowledge… Teach me and I gain nothing."

Enough

"Push me, I will fall... Push me, I will push back."

It was about this time when I finally realized why J.C. was not employed. He was illiterate! I found this out one day when I saw him practicing how to write his name on a piece of scratch paper. Later that same day, I saw my mother teaching him how to form the letters. I was then able to put the pieces together. My mother was teaching him basic handwriting skills! I didn't really care for J.C., so I thought that maybe his dumb ass could just sign everything with an 'X.' I found it disturbing that J.C. was a grown man, and he was unable to write his own name. I found it even more disturbing that my mother, for as far back as I could remember, had not once sat down beside me to help me with a homework assignment. Yet she took joy in teaching a man who abused her constantly how to write. I just watched in disbelief.

It occurred to me that J.C. most likely felt insecure around me. Just think: I was in the fifth grade; I could write my name, and I was more educated than he was. No wonder he bossed me around and disliked me. Regardless, I made it my business to never challenge his intelligence. As a matter of fact, I never really talked to him at all, even if we were in the same room. When we did communicate, our conversations were limited. It was usually him telling me to go to the store to get him a pack of cigarettes or to go into the kitchen and wash the dishes. He obviously took pleasure in making me do chores. Every time he would tell me to do

44

the dishes, he would say, "Time to go bust the suds," and then he would laugh out loud. I never thought it was funny and felt ridiculed. Since my mother had shown me on several occasions that she would not fend for me, I just did as I was told. For years J.C. was able to compensate for his shortcomings at my expense. He had his fun, but this all came to an end on my tenth birthday.

I was having a good day. There was no birthday party, no presents and such, but I did not expect those things anyway. I was happy, and I felt great. My school day had gone well, and I didn't have any problems with any of the neighborhood bullies. The day was perfect. It was close to seven-thirty at night. I remember the time because that was when the English comedian Benny Hill appeared on TV as the star of "The Benny Hill Show." We didn't miss a show. When it aired, we would all gather around the twenty-five-inch floor model TV that we had in the living room.

As the opening credits were rolling, I heard J.C. say, "Go bust the suds!" I replied, "Okay, as soon as the show is over." He said, "Go do them now!" I said in an annoyed tone, "Man, why don't you just leave me alone?" As the words left my mouth, I realized that I had had enough. I wasn't afraid anymore. I just didn't care. As he got up to go get his belt, he said, "Boy, you better get in there and wash those dishes." As I walked to the kitchen, I called to my mother, who was lying in bed, and asked her to tell J.C. to stop bothering me. She did not respond. I didn't really expect her to anyway. I started to run the dishwater in the sink, and J.C. came up behind me and swung his belt to hit me. As it struck me, I ignored the pain, grabbed it with one hand, and moved my hand in a circular motion so the belt would wrap around my arm. This prevented him from swinging it again. In an annoyed, agitated voice, I said, "Stop playing!" Then I threw the belt off my arm down toward the ground, and I looked him right in the eye. He had a look that was composed of shock and confusion. Something had occurred that he hadn't expected. I guess this is why he didn't swing the belt again. His commanding tone had drastically diminished as he said his last words before he left the kitchen. "You better do those dishes."

That's how I spent my tenth birthday. As far as I was concerned, it had not been a total loss. I regret missing "The Benny Hill Show," but at least I was able to show J.C. that I deserved respect. From that day on, he treated me differently. No, we didn't become buddy-buddy, but going to get his belt to discipline me was now a thing of the past.

J.C. never found a job. I don't think he was really looking for one. He would spend his days visiting the couple who lived across the street from our house. Their names were Buddy and Peggy. They were both unemployed alcoholics. They were always home, so their house became the meeting spot for anyone who was not tied to a definitive schedule—you know, like a work schedule. They hosted nonstop alcoholic festivals, and they always had a house full of people. This made them a perfect fit for J.C.

The best-kept secret on our street for a while had to do with J.C. and a twenty-three-year-old-girl who lived above Buddy and Peggy. She had taken an interest in J.C., and she let him know it. He had it made. He was thirty-two and my mother paid all of his bills. He stayed home all day, watched TV, ate all the food in the house, bossed me around (until my tenth birthday), and drank a beer whenever he wanted. Now a younger woman was interested in him. What else could a guy want? Of course he took her up on the offer and continued to see her anytime he could while my mother was working. J.C. was not only illiterate; he was stupid too. He was cheating with the girl right across the street from where we lived, and he had stopped being discrete about it. Eventually, word of his indiscretion got back to my mother. She chose to deal with the situation by challenging the girl to a street fight. I hadn't seen my mother openly challenge someone to a street fight before, but knowing that she would grab a knife at the drop of a dime, I guess I shouldn't have been surprised. I think the girl was too scared to come out of the house, so she and my mother never fought.

Instead of giving J.C. a beat down, she chose to lash out at the twenty-three-year-old neighbor. I don't quite get it because J.C. was obligated to my mother; the girl was not. I guess I shouldn't have expected the outcome to be any different, though. J.C. had done much worse to her, and she allowed it to continue.

A short time after finding out J.C. was cheating on her, my mother started losing weight. This was the thinnest I had ever seen her. She also started having my cousins do her hair in a style that a twenty-year-old girl would wear. The weight loss and hairstyle looked nice on her, but something just didn't seem right. She had dropped about thirty-five pounds in what seemed like a month. I tried to figure out the reason for the drastic changes. Maybe this had something to do with J.C.'s infidelity with the twenty-three-year-old girl who lived across the street. Perhaps this was my mother's way of emulating what she thought J.C. wanted. I just wasn't sure.

Sometime later, word got back to me that my brother Haven had smacked my mom around. I became angry, confused, and upset. I instantaneously began to feel hatred toward my brother. I couldn't think of any reason he would hit my mother, and at the time I didn't care if he had one. Before hearing about this, my brother Haven was my idol—a superhero who could do anything. Now I just wasn't sure I wanted to talk to him or be anything like him. In my eyes, Haven was no different from Trip, Butchy, or J.C., who had all abused my mom.

A few days later I found out why Haven assaulted our mom. I received the information while Haven and I were having a discussion about nothing in particular. Haven told me that he caught our mother doing cocaine. Now it all fit together: the strange behavior, the teenage hairstyle, and the weight loss. As I thought back, I also remembered noticing a change in my mother's hands. They were swollen and had the same sores as the people who bought drugs from my father. It was true; she had been doing drugs.

Haven was my superhero again. He was back in my good graces. I was glad he gave our mother some tough love to motivate her to stop using drugs. I had seen the mental and physical trauma drugs had caused other people. I thought back to how drugs had ruined Yvonne's (my father's girlfriend) health and had stolen her youth to make her look ten years older than her actual age. I thought back to how drugs had killed my aunt Pinky and my aunt Brenda. Haven had prevented this from happening to our mom. I was grateful and in his debt. A few months after the *hand* of persuasion spoke, my mother regained the weight she had lost, the swelling of her hands went down, the sores on her hands disappeared, and she stopped wearing the teenage hairstyles. Everything seemed to be going in the right direction. Now all she needed to do was get rid of J.C.

The affair J.C. was having eventually ended, but as you might imagine, he was still a resident in our home. I'm not sure how he worked things out with my mom. If it was anything like I had seen before, it probably went like this: "Aw, baby, you know I love you. I swear 'fo' God I won't do it again." J.C. knew my mother couldn't resist his feces-laced charm, typically known as bullshit! He would lay it down real nice, and by the next morning he knew my mother would be pacified and everything would be back to normal on the home front. He followed up the meaningless love chatter by riding the straight and narrow for a few days. Once he was sure my mother truly forgave him for his moment of weakness, he was back to no good as usual.

A few days after he reconciled with my mother, J.C. really decided to flex his muscle. He probably just needed to let everyone know that he still ruled the roost and was still king of his castle. Unfortunately, he had pretty bad timing. I was ten now and had finally decided to stand up to him. Ervin was thirteen, and on this rare occasion he was home. Haven was home too. He had come from my grandfather's to visit for a few days. He was sixteen.

From my bedroom I heard J.C. and my mother having an argument. This was a bad one because their voices filled my room, which was all the way at the rear of the house. I ran to my mother's bedroom to find that Haven and Ervin were already there. We all watched as J.C. walked from the bedroom into the living room with his shotgun in one hand. With an angry scowl, he turned back toward the bedroom and yelled, "I swear 'fo' God! I will plant you!" As soon as he said those words, Haven grabbed the shotgun from his hand, and Ervin threw a lightning-quick punch to J.C.'s throat. Once Ervin's fist hit J.C.'s Adam's apple, I watched J.C. grimace in pain. He grabbed his throat like he was trying to soften the effects of the blow. The angry pit bull scowl he previously had on his face changed to the look of an injured puppy. The only thing I was sure about at this point was that the fight he was having with my mother was over. J.C. sat on the couch in the living room holding his throat and didn't say a word. I felt no sorrow for this man. At that moment, I actually felt like saying, "Now go bust the suds!"

J.C. was unable to talk for about a day, and then he was hoarse for about a week. As expected, my mother allowed him to continue living with us. This was just a day in the life of my family, nothing new, and nothing we weren't familiar with. When it was over, everyone just resumed doing whatever they had been doing before the argument. I think I went outside to play with my friends. This dispute was also another testament to why I knew J.C. was a pure idiot. Why else would he start a fight with the mother of three teenage sons who were all home that evening and had all grown up around violence? Not the smartest thing to do.

As an observer during this incident, I noticed that throughout the entire altercation between J.C. and her children, my mother had not said one word. She just let the situation work itself out. It didn't matter that she was the reason we were in this dangerous predicament and had to deal with an egotistical abuser with a shotgun. This time I think we were all lucky. No one was hurt or killed. But what if J.C. had decided to murder our entire family? I could visualize the front-page report that would have been printed in the newspaper: "**Woman, Sons Murdered by Boyfriend.**"

It didn't surprise me that Ervin was the first one to throw a punch at J.C., since he was always involved in altercations. I remember him getting into fights all the time with people in the neighborhood. Every time

I saw him fighting, it caused me turmoil and pain. I did not like to see my brother in any situation where he might get hurt.

The front porch of our home was located directly across the street from the project basketball court. This was convenient because I could see if there was anyone playing basketball without leaving the house. There was one time when I went to see if there was anyone on the court when I saw a group of about thirty people in a semicircle. It was a fight! In my neighborhood a fight was entertainment that was synonymous with going to the movies. This is why the thirty people had gathered, and now I had a seat to watch too. There were two people in the center, a male and a female who were punching another person who was on the ground. When I finally made out the figure on the ground, it turned out to be Ervin! He was in an almost fetal position getting kicked and punched by a larger, older male and female whom I recognized from the neighborhood. Because I was only ten, I knew I would not be able to help. I just stayed on the porch and watched one of my worst fears unfold before my eyes. My brother was getting beaten up, and there was nothing I could do.

Ervin somehow managed to get up to run into the house. I stayed on the porch and watched the crowd outside wait around to see what was going to happen next. Two minutes later, Ervin came to the porch with a shotgun! It was the same shotgun that J.C. had used to threaten my mom. He had tears in his eyes, and he was trying to pump the handle on the body of the shotgun to load it. As he did this, I could tell that he didn't know how to use it.

At first the group near the basketball court didn't believe that Ervin had a real gun or that he would use it. They were wrong. I knew that if Ervin was able to get the shotgun loaded, several people were going to die. They just stood and watched as he tried to figure out how to load the gun.

I watched as Ervin put the stock on his shoulder and aim it at the mob near the court. As he did this, they finally realized this was not a game, and they started to run frantically in every direction to find cover.

Ervin pulled the trigger twice. Fortunately, the shotgun did not fire. From the clicking sound the shotgun made when he pulled the trigger, I knew that the safety was still engaged. I only knew this because I would listen to the conversations at my grandfather's house. They would talk about the type of gun and ammunition they liked. I heard them say things like "Those hollow points are *bad news*!" I also heard them mention the safety and how it prevents the gun from shooting.

Ervin kept trying to figure out how to get the shotgun to fire. I knew he wasn't going to give up until someone in the mob was the host of a funeral, but he was out of time. In the distance, we heard a police siren getting louder and louder. We knew it was headed toward our house. My guess was that even though Ervin never fired a shot, someone from the mob of people had gotten scared and called the cops.

When the cops showed up, they came upstairs and began asking a lot of questions about a shotgun and if we had one. There were three cops. One was questioning me, another was questioning Ervin, and the third was looking around in the rooms and closets. I heard Ervin tell the cops that we didn't have a shotgun, so I told them the same thing. I lied because I didn't want Ervin to get into trouble. In fact, I knew exactly where the shotgun was. Ervin had hid it in the basement before they arrived.

The policeman who was searching the house found a small plastic rifle that was part of our Nintendo "Duck Hunt" game. He asked Ervin if it was what he used to scare the people near the basketball court. Ervin replied yes. This is when the officers began to lecture us about how from a distance the gun looks real and that we should not pretend to have a rifle. Their lecture was a bunch of crap that they probably told the kids from the suburbs on a daily basis. Death and danger were our lives. Their "stay out of trouble" speech was useless to us. They finished their lecture, and then they left. We dodged a bullet that day, no pun intended!

Sometimes I flashback to that day to see Ervin release the safety on the shotgun and fire into the crowd. Then I visualize the front-page report that would have been printed in the newspaper: *"Thirteen-Year-Old Kills Several People with Shotgun in Street Brawl."*

In the days to come, I began to see Ervin less and less. There were nights when he didn't come home. I had no idea where he was and constantly worried about him. His presence in my life was minimal and this had a direct correlation to how close we were. I would have done anything to cultivate a strong relationship with my brother. But I had no confidence that it would ever happen because Ervin would never allow me in his inner circle. I didn't meet his standard of being a *cool* little brother.

Ervin wholeheartedly embraced the materialistic culture that propagated through our neighborhood. In order for him to accept you or befriend you, you needed to be the best "this" and have the best "that." The younger boys that he thought were cool always had talent, good hair, or nice clothes. These were things that I could only dream of having. Their talent had been cultivated by an older brother or elder who spent time teaching them how to play sports. Some of them had perfect blowout afros. I didn't—we couldn't afford the hair products. All of them wore better clothes and had better sneakers than I had. My mom couldn't afford to buy me anything better. This put me at a loss and solidified the dividing line that would always exist between me and my brother. The irony of my dilemma is that Ervin's admiration for other little boys occurred because their siblings had taken time to teach them how to do things. Ervin was *my* big brother, and he hadn't taught me a thing! If he had, I could have probably met his standards in order to win his graces.

I can probably remember a handful of occurrences when Ervin let me hang around him. These would have been times that I would have treasured if it wasn't for the fact that they were only when Ervin was up to no good. I remember a time when Ervin convinced me to skip school and follow him to Springfield College. The campus was about twenty minutes from our house. If you had taken the walk with us, you would have probably noticed the gradual improvements in landscape maintenance, residential upkeep, and the overall quality of life. I've seen this several times, like when I lived two blocks from Yale in New Haven. If you walk a few blocks in the wrong direction, you are back in the ghetto. In thinking about this, I decided to give this phenomenon a name—I call it the invisible line theory. The theory relates to an invisible boundary on a map that defines the poor and affluent areas of a community. I imagine that the invisible lines are drawn by somebody like a city board member who makes sure schools, libraries, and banks mostly end up on the good side of the line. Once the invisible lines are in place, noticeable environmental improvements follow.

Another view on this is that the city perhaps decided that it was futile to fix up certain areas, such as the ghettos of America. The thought might have been that every time they fix things up, they get destroyed anyway. I would have to say that I agree with this assertion. I lived it. I've seen it. Remember the old rusty car and the broken refrigerator in the field. Remember the garbage that was freely thrown about the residential area. *I* probably put the refrigerator there. I make no excuses for my struggle through life. But just like when I was unable to focus in school because I was hungry, the struggle through life makes people living in ghetto environments value the acquisition of shelter and food over having a nice lawn, or caring how clean the street is, where they live.

After walking around the college for about thirty minutes, Ervin broke into a car and stole an umbrella. I'm not even sure why. It wasn't even raining. As we were leaving to go back home, we were met by the campus police. They didn't arrest us, but they took us to the booking area of the campus police department. They held us in separate rooms until our mother arrived to take us home. The strange thing is that I don't recall being scared at all during the ordeal—not even when my mom picked us up. I knew she was upset because she didn't say a word on the way back home. That meant we were going to get a real good whippin'. Even though I knew this, I still wasn't scared.

My mother made sure we would not forget this whipping. In the flood of her anger, she was unable to find a belt, so she used an extension cord. Take my word on this: you do not want to be hit with an extension cord. The sting is so bad that your entire nervous system goes into shock. I remember the sixth blow she delivered; I almost passed out. I braced myself for the seventh blow, but it never came. What did come was a lingering sting from blood-filled welts that swelled up right before my eyes. They were all over my legs, but I had more on my arms as I tried to block the blows as they were delivered. I had Ervin to thank for the whippin' we got that night. I guess I was wrong. Ervin did spend time to teach me things. Unfortunately, he taught me the wrong things.

Regardless of all the things Ervin had done to me, and despite the fact that he never showed that he liked me, I still loved him dearly. I never told him this because he would have laughed at me. He always laughed at me when I showed compassion, pain, or fear. I remember when I turned thirteen and my body began to change. It seemed in the middle of the night I released a substance from a part of my body that as far as I knew was only used for urinating. When I first saw it, it scared me to death. I thought I was sick and might die or something. I never even gave it a thought to go ask my mom what was happening; that would have been too embarrassing. I couldn't ask Haven because he was government property now and living on a military base. He had joined the Army to become an ear, nose, and throat specialist. I had no choice but to ask Ervin about it. I was still embarrassed even though he was a male. All he did was make matters worse. He started laughing at me while saying, "You went off on yourself! You went off on yourself!" I just went and cleaned myself up and decided I would never attempt to discuss it with anyone else. At that moment I realized how bad I needed a mentor, someone to talk to, a real big brother. This would be the last time I was going to be humiliated by Ervin. Then and there I made the decision to never ask him to explain anything else to me.

After a time, the occurrences of abuse Ervin subjected me to must have begun to affect me. I found myself no longer worrying whether he was safe, hurt, or in trouble. I think I finally accepted that the distress I was feeling was one-sided. Why was I worrying when Ervin himself did not care about his own welfare? Not only that. I always knew Ervin never cared about me. As I grew to an adult, I realized that it is impossible for a person who does not care about himself to care about anyone else.

I had been around drugs all my life. Now it was my turn to experiment with them. I don't remember this being a conscious decision. It was almost like it just happened, and I wasn't in control. My use of drugs started when I began to hang around some of Ervin's friends who were high-school dropouts. I don't know what attracted me to these guys. Perhaps this was a way for me to get closer to Ervin. If his friends liked me then maybe he would too. Perhaps this was a way for me to feel like I was really part of a group. I didn't know what that felt like since I didn't fit in any groups in middle school. Whatever the reason, I embraced my new vice wholeheartedly. My father had sold drugs and used them, my mother had used them, and Ervin had just started getting into trouble for smoking marijuana. Up to this point no one had ever told me that drugs were bad, not even my grandmother.

The choice drug that we used to get "high" was airplane glue. One of Ervin's friends named Larry showed me how to squeeze the tube of glue into a paper bag and how to inhale and exhale the fumes. The street name for what we were doing was snuffing. I remember feeling calm and disoriented the first time I snuffed. It was the strangest feeling. My head would spin continuously, and it felt like nothing mattered. I remember trying to cross a busy street after we took a hit. It seemed like the cars were moving in slow motion. Then they would speed up and then go back to slow motion. It was crazy.

It must be true that snuffing causes memory loss because I don't remember all the day-to-day details of what we did. Many days were a blur. I had stopped going to school, and I was violating all the knowledge I learned from my grandmother. At the time, her teachings did not matter.

One time we ran out of glue, and Larry told me to go into the convenience store to buy a new tube. He said I should buy it because I was the youngest in the group. He said I looked innocent, and no one would question why I was buying it.

Larry and the rest of the group waited a block away from the convenience store as I went inside to buy the glue. The clerk on duty was a forty-year-old white man. I remember his face clearly because he did me a favor that day. I went up to the counter and told him that I need to buy a tube of airplane glue. At the time I didn't understand why all the stores kept the glue behind the counter—it became clear why. It was to keep kids like me who would abuse it as a drug from stealing it. The clerk asked me, "What are you doing with it?" I told him that I had some model planes that I was putting together. He somehow knew I was lying and growled, "You don't have any model planes. Get outta here!" As he yelled at me, he made a move like he was going to come from behind the counter and grab me. That's when I took off running out of the store. As I was running, it finally occurred to me that something was wrong with sniffing glue. Why else would the clerk get so upset with me?

Later that day I was walking home with my brother Haven. I'm not sure how he knew, but somehow he was aware that I was sniffing glue. He didn't really yell at me, but in a sharp tone he said, "I know you're sniffing glue. Are you stupid? Don't you know that doing that kills brain cells? If you do it again after today I'm going to tell Ma!" That was it. Those words were magic. This was exactly what I needed to hear. Finally! Someone told me that drugs were bad. As Haven was verbally chastising me, I started to feel like I had let him, my grandmother, and Allan down. They had invested time in me and had given me their wisdom. In return, I ended up hanging with a group of idiots and sniffing glue from a bag. This thought had a drastic impact on me. I vowed that after that day I would never touch a single drug again.

Regardless what is going on in life, it seems like people always have time for love making. Somehow between the drama with the twenty-three-year-old girl, the drugs, arguments, and death threats, my mother had gotten pregnant by J.C. This was going to be her fourth child from a fourth man. I don't remember much of the time that passed when my mother was pregnant, but I do remember the first time I visited the hospital and saw my little sister, Serena. She was in a plastic-looking incubator with some type of gadget in her nose with hoses running out of both sides. I remember my mom asking me, "Isn't she pretty?" All I remember thinking was, *No, look at her ears. They look pointy and are really dark at the top like they had been left in the oven too long.* I didn't say that, though. I simply shook my head yes.

I initially remember feeling indifferent about my mother being pregnant by J.C. It wasn't a big deal for me. I wasn't impacted until the day I was standing in front of my little sister, staring at her through a glass window. At the time, I had no idea how significant her birth was going to be. I had no idea how much she would influence me in ways that I couldn't have imagined. The gift of her life would keep me following a righteous path.

As I was staring at her in the incubator, I knew that our relationship would be nothing like the one Ervin and I had. It was *my* time to be the big brother. I would be there when she needed me. I would have her back and influence her to do great things. I would be a real big brother.

By the time my mother brought Serena home from the hospital, her skin had darkened a bit, and the dark crust around her ears was gone. Now she really was pretty. In fact, she was so pretty that she later won a cute baby contest and had her picture posted in a magazine. When she won this contest I was so proud of her. She was light-years ahead of me when I was her age. Before she turned two years old, she was already showing that she was a winner.

It had taken me about thirty years to finally confirm that Butchy was my father, but there was no dispute that J.C. was Serena's dad. This was unequivocally confirmed once her baby teeth grew in. My mother noticed that, like J.C., Serena had two teeth that were fused together. They both had an incisor on the right sides of their mouths that grew as one with the tooth next to it. When J.C. or Serena smiled or laughed, the fused teeth were visible. There was no dispute that Serena was J.C.'s daughter.

The bond that I was building with Serena grew exponentially every day. I used to look forward to going outside to play when I came home from school. Now I looked forward to playing with Serena when my school day ended. My mother always placed her in a beanbag chair in our living room. She looked so comfortable. She would sit in the beanbag making squeaks and baby noises while kicking her legs. I would sit on the floor next to the beanbag and play with her for what seemed like hours. It was great. I had so much fun with her when she was a baby.

Three more years had passed, and it was time to move again—another eviction. This time we moved to a different apartment on Eastern Avenue. J.C. went back into his routine of eating and watching TV. When he wasn't doing this, he was across the street at the blacktop. The blacktop was an area located about two hundred feet from our front door. It was a five-hundred-square-foot paved asphalt parking lot adjacent to Blacktop Liquors. The blacktop had been adopted by all the neighborhood alcoholics as their second home. They would buy liquor at the store and just hang in the parking lot drinking all day. There were usually about fifteen parked cars and anywhere between forty to fifty alcoholics on the blacktop. The package store owner didn't seem to mind the intrusion on his property since they were all true-blue customers. This was a good thing for the store owner but not so good for the neighborhood. Whenever a group of alcoholics assembled, arguments and fights were inevitable. Just about every one of them carried a knife, and a few carried guns. Sometimes people would not only get hurt, they would get killed.

I could see the blacktop from my front porch, so anytime something happened I had my own front row seat at the "Blacktop Theatre." Showtime was from sun up to sun down, and the feature was entitled *Alcohol, Murder, and Mayhem.*

One day while I was sitting on the porch watching an episode, I saw two men running from the blacktop toward our house. One of them was J.C., and he was getting chased by a man who had a knife. J.C. was six-four, and it looked like the other guy was five-five. He was running behind J.C. stride for stride. Every time the man took a step, his arm made a big circular motion. The knife swept through the air as he tried to cut J.C. The knife never made contact because J.C. was too fast. If the man was a half-step faster, he would have inflicted a long open wound from the top of J.C.'s neck to the small of his back. The man stopped chasing J.C. a few feet from our front porch and turned around to walk back toward the blacktop. J.C. took a minute to catch his breath at the gate to our house then he walked up the porch and passed me without saying a word. He went into the house to get a steak knife and concealed it under his shirt. Then he went back to the exact same spot he had gotten chased from. I'm not sure what J.C. was thinking, but I could hear my subconscious saying, *I wouldn't go back down there. It just don't seem smart.* But, then again, J.C. wasn't in line the day that smarts were handed out.

The years passed in a blur, and the next thing I knew, Serena was three. My mother had given me the responsibility of dropping her off at the Headstart Child Care program before I left for school. I was also responsible for picking her up and bringing her home. There, I would watch her until my mother returned home from work.

The child care program she attended was about a quarter-mile from where we lived and just down the street from my bus stop. This was convenient for everyone. My mother would have Serena ready to go by seven o'clock in the morning. It would take me five minutes to walk her to Headstart, and then it would take me five minutes to get to my bus stop. The timing worked out perfectly. I would arrive at my bus stop at seven-fifteen in the morning, and my bus would arrive at seven-thirty.

I looked forward to dropping Serena off at Headstart because she was always dressed in cute outfits and always looked polished and clean. I had no idea how my mother was able to afford Serena's clothes (which all looked new) or where she was getting them from. I was just happy to see that Serena had all the clothes she needed and that my mother wasn't going to let her go without. After a couple of months of dropping Serena off at Headstart, her teacher began to recognize me. When we would see each other, she would address me by name. She was so nice that I would look forward to dropping my sister off to have that moment of kindness to offset my days filled with turmoil. Her kindness felt like a big hug that helped to compensate for the affection I did not receive at home.

It was winter now, and my routine was the same. I would drop Serena off then go to my bus stop and wait for the seventh-grade school bus. I had my books, my shirt and slacks, but no coat. I didn't have one. This was not by choice. It was just the way things were. I'm not sure whether my mother knew that I was going to school without a coat, and there was no way I was going to tell her. People in my family dealt with their own problems and issues the best way they could. Asking for help was futile. Just like when I asked my mother for help when J.C. was going to hit me with a belt and she did nothing.

The third time I showed up to get on the bus, the bus monitor, who coincidentally was my friend's mom, asked me if I was cold. I said, "No, I'm fine" and went to take my seat. As the bus was headed to school, I could hear her and the bus driver talking about me. They were discussing whether they should buy me a coat after seeing me without one for the third time in the cold weather. Ultimately they did not buy me one, but I thought it was a nice gesture. I certainly would have appreciated it, but at the time it didn't matter. My grandmother had told me, "You get to school, get to class, and listen to the teacher," so that's what I was doing, coat or no coat.

Believe it or not, I loved going to school. It was a place that provided me with many benefits. For example, many of my white classmates brought lunch from home because, as I had heard them say, "School lunch sucks!" After hearing this over and over, I concluded that they wouldn't need their lunch tickets. I also found out that many of them ate breakfast before they arrived at school, so I knew their breakfast tickets were up for grabs too.

The breakfast tickets were blue, and the lunch tickets were yellow. They came in a strip of five, and they were labeled with the day of the week and the date stamped on the back. Time was a factor. I devised a plan to commandeer as many breakfast and lunch tickets as possible. On Monday mornings I would walk around and ask my classmates who disliked the food the school provided for their breakfast and lunch tickets. On the weeks when I was lucky, I would end up with two sets of breakfast tickets and two sets of lunch tickets. Having those extra tickets would make my days a lot easier. I could focus on my school work and forget that I had come to school hungry.

There must have been something wrong with my classmates' taste buds because to me the breakfast and lunch the school provided tasted just like it had been prepared by a gourmet chef. Breakfast was always a serving of cereal. Most times it was the healthy stuff like Special K, Kix, and Corn Flakes. On the days when I was lucky, they served Apple Jacks or my favorite, Cocoa Krispies. These were my favorite because when I was done eating them, I was left with chocolate milk to drink. Fantastic!

Lunch was even better. Sandwiches, meatloaf, and shepherd's pie would typically be served. On my lucky days, spaghetti was served with a stick of cheese and a peanut butter sandwich that was cut so the pieces made two triangles. I know other kids hated it, but I loved and appreciated the school lunch. The school provided other benefits for me as well. The school furnace always worked, and I didn't have to worry about being cold, especially during the winter. It was almost like school was my better home away from home.

I did fair in most classes. I earned Cs and occasionally Bs, but I don't think this was an accurate reflection of my true ability or my capacity to learn. Maybe I could have done better if I weren't faced with the hardships of poverty. That's one thought, but my life and the circumstances I was dealing with did not allow room for excuses. One thing I am sure of above everything is that I did my best and gave it my all, just like my grandmother told me to do.

I didn't think it would ever happen, but by some miracle J.C. made a connection and was finally able to get a job. He had met Gregory Finch and Alphonso Click, who both worked at a foundry in Windsor, Connecticut. Greg's nickname was Finch, and Alphonso had three nicknames. I remember Finch using them for different purposes. When he was being polite, he would address Alphonso as Al. When he was trying to insult Al, he would call him Hardrock, and when he wanted to agitate Al, he would call him Clickety, Clickety. I am not quite sure how J.C. met these men, but they were somehow able to get him employed, despite his illiteracy. J.C.'s new job was labor-intensive grunt work—moving heavy iron molds that had been created by pouring molten steel into sand and plastic templates. The end products were commercial- and aerospace-grade steel casts that were used for bushings, fittings, shock and vibration fixtures, and high-pressure valves.

J.C.'s illiteracy and his acquisition of the labor-intensive work remind me of something my third-grade teacher Mr. Zamaha said. His voice still rings in my head so clearly that it seems like a miniature version of him is standing on my shoulder, talking in my ear.

I remember he was in the front of the class preparing for his lecture. He was patient as he waited for the classroom of about twenty-five eight-year-olds to settle down. The only reason he wasn't waiting for me was because of my grandmother. She was standing on my other shoulder saying, "You get to class and listen to the teacher," so I was ready to hear what he had to say. He didn't yell or raise his voice at all but calmly addressed the class and said, "Okay…keep talking. There are only two ways to work: one is with your brain, and the other is with your back. Those of you talking will be working with your backs." Wow! How right was he! I couldn't appreciate the truth in his words at the time, but now I get it. J.C.'s fate was what he was talking about.

Finch and Al would come over to our house and sit around with J.C. and my mom and drink on a regular basis. Finch was about six-four and weighed three hundred-plus pounds, and Al was five-seven and weighed one-thirty. Even though Al was small, his liquor intake was at least twice as much as Finch's. The outlandish behavior he displayed once he was intoxicated was evidence that he had drunk more than Finch and everyone else too. I will go out on a limb and make a wild guess that this was probably why he was given the nickname Hardrock, short for Hard Rock head! I'm pretty confident that I was right about this because I wasn't allowed to call Al by his nickname. Hardrock had to be one of those insulting nicknames that just stuck over time.

I was introduced to Finch and Al, but I wasn't allowed to stay around while they drank. Frankly, I didn't want to be around anyway. I had been around my share of alcoholics already and realized that there was nothing I could learn from them. Plus, I had a clear view of about fifty alcoholics if I just sat on my porch and looked in the direction of the blacktop.

I didn't really have an opinion about J.C.'s friends, but Haven did. He became familiar with who they were while he was home for a month-long visit. In a conversation we had after Finch and Al first starting visiting,

Haven told me that he had told J.C., "I don't like that guy [Finch]. He's out to get something you got." Haven never told me why he felt this way, but my guess is that he made some observations that gave him concern. At the time I couldn't see what he was talking about, so I didn't really pay it any attention. Neither did J.C.

After working for two months, J.C. "hurt" his back. The story was that he had lifted one of the heavy casts incorrectly. He was eventually let go because he had missed too many days of work. I bet he was thinking, *At least I gave it the good old college try*, or, in his case, *the good old high school drop-out try*. Losing his job was no stress for J.C. He knew he could count on my mother to pay all the bills and to fund the drinking get-togethers with Finch and Al. A few days later, he was back on the couch with a sandwich in one hand and the remote in the other.

My mother worked at a good company, Digital Equipment Corporation, better known as DEC. At the time, it was one of the largest computer manufacturers. My mother was an assembly technician. Her job was to touch up the computer boards and assemble the computer components. As a child, I loved to go visit her at work. Her site spanned a full block and had three large buildings that were protected by a seven-foot wrought-iron fence. There were three security shacks, one at every building, and there were also security stations inside the lobby of every building.

Whenever I visited my mother I would have to wait in the lobby of the main building while security paged her. I always turned my wait into a game. There were three internal entrances into the lobby—two from upstairs and one on the level where I waited. My game was to guess which way my mother would enter the lobby. I would guess correctly most of the time. My little game kept me occupied, but it was not really that important. I was just happy to see my mother when she arrived. She would always have on her powder-blue smock that had her name, Mattie, embroidered above the upper left pocket. She would have to sign out then she could go outside on her break, and I could see her for about a half hour before she had to go back to work.

For years I didn't know why visits to my mother's job left me confused, upset, and angry about things that just did not seem to add up. I was confused because I could not understand why my mother had to be at work all day while J.C. sat at home. Something just felt wrong about that. I could not understand why my mother had to bear the full load of taking care of her children and supporting J.C. too. I was upset because of all the abuse my mother went through. It was the same thing over and over. Trip, my father, and J.C. had all verbally and physically abused my mom. I was angry because my mother kept letting this happen. I wanted it to stop. I wanted her to make one final decision to not form relationships with alcoholic abusers.

Working for a company of the size and prestige of DEC certainly had its benefits. Once a year, every year, Digital would sponsor an employee appreciation day that was held at the High Meadows recreation grounds. They were even kind enough to provide free bus rides from the city to this beautiful rural location. I remember the things that I would see on the thirty-five-minute bus ride to High Meadows. I saw long, beautiful, deep green lawns, homes that seemed to be a half mile apart. Every home had its own garage, and almost every single one was flying an American flag on the front porch canopy. The homes and scenery were beautiful but nothing I could really relate to or truly understand. They just became visual snapshots that I took on the way to the outing. High Meadows was a beautiful recreational ground that had an Olympic-size swimming pool, horseback rides, bocce ball, shuffleboard, and relay games. There was kite flying, bingo, card games, and, last but not least, free food! Any kind and as much as you wanted! Hot dogs, hamburgers, fried chicken, French fries, and enough ribs to feed an Army. They had all types of breads, fruits, and any dessert you could think of or dream of. For me, this was simply unbelievable. At that time I had never been to Disneyland, but if I knew one thing it was that it couldn't be better than this. I'm not sure whether the event planners knew, but in my world the High Meadows event became legendary. Word about its yearly arrival spread in my neighborhood. Every year, a few weeks before the event, I would inevitably be asked by friends and acquaintances whether my mom was going to have any extra High Meadows tickets.

The arrival of the High Meadows event was an indication that it was time for our summer vacation. Every year when we had enough money, J.C., Ervin, my mom, and I would pile in the car, get on I-91 South, and head to New Haven. We would see everybody. My grandfather, my brother Haven, my uncle Ike, my cousins, and I would get to go see my grandmother and dad in West Haven. Our first stop when we got off the highway was to my grandfather's house. His place coincidentally was right down the street from the Ashmun Street projects, where we lived until I was almost five years old.

Without fail, every time we showed up, my grandfather would be sitting on the front porch in his wheelchair. He always had on a pair of the coolest dark-brown tinted sunglasses and a white Kangol hat. He had an air about him that always brought to mind the words "Yeah, that's right; I got this!" He was the coolest, most confident single-leg amputee that I have ever known.

When we would arrive on his street, it was fun seeing him sitting on the porch outside enjoying the weather. My grandfather wasn't one to show a lot of emotion, but somehow I knew he was happy and excited to see us all, even if he didn't say it. Most times his nonverbal indication of happiness was a slow nod of his head, which looked like he was responding "yes" to a question he had just been asked.

Being hungry was never a concern at my grandfather's because he loved to cook. There was always a pot on the stove simmering cubed-sized pieces of beef and pork with corn and potatoes in a vinegar and mustard broth with crushed red pepper. It was either that or maybe he was making hogs' head cheese, hog maws, pigs' feet, or shredded beef. The meal wasn't complete until he created one of his dessert masterpieces. Some of his favorites were sweet potato pie and upside-down pineapple cake. You name it, he cooked it. When he really wanted to enjoy himself, he would get Haven to dig a pit in his backyard so that he could slow roast a whole pig. Cooking—that was his passion. The guns and bootleg business was only his livelihood.

We were in the town where my mother grew up, so she knew lots of people. This meant that the time she spent visiting my grandfather was brief. It was typical that I would only see her when we were greeting my grandfather hello and when we were saying goodbye to him and leaving to go back home. I didn't mind not seeing my mother because this gave me a chance to hang around my brother Haven. He would usually have me assist him with cooking or with chores, and sometimes he would take me to the store with him. If I wasn't doing that, I was being entertained by the people coming and going through the revolving door of my grandfather's bootleg business. Sometimes the customers appeared to be good friends of my grandfather's, and sometimes the customer would be pissy drunk strangers looking for their next drink. Other forms of entertainment in my grandfather's living room included seeing him watch a Cassius Clay boxing match (he hadn't changed his name to Mohammed Ali yet) or seeing him cuss and swear at the players in the football game who made a bad play. I had a great time whenever I visited.

My mother and J.C. would always go visit one of my mother's best friends, who I came to know as Aunt Maggie. However, she and my mom were not related at all. I had visited Aunt Maggie with my mother several times, so I knew that her apartment was about a quarter-mile from my grandfather's house. I had seen my mother and J.C. there playing cards, smoking, and drinking every time they visited. There was always music playing in the background: Al Green, Teddy Pendergrass, and some foul-mouthed lady named Millie Jackson. I remember the kind of things she would say on her records. It was always stuff like "oh, baby, do this to me, do that to me." Then she would say stuff like "Millie don't give a @#!!" Very unhealthy music for a young child, but I had already been exposed to so much that it really had no impact. It was party time when my mother and J.C. visited Aunt Maggie. First she would greet them, and then she would get on the phone and invite as many people as she could over to her place to join the party.

My aunt Maggie was really nice to me all the time. When she addressed me, she would never call me by my name. She would always say, "How you doing, baby?" or "You want something, baby?" That was my aunt Maggie, sweet as can be. She was so nice to me that sometimes I felt like I wanted her to be my mom.

Just like every one of my mother's friends, Aunt Maggie by definition was an alcoholic too. She wasn't a rude drunk, though. Under the influence she became calm and peaceful, but she was still quick to react if she thought someone was being disrespectful. I saw it firsthand during a time when my mother asked Aunt Maggie to watch me.

I remember we needed to go to a department store so she could buy some things for her home. As she selected the items she needed, she let me push the carriage down the aisles. When she was finished picking her items, we went to checkout. I hadn't been paying attention to the interaction between her and the cashier, so I was caught off guard when I heard my aunt Maggie say, "Next time you snatch my money, Im'a reach over this counter and snatch you!" My ears stung in disbelief only because I had never seen Aunt Maggie this way, but she quickly returned back to the sweet lady I knew. Seconds after she finished putting the verbal lashing on the cashier, she turned to me and in the sweetest voice said, "Baby, you want a hotdog?" I said, "Yes, Aunt Maggie" as I watched the cashier carefully give her back the change from the sale. And that was that.

It was this visit to New Haven that finally separated J.C. and my mother. During one of the get-togethers at *Aunt Maggie's*, a man named Larry was killed. The story I received indirectly was that a mistake occurred while showing or handling a gun. The result was that Larry ended up dead. I didn't believe this story then, and I don't believe it now. At the time, I had a feeling that there had been an argument and someone, probably J.C., shot Larry dead. After this happened, I believe my aunt Maggie panicked and demanded that J.C. and two other men move Larry's body from her home before it was discovered. This is what I believe happened from the small pieces of information I received.

The part of the story that I am absolutely sure of is that detectives showed up, did an investigation, and, in the end, the jury decided that J.C. would spend the next ten years of his life in prison. Since J.C. and I were barely acquaintances, his absence was not going to be anything that I would notice. Serena was too young to understand what was going on with her father, and my mother was resilient and would always quickly fill the empty space of her disposable suitors. For J.C., this meant that no tears were going to be shed for him.

J.C.'s misfortune had started an epidemic. As he was taking the bus ride to his new home where he would receive his new black-and-white-striped two-piece outfit, the court notified Ervin that he would now be living in a group home detention center for the next year. Ervin had finally done it. He had worked so very hard to become a group home resident. The court granted his wish and gave Ervin his prison starter kit. Real prison would be next. I wasn't privy to the exact reasons Ervin now had to live at the detention center, but I had an idea. My guess was that all those meetings he had missed with his case worker, Tyrone, and his thievery had finally caught up with him. Now it was time to pay the consequences.

My mom waited about six months before she decided to move on with her life and fill the void J.C. had left. With no moral compass, she began dating J.C.'s friend Finch. Now I understood what my brother

Haven meant when he told J.C., "I don't like that guy; he's out to get something you got." Once I realized that Finch would now be part of my mother's life, I lost all hope for her. With another bad choice for a male companion, I knew my mother was never going to realize where she went wrong with Trip, Butchy, and J.C. J.C.'s prison sentence was a blessing in disguise. This was her chance to purge herself of the ignorant, alcoholic, women abusers, but she was not going to capitalize. Her choice to date Finch was actually a giant step in the wrong direction.

It didn't take me long to realize that Finch's self-worth started and ended with having power over everything and everyone that resided in *his* house. I bet he sized up his goal of taking over his new domain and realized that it should be fairly easy to achieve. Ervin was living in a group home, and Haven was living in New Haven with my grandfather. He would not have them to deal with. This left Serena and me as potential obstacles, but we were both powerless and had no say in our destinies. Serena was four, I was fourteen, and we both relied on our mother to make decisions for us.

Finch wasted no time as he started building his empire of control. Two things that he quickly realized were that my mother was an easily influenced, co-dependent woman and that she did not consider the impact of her decisions on her children. Armed with this information, Finch put his plan into effect. The first change he made without a lot of thought or planning was convincing my mom to buy a home in Sixteen Acres. Wow! The Acres, as it was called, was a suburb of Springfield, and most of the well-to-do people lived there. I didn't know about mortgages, budgets, or how the bank system worked, but even at the age of fourteen I knew something seemed wrong with the decision they were making. We had lived at or below the poverty line all my life, so it wasn't reasonable to think that the addition of Finch's modest salary would make it possible for us to all of a sudden afford to buy a home in the Acres. This was my personal opinion of the situation. If I had voiced this opinion, it would have been taken as though I was being disrespectful. At the rate decisions were being made, I wouldn't have had time to speak up anyway. The decision to buy a home in the Acres had been made.

I remember initially feeling indifferent about the move to the Acres. I started to get sad once I realized that I would no longer be within walking distance of my friends. When I told them I was moving, they also became unhappy. We started thinking that we wouldn't see each other very much because none of us were old enough to drive, and my new house was going to be about ten miles away from where they lived. In anticipation of my move we saw each other every day, and we made an agreement to keep in touch any way we could.

Moving day finally arrived, and I saw our new home for the first time. I'm not sure I really appreciated the lifestyle upgrade, perhaps because I was still only fourteen. However, I did notice the drastic improvement. We had a yard with grass that had to get cut. We had our own driveway on the side of the house. The exterior of the house had weather-proof siding. I had my own bedroom. We had a basement where I could set up my own living area and be as noisy as I wanted. We had a washer and dryer. I no longer had to lug garbage bags of clothes to the Merri-Maid Laundromat. We had a dishwasher. The sink had a garbage disposal. The bathroom had a tub and a shower. Every room except the kitchen and bathrooms had a carpeted floor. I almost forgot: the living room had a real fireplace! This house was too good to be true, especially compared to our apartment in the Ashmun Street projects.

These new accommodations were amazing, but Finch wasn't finished yet. He also convinced my mother that they could afford to purchase a practically new automobile. One day it just appeared in the driveway, and my mother told me that it was our new car. She and Finch had gone to the Mutual Ford car dealership and purchased a one-owner, metallic green Ford Crown Victoria. This was the best car we ever had! It was dent-free, the paint job was immaculate, it had power everything—windows, seats, sunroof, key locks, etc. The inside was spotless, and the seats were made of a plush material that gave each passenger a custom-contoured feeling. This car was absolutely amazing!

Finch had his kingdom all set up now. He had a nice home; he had a nice car. All he had left to do was to *take* the respect that he was due.

Finch had a suspicious air that followed him. He gave off an untrustworthy vibe. Anytime I walked just outside his personal space I could see him looking at me using his peripheral vision. It was like he was continuously on guard waiting for me to make the wrong move. I wasn't sure why he was like this. The only reasonable explanation was that he had done something that he knew he would have to pay for one day. It made me wonder.

Finch was the type of guy that absolutely demanded respect. He made this known to everyone in his house and was not shy about it. One of his favorite phrases was "I pay the cost to be the boss." Most of the time, he would use it as leverage to get me to do things. Sometime he would just say it to reaffirm his dominant posture, and other times he would say it just to say it. His other favorite phrase was "I laugh and joke, but I don't play." I would hear this constantly, even when he had no reason or basis to say it. The first few times he blurted his power statements I checked to see if he was joking or half serious, but this wasn't the case. His face was stone cold. He did not laugh; he did not smile. That's when I knew he was warning me that I would have to deal with him if I got out of line.

My bedroom was upstairs, so I needed to walk down a flight of stairs in order to get to the kitchen. When I would come downstairs in the mornings, I would usually see Finch in the kitchen preparing to go to work. Every time I would reach the bottom of the stairs, Finch and I would make eye contact for a brief moment, and he wouldn't say a word. He always waited for me to show respect. This meant that I had to say good morning first. It was clear to me that Finch did not know anything about me. My grandmother had raised me to respect adults. For that fact alone I was already prepared to give him respect—he did not need to take it. I never bothered to tell my mother about the constant power plays that Finch made because she would have done nothing. She had already shown me that when I asked for her help in dealing with J.C.

I don't know if Finch just wanted to make things difficult for me, but I remember a time when he purchased a manual grass cutter, the kind that you had to push. It had the twisted metal blades and the wood roller that would push the grass down. He bought this so that I could cut the grass in our backyard. There was a small problem, though. The grass was about four feet high, and the blades of the grass cutter had not been sharpened in a millennium. I could tell because they were rusty. I guess Finch figured a little elbow grease and lower back power could make up for the shortcomings of the cutter. I watched as he struggled to cut down a four-square-foot patch of grass as he gave me a demonstration of how to use the cutter. It took him ten minutes to get the area he was cutting to look decent. I'm sure he realized that it took too much effort and time to get this done. Yet now he wanted me to cut the entire yard, which was about fifty square feet. He said, "There you go" and gave me the cutter. Then he went to sit on the porch and sipped a beer as he watched me struggle with the absolutely inappropriate tool.

I did my best, but my effort was futile. The grass cutter was just flattening the grass and not cutting very much, but I was still trying. Sweat was dripping in my eyes, and my arms were tired, but somehow

I managed to get the yard looking decent after about an hour and a half. Once I was finished Finch said, "You did good. I'm proud of you." This was another one of the things he liked to say. One might think that his comment was made to acknowledge the good job I did, but the vibe that followed the words gave me a feeling that he wasn't proud of me at all. What the words really conveyed was that he was proud that I obeyed his command. We should always remember that *he paid the cost to be the boss.*

Finch had a passive-aggressive personality that he used to control people, render them powerless, and establish his dominance. One of his passive-aggressive actions was leaving Comet scouring powder in the tub when he finished using it. The first time he did this I figured he was going to come back and wash out the tub once he was dressed, but he never did. I thought this was pretty inconsiderate and forced everyone into his game of manipulation. Others who wanted to take a bath after Finch were now forced to wash out the tub first. I was taught that it was my responsibility to clean up behind myself—I'm not sure what Finch was taught.

Ervin had now been in the group home for a year, and it was time for him to come home. While Ervin was away, Finch did everything he could to provoke me to start trouble with him. Finch tried the same "I pay the cost to be the boss" power plays with Ervin when he returned home. This time Finch found the trouble he was looking for.

I had already thought about Ervin and Finch living in the same home and knew it just couldn't work. Ervin was now seventeen. He had gone through the crucible of hate, neglect, and abuse and was transformed into a temperamental, troublesome young adult. For a long time I had thought that trouble followed Ervin wherever he went, until I finally realized that Ervin *was* the trouble.

The first morning Ervin was back, he and Finch got into it. I caught the tail end of the interaction when I entered the kitchen. Finch and Ervin were face to face, staring each other down. They were in a stand-off. Then the next thing I knew they were locked up like they were in a wrestling match. I knew there was no way Ervin was going to win this fight because Finch was six-four and weighed three hundred-plus pounds, and Ervin was six-one and weighed one-fifty.

My thought was that they were in this wrestling match to establish dominance and determine who was the king of the castle, the boss, the head honcho. I likened it to a National Geographic documentary in which a rogue gorilla tried to get acceptance from an already established gorilla family and was rejected. His next move, which was foolish, was to challenge the alpha male's dominant position to see if he could take over the gorilla family. The outcome of the battle was that the rogue gorilla had to settle for second in command. He had put up a good fight, but in the end he lost the battle with the alpha male. In the battle between Ervin and Finch, Ervin was going to have to settle for second in command as well.

Finch put Ervin in a full nelson just before they fell to the floor. He ended up on top of Ervin and kept him trapped so that he could not move. He lay on Ervin for a few seconds to confirm his status as the alpha male in the house. Once he felt the message was clear, he let Ervin up, and they both went their separate ways. I went outside to play.

Of course there was no intervention from my mother when she heard about this incident. She didn't intervene when my father made me feel bad and cry, she didn't intervene when J.C. bossed me around like I was his personal servant, and she didn't say a word to Finch about the strong arm and manipulation tactics he subjected me to. It made sense that she would not get involved or be concerned with her boyfriend beating up her seventeen-year-old son either. This is probably why Ervin only stayed with us for about a week after that. Once he left, he and I had no contact. I had no idea where he found shelter, how he got fed, or how he was able to survive, but I would find out later.

We had been in the Acres for about five months when my mother decided that it was time to see my grandfather in New Haven. She, Finch, Serena, and I took a road trip to go visit him. Trips to New Haven always made me happy because I knew I would see my big brother Haven. I was even happier this trip because we were going to meet his girlfriend for the first time. This was thrilling enough, but there was one more thing: she was pregnant. I was ecstatic!

When we arrived in New Haven, my mother introduced Finch to my grandfather, and then we met Haven's girlfriend, Sherry. I think everyone including myself had several expectations that Sherry unfortunately did not meet. I don't think she was an equal to Haven in any area. Physically and mentally she fell extremely short. The one redeeming attribute she did have was she was nice, and I guess that counts for something. Even though I had my opinion, I kept it to myself. I realized that I was not in a position to judge anyone's choices, not even my brother's.

We stayed for the weekend and returned back home. It was then that I learned that my mother and Finch both felt that Haven's choice to be with Sherry was so disturbing that they made contact with him and insisted that he move back to Springfield. I don't know what was said in the conversation, but it must have been compelling because he packed his things, moved back to Springfield, and let our cousin Rodney take over his job of assisting my grandfather.

It was nice having my big brother back home. He seemed to settle right in from what I could see and didn't have the same power struggles with Finch that I had. That put me at ease. I didn't want anything to threaten my plan to rebuild my splintered family.

Haven and Serena were with me, and we were living as "family." All we were missing was my brother Ervin. If he could have been home with us I would have been truly happy. That wasn't going to happen because Ervin had gotten into more trouble. I didn't have any details; all I knew was that he was involved in some bad things and wasn't coming home anytime soon.

My mother and Finch told Haven to take his time finding work so that he could consider his options. He wasn't under any pressure to take the first job he found. I'm not sure what his plan was at this point, but it was great seeing him every day when I got home from school.

We spent a lot of time playing videogames at a little convenience store that wasn't too far from where we lived. Our favorite game was Q-bert. The video display showed a three-dimensional pyramid that had multicolored squares. Players had control of Q-bert, an orange aardvark-looking critter that could bounce from each landing with the goal of getting to the top of the pyramid. Reaching this goal was incredibly difficult because there were many things falling out of the sky that could kill Q-bert and end your game. There was also a very dangerous snake named Coily that would chase you around the pyramid. Coily's sole purpose was to kill Q-bert and end your game. Running out of time was another way that your game could end. The only way to extend time was to get Q-bert food by chasing different shaped items and bouncing on top of them. I think the main reason we liked playing Qbert was because we saw ourselves as Q-bert. The little orange critter had to overcome many obstacles and was always faced with the imminent threat of death. Symbolically, the game represented a microcosm of our real lives.

I knew it would only be a matter of time before Finch would get the urge to flex his muscle again to show me who was boss. This time when he did it, my brother Haven was present.

Haven and I were playing cards at the kitchen table, and Finch was in the kitchen near the sink straightening up. He removed a trash bag from the garbage container under the kitchen sink, closed it with a twist tie, and told me to take it outside. Most of the time when Finch told me to do something I did it immediately in order to satisfy his need to feel powerful.

I began to stand up to take the garbage outside right in the middle of our hand. I started to sit back down once I heard Haven tell Finch that as soon as we were finished with the hand he would take it out. Unfortunately that wasn't good enough. Finch replied, "I told Maurice to do it."

From the look on Haven's face I could tell that he did not like the fact that Finch wanted me to jump when he said jump. To avoid problems I told Haven not to worry about it and asked him to wait a minute while I took the garbage out real quick. That's it; it was over. The trash was put out, and Finch's need to feel like the all-powerful was satisfied. For once I just wanted us to all get along. Seven years later Rodney King would utter this same sentiment on CNN to the entire country.

A few months had passed. It was winter now, and Christmas was coming. My brother Haven took advantage of the inclement weather and went snow shoveling to earn money as he had always done when we were younger. I remember that he would always take me with him and share his earnings with me. I was always excited to help, but my winter clothing was never adequate. My boots and gloves were never waterproof, so when the snow would melt, the ice-cold wetness would penetrate to my fingers and toes. Every time this happened, I became a burden because I could no longer help. Unfortunately, this usually wouldn't happen until we were far from home and when business started to get good. I think that if I would have asked, Haven would have stopped snow shoveling and would have taken me home, but I didn't want to interrupt his opportunity to make money. Instead, I would tolerate the cold and just wait for him to finish shoveling as many driveways and walkways as he could. Even though I never really helped much, Haven never became upset with me. He would just tell me what to do to stay warm while I waited. This was the scenario every time I went snow shoveling, yet I still decided to go. For me, the best part of snow shoveling was getting home so that I could take off my cold, wet boots and gloves. Then I would snuggle up to the radiator to get warm and let my frost bitten fingers and toes thaw out.

We received news from New Haven that my grandfather's health had taken a turn for the worse. His diabetes had started to debilitate his functionality, which made it impossible for him to sustain his bootleg business. He was now living in the first-floor apartment of my uncle Ike's house. If my grandfather needed assistance with anything, help would just be upstairs on the second floor.

The update they received was that my grandfather was essentially being neglected. This bothered my mother so badly that she wanted to move my grandfather to Springfield so that she could take care of him. She discussed it with Finch, and he agreed that we should go to Connecticut to get him.

When we arrived at my uncle's house, I remember being the first one to run inside to the see my grandfather. As I entered the apartment on the first floor, I noticed that all the lights were out and that it was cold. The temperature in the room felt like the heat had not been turned on. Something was wrong. It was the middle of February in Connecticut and people still had their furnaces going.

When I opened the bedroom door I saw my grandfather huddled under two light sheets that he had pulled over his head to stay warm. When I saw him, I felt like crying, but I held it together as I stood in the doorway and said, "Hi, Granddad." He slowly lifted his head, looked at me, and said, "Hey, boy." Then he lay back down. This was the first time I saw my grandfather outside his tough exterior. He wasn't angry, he wasn't swinging his crutch or cane at anyone, and he wasn't threatening anyone with a gun. The spark of life and vigor my grandfather once had was gone. He was unable to protect himself. He was vulnerable. Seeing him like this was a humbling experience.

I had regained my composure by the time everyone else had come in to see him. We stayed and visited for a while then we packed everything up and headed back to Springfield. I was in my glory. Moving my grandfather back to Springfield to live with us was great. Pieces of my broken family were being glued back together one by one. Everyone except

Ervin would be together for Christmas. I knew that having him with us would have been the answer to all my wishes, but instead of focusing on his absence, I remained thankful for the family that was there.

It was a fantastic Christmas. Everyone received gifts, but Serena received the most. I felt more joy when she opened her gifts than I did when I opened mine. I was living through her excitement. Her happiness, joy, and smile were recompense for the years I went without.

Two months had passed, and my grandfather settled right in to his new home. I had never seen him so happy. He was the nicest man you could imagine. He smiled all the time and even tried to go out of his way to have a conversation if you were in his presence. He was absolutely in love with Serena—she was his pride and joy. He would hold her in his lap as he sat in his wheelchair and entertain her. He played peek-a-boo with her, he would give her little baby kisses, and pretend to have baby talk conversations with her. It was a good feeling to see my grandfather happy for once. This by itself was great, but there were more positive changes. It seemed as though my grandfather's presence had a positive effect on Finch's "king of the castle" attitude. He didn't boss me around as much, and it seemed like he stopped instigating trouble between us. I was enjoying the harmony among everyone in my household. Things were absolutely fantastic, but the black cloud of despair was not finished with my family yet. Things were just getting started.

I saw the whole thing and had no idea what to do. We had just finished dinner. My grandfather started to convulse and began to jerk back and forth in his wheelchair. His movements were so erratic that he tipped his chair over and fell to the floor. Frantically, my brother Haven yelled, "What did he eat? What did he eat?" As he was shouting his question, he put two fingers in my grandfather's mouth to try to remove whatever might be choking him. His effort didn't help. My grandfather just kept thrashing around, and his whole body was shaking. Haven yelled "ouch!" and quickly pulled his fingers out of my grandfather's mouth. If he hadn't removed his fingers when he did, my grandfather would have bitten them off. His mouth was quickly moving up and down, and his eyes rolled to the back of his head. It looked like he was having a seizure.

My mother called for an ambulance and notified us that it was on the way. Finch was holding my mom to comfort her. Once I realized that Serena was watching my grandfather kick and convulse on the floor, I took her into the living room so she couldn't see what was happening. By the time the ambulance arrived and the paramedics entered to check my grandfather's vital signs, he had stopped moving. I overheard one of them tell my mother that it looked like he had a massive coronary and that it did not look good. I knew he was breaking it to my mom gently. I knew exactly what his words meant: my grandfather was dead, and he wasn't coming back.

I began thinking about why my grandfather was dead and what could have been done to save him. I had a thought that he would have probably lived twenty more years if we would have left him alone in that cold, dark room in my uncle's house. My brother Haven must have been thinking the same thing. He told me not to be surprised if people blame my grandfather's death on my mother. It was her idea to move him to Springfield. He said it was the nature of people. He said that they would all probably say that my grandfather was doing fine in Connecticut and that we should have left him alone. I would have never believed such a ridiculous assertion. I had seen his previous living conditions firsthand, and I had witnessed him happier than he had ever been in his life during the two months he had lived with us. I knew exactly what killed my grandfather—happiness.

We had my grandfather's body sent back to New Haven to be buried since he had spent most of his life there. I only have scattered memories of the burial, but words that my brother said to me at his funeral have forever been burned into my mind. As Haven and I watched my grandfather get lowered into the ground, Haven said, "I just lost my best friend."

My luck with rebuilding my family had run out. I didn't know it at the time, but the loss of my grandfather was the beginning of a domino effect. His death represented the first domino that was tipped over into a labyrinth of other dominoes waiting to fall.

Shortly after we buried my grandfather, I noticed an eerie silence in my house. I knew that the loss of my grandfather had something to do with it, but it wasn't the only thing I was sensing. I overheard several conversations between Finch and my mom, and I was able to surmise that we were going to lose our home. My guess was that they didn't tell me about it directly because they were too embarrassed. I don't think they would have admitted that to themselves. They probably rationalized it by thinking that they were *protecting* me by withholding the bad news, but my life was a constant procession of bad news. No pun intended. Losing our home was not going to impact me at all.

The nonexistent financial planning had caught up to them. They were finally finding out that the monthly mortgage for the house in the Acres and the monthly payments for the new car were too much. Finch and my mom were taken to housing court and were evicted. Under the terms of the eviction they were ordered to move out of the house, to pay rent that was owed, and to pay restitution to the landlord. The court gave us thirty days to move on our own. After that, people with badges would come give us a hand.

It was back to reality. The pipedream of sustaining the lifestyle that the Acres brought was over. My mother found an apartment three blocks from our old neighborhood. It was back to life in the ghetto, and this time we took two giant steps backward. This was the second domino to fall. Our new second-floor apartment on Union Street was just as bad as our first apartment on Eastern Avenue, the one that had all the plumbing problems. I hated this place not because I was spoiled by living in the Acres but because it just never felt like home.

After losing in housing court, my mother and Finch had no money left to turn on the heat in our apartment. It was the dead of winter, and every room was cold. It was so cold inside the house that I could see the fog my breath created when I talked. The back door of the apartment was broken. It had to stay that way because there was no money to get it fixed. I felt paranoid and unsafe every night at bedtime. I would lie in bed unable to get to sleep, thinking that someone was going to sneak in the backdoor and kill us all.

We did not have a phone, so we had to walk to the payphone if we wanted to make a call. The refrigerator did not work because the high-voltage line in the kitchen was defective. We lived on fast food because there was no food in the kitchen, and the cupboards were bare. If my mother wasn't around to buy something to eat I would just have to figure it out. Sometimes this meant microwaving a pack of Ramen noodles for dinner or making a box of macaroni and cheese without adding milk and butter.

This was my new home; this was my new life. I hated this place, but, ironically, I wasn't inconvenienced too much because I had already experienced a life with less. You know the saying—*been there, done that.* I also thought that even though I was back living in these conditions, I could now say that I experienced what it was like to have lived in the Acres, even if it had been temporary.

When pushed, there are people who fall; there are others who push back. I now realize this—there is an appropriate reaction for every action.

"Push me, I will fall… Push me, I will push back."

Family

"Together we fall... Divided we stand"

The only good thing about moving to Union Street was that I once again lived right around the corner from the friends I had left seven months earlier. We were back within walking distance of each other and instantly reconnected. We were together all the time. Our favorite activities were playing basketball and attending the local teen parties. My friends made my reintroduction back to ghetto life easier, but they could not prevent what was going to happen next. Domino three was about to fall.

My friends and I had been out all night at one of the teen parties that was held at a local college auditorium. We listened to the music and challenged each other to approach girls that the other two picked out. This game was exciting and scary at the same time. We probably only played it because, at fourteen, we were all still terrified of approaching girls. Most of the time, whoever was challenged chickened out. The party ended at 10:00 p.m., and it was time to go home. We left the auditorium and walked back to our neighborhood. My street was the first one we reached. When we got there, I said, "Catch you later," and headed down the street to my house.

When I reached my house, I noticed that the front door was wide open. I could also see that the light that illuminated the hallway and staircase was on. This sent up red flags in my mind. We never left the door open at night, and we never left the light on. I started to think that maybe someone in my family was moving furniture or something in or out of the house. My thoughts changed quickly as I started walking up the stairs. I was about halfway to the top when I noticed the blood streaks on the walls. At that moment, my brain signals went haywire. A billion thoughts crossed my mind: *Who was hurt? Did someone break in and hurt one of my family members? Are they still here?* I looked up and then down the stairs and noticed that the blood streaks started at the top of the stairs and ended at the bottom. When I first entered the hallway I hadn't noticed this. I wasn't afraid, but I was on alert in case I ran into the intruder. I continued up the stairs. I needed to find out what had happened.

The first room at the top of the stairs was the living room. I noticed all the lights were on and it was eerily quiet. I called out, "Hello, hello?" No one answered, so I assumed that nobody was home. As I walked toward my mother's room, I noticed a crimson red spot about the size of a small plate on the living room floor. From what I had seen in the hallway, I knew that it was blood. I still was trying to piece things together. Was my mother hurt? What happened?

What caught my attention was not only how quiet it was inside the house but how quiet it was, period. On any given night a police car siren could be heard in the distance, or the sound of children playing in the street would fill the air. Not that night. I wasn't sure what to do next, so I walked back downstairs and stood at the front gate for a few minutes. I looked up and down the street and still had no answers.

I started slowly walking to the end of the street when a car pulled up alongside the curb next to me. Finch's brother was in the passenger seat, and his friend Joey was driving the car. I had met Joey through his visits to see Finch. The first thing I noticed was that Finch's brother was crying. Before I could ask what happened, Joey asked me if I had seen my brother Haven. I said, "No, I haven't." Then he said, "Your brother hurt Finch. He hurt him real bad." At that moment I put it all together: the blood on the walls, the empty house. I was instantly on guard.

The first thought in my mind was that Finch's brother had a gun and was going to try to kill me, so I made sure I wasn't in his direct view by standing closer to the back door of the car. I had noticed that the police do this when they stop motorists to give them traffic tickets. I figured that they did this so that it would be difficult for a person in the front seat to take a shot at them. Standing in this position would make it so that the shooter was in an awkward aiming position. It was probably a good thing I was thinking this way, but I was way off. Finch's brother and Joey were not there to kill or hurt me; they wanted to retaliate against my brother Haven. As they pulled away from the curb, Finch's brother just kept crying, and they drove off into the night. After they left, I just stood at the end of my street on the corner thinking about what I should do next. I had nowhere else to go, so my only choice was to go back home.

As I approached the house, I noticed a dark-blue Crown Victoria that was parked in front. I started to walk up the front porch when a man got out of the car and asked, "Do you live here?" I replied, "Yes." I figured that he was a detective. A moment later, another detective got out of the car. They both began to ask me several questions. It felt like I was being interrogated. They asked me if I had seen my brother. They wanted to know if he had any friends, and they wanted to know where his friends lived.

I only knew one of Haven's friends. His name was Tom. He and Haven used to play chess regularly at our house when we lived on Chester Street. The detectives made me get in the back of the Crown Victoria and told me to show them the way to Tom's house. When we arrived, they brought me with them to the front door. They knocked on the door, and when Tom's dad answered, they asked if Tom was home. Tom's dad called for him, and they both stood in the doorway as they spoke with the detectives. I looked up to see Tom and his dad staring at me as if I should not have brought the detectives to their house. I felt my face flush because I was embarrassed to be there. When the police finished their inquisition, they took me back to my house.

I waited at home alone for two hours until my mother, Serena, and Finch's friend Al arrived at the apartment. This was when I finally heard the story of what had happened. My mother told me that Finch and Haven had an argument and that Haven went to get his gun and shot and killed Finch.

When I first heard the story I became angry, confused, and distraught. I kept picturing Finch's face. Every time I visualized it, there was no smile, and it looked like he had just finished saying, "I pay the cost to be the boss." I wasn't sad that Finch was dead. He had not made any positive contributions to my adolescent development; he had done exactly the opposite. I felt the same way I did when J.C. went to prison—I really didn't care.

As my mother continued telling me the details of what had happened, my emotions fluctuated between worry about what was going to happen to my brother and anger for the things he had been taught. Destiny was upon us. My brother, once a young, naïve child, had been raised to put no value on human life. His seven-year-old hands were dirtied when he was instructed to bring a knife to my mother so she could hurt someone. At fifteen he was persuaded to live the life of a bootlegger's assistant. He was encouraged to carry a gun and taught how to use it as means of self-preservation. He learned that anger justified violence and death. It was no surprise to me that I was standing in my living room near a small pool of blood, in the middle of a crime scene.

We had seen our mother threaten every man in her life. Each of us received a personal request from our mother to help her kill or hurt these men. It was foreseeable that my mother or one of us would one day take a life.

According to my mother, Finch and Haven had gone out gambling together. When they came back home, Finch said something that insulted Haven. After a verbal altercation, Haven went to his bedroom to get his gun. She tried to stop Haven as he rushed back in Finch's direction with his loaded gun. She pleaded with Haven not to retaliate and even blocked his path. Her efforts were in vain. She said Haven pushed by her and went into the bedroom where Finch was sitting and shot him. Finch tried to rise to his feet and follow Haven out of the bedroom, but he collapsed in the living room after a few steps. She said Haven then shot Finch twice more before he fled the scene.

(News articles that you will read have been retyped because the original articles are of poor quality. No content has been changed. The provided articles might have published errors about the actual facts. For example, in the article you are about to read, the publisher reports that Haven was the brother and not the son of Ms. Triplett.)

Springfield Union
Friday, April 20, 1984
Police seek gunman in slaying
By RICHARD NADOLSKI (Union Staff)

Springfield detectives were searching early today for a gunman who killed a 26-year old man by shooting him in the face with a .44 caliber revolver during an altercation in his second-floor apartment on Union Street late Thursday. Gregory Finch was shot in the living room of his apartment, part of a two family-frame house at 650 Union St. shortly before 8:35 p.m., police said. Finch was rushed to Baystate Medical Center, Wesson Unit by Baystate Ambulance Service. Doctors spent an hour attempting to revive him and Finch was pronounced dead in the emergency room at 9:35 p.m, according to a nursing supervisor. Police said Finch's girlfriend, Mattie Triplett, of the same address, was in the apartment at the time of the shooting and they were questioning her at police headquarters late Thursday. Police broadcast a lookout for Ms. Triplett's brother, Haven Triplett, for questioning in the shooting. The high-powered handgun was not recovered and it was believed that it was still in the possession of Finch's assailant.

⌘ ⌘ ⌘

Police received a report that a man wanted in the shooting was seen shortly after the incident inside Phelan's Package store at 166 Eastern Ave. Police rushed to the store but the suspect had left. "Apparently there was an argument," said Detective Sgt. Andrew Canevari. Canevari declined comment on what the argument was about. A neighbor, who asked not to be identified, said she heard two loud gunshots come from Finch's apartment. "I heard two loud bangs. Boom. Boom. Next thing I know, I heard sirens," she said. A man who identified himself as a relative of Finch said he worked for the Yankee Casting Co. of 243 Shaker Road, Enfield, Conn.

As I listened to my mother's story I immediately began to doubt her recollection of the tragic incident. There were lots of gaps in the story. From what I knew about Haven and from what I knew about Finch, things did not add up. I knew that Haven was not a troublemaker. In my entire lifetime I had never seen him start a fight or instigate trouble. On many occasions, though, I had seen him finish trouble that others started. What I heard just didn't sound like the Haven I knew. On the other hand, I knew Finch as the type of person who loved power, demanded respect, and welcomed confrontation. I had seen him use his size and presence to intimidate and manipulate others to get what he wanted. I was one of the people that he did this to constantly. To him, this was synonymous with receiving respect.

Even though I did not have all the details yet, I suspected that Finch probably had tried to intimidate or manipulate Haven to do something and Haven did not comply. I was sure a scenario like this is what led up to Finch's death.

All through the night and into the next morning, the television and radio stations kept announcing that there was a manhunt for Haven Triplett. A manhunt! I was certain my brother was going to end up dead. I wanted this to be over. I wanted everyone to leave my brother alone. I wanted him to be safe.

For two more days straight, I heard Haven's name echoed over every television station. The search for Haven was the top story on the "Morning News," "Mid-Morning Update," "Evening News Update," and "News Watch" programs. I tried to ignore these updates, but I couldn't. It was the only way for me to know what was happening with my brother. With all the publicity surrounding the murder, there was one thing I was sure of: my brother was not going to escape the authorities.

On the second day of the manhunt, Haven walked into the New Haven Police Department and surrendered. When the news story aired, I was relieved. I was glad that he was alive and had not decided to get into a shootout with the police.

On April 19, 1984 Mr. Triplett shot and killed Finch in the Triplett apartment. The killing followed hot on the heels of an argument started by Finch, which became violent when Finch pulled a knife and threatened Mr. Triplett with it. Mr. Triplett left his mother's bedroom, went to his room, and confronted Finch with a loaded pistol. He fired once as he stood in or near the bedroom doorway, then retreated across the living room with Finch coming after him. He shot Finch in the shoulder as Finch came across the living room; Finch fell to the floor, where he was shot in the back of the head as he lay face down on the living room floor. Mr. Triplett ran out of the house and fled to New Haven, where he surrendered to police on June 6, 1984.

In the next few weeks, I would have to deal with issues that would begin damaging the already fragile relationship that I had with my mother. I'm not sure if she thought it all the way through, but my mom decided to attend Finch's wake. She took Finch's best friend, Al, and me with her. To me, her choice to attend the wake indicated that she felt Finch had done nothing wrong the night he was killed. It was like she was saying that the argument and the outcome were all Haven's fault. The fact that she felt this way was bad enough; to make things worse, she was taking me to the wake of the man that my brother had just killed.

As we entered the wake, I felt like a zebra walking into a den of lions. I remember all the eyes that looked at us as we entered. The focus was now on us rather than the casket at the front of the room. At this time, I visualized someone standing up and shouting, "That's his brother...get him!" I was on edge and paranoid. Things got worse when I was seated next to Finch's brother. This is the same guy who was looking for Haven the night Finch was killed, the same guy who was in the front seat of the car crying, the same guy whom I thought might try to kill me. Now I was sitting next to him!

If I had had a white canvas at the time and someone said, "Paint a picture to describe the emotional turmoil that you feel," the resulting picture would have been a psychedelic swirl of color with a splattered blotch of black and red dead center.

I didn't want to be at this wake. I didn't even like Finch. I didn't know Finch's brother that well, but I did know that he had a different personality than Finch had. Even still, I didn't like him either. So someone tell me again why I was at this wake! There was no way I could leave. It was too late, so I made the best of it. I sat down next to Finch's brother and just kept my head down most of the time.

The only time I looked up toward the casket was when my mother went up to the podium to speak. I remember seeing the tears stream down her face as she spoke. She let everyone know that no one could be more hurt by Finch's death than she was. She spoke of how important Finch was in her life and how she was going to miss him. As she was speaking, my mind wandered again, and I could see the same guy who potentially stood up and said, "That's his brother...get him!" This time he stood up and yelled at my mother, "It's your fault Finch is dead! Your son killed him. Why are you here? You are not really sorry." I was relieved when it was finally time for us to leave.

As we left out of the front door of the funeral home, my daydreaming became reality. A man I had never seen before stopped and yelled at my mother, "I'm going to kill you if it's the last thing I do!" In any other environment, those words would have caused an altercation that would have possibly left someone badly injured or dead.

At a wake, no one expects to be threatened. This is probably why the words didn't really affect me until we were about a mile down the street. I instantly became angry. I started crying then I yelled, "Take me back to the wake! Take me back!" But my mother pleaded for Al to keep driving. They both attempted to calm me down by talking and reasoning with me. It took a few minutes, but I eventually came to my senses. Today, I'm glad we didn't go back. I'm not exactly sure what I would have done or what might have happened to me.

Days later, I imagined that Al turned the car around to give me the opportunity to approach the gentleman who threatened my mom. As

I pictured the events that followed, I could see the man lying on the ground dead. This would have been tragic. My mother had already had one son who was probably in prison somewhere and another son who was going to be charged with murdering her boyfriend. I pictured myself being brought up on murder charges for killing Finch's family member. I imagined that this would have been too much for my mother to manage. In the final image I saw my mother sitting on a couch. She was motionless and staring off into space after having a nervous breakdown.

It was clear that my mother and brother had different viewpoints on what happened the night Finch was killed. Years later, Haven explained it to me this way. He told me that he and Finch decided to go gamble at someone's house. I'm not sure if they were playing cards or shooting dice. As far as Haven was concerned, it didn't matter which. His days living with my grandfather had made him a well-seasoned gambler. While they were gambling, Finch lost a significant amount of money while Haven won a substantial amount. He went on to tell me that when they arrived home, Finch said in a demanding tone, "Ain't you gonna give your mother some of that money you won?" My thought was that this was probably a clever way for Finch to get back his losses. He knew that once Haven gave any money to my mother, he would have access to it. Haven told me that he was absolutely planning to give my mother some of his winnings because she had opened her home to him. He told me that he was going to do this on his own accord. He wasn't going to do it under duress because Finch bullied him. This is when I learned that my assumption of what had happened was correct. I knew that the problem had to start with Finch trying to manipulate Haven. A verbal argument ensued, and Finch threatened Haven by pulling out a knife. Finch should have known that as a bootlegger's keeper, Haven absolutely had to have a gun for protection. He also should have known the code of the street: *If you pull out a weapon, you must use it.*

Springfield Union
Thursday, January 10, 1985
Murder suspect panicked
By HELAYNE LIGHTSTONE (Union Staff)

Murder suspect Haven Triplett took the witness stand in his own defense Wednesday and said he shot Gregory Finch to death out of fear for his own life and the life of his mother. But Triplett said he did not intend to kill Finch when he got a gun and began shooting after Finch lunged at him with a knife. "I panicked. I freaked out and lost my mind. I didn't mean for Gregory to be killed. It just happened," Triplett said.

Triplett was the final witness during his three-day trial in Hampden Superior Court on a charge of first-degree murder. Jurors are scheduled to begin deliberations today.

Triplett, 21, is accused of killing Finch, his mother's fiancé, during a dispute in his mother's apartment at 650 Union St. on April 19.

⌘   ⌘   ⌘

Triplett's mother, Mattie Triplett, took the witness stand Tuesday and tearfully testified against her son. She said Finch flashed a knife at Haven during an argument, and then Haven left the room and returned with a gun. She said Haven shot Finch in the face and then fired two more shots after he was on the floor defenseless. On Wednesday, Triplett repeatedly contradicted his mother's testimony. Mattie Triplett said Finch never abused her, but Triplett said the day of the shooting Finch had stabbed her with the knife. He also said he had seen Finch abuse his younger sister.

Triplett was questioned by defense lawyer Philip N. Lauro and cross-examined by Assistant District Attorney Francis Bloom. Triplett said after Finch flashed the knife, "I ran toward my room. I grabbed a gun that was in my room...I saw my mother in the hallway. She had been cut; she was bleeding. I ran back towards her room...Gregory lunged at me and I fired a shot. I backed out of the room. He kept coming at me. I fired another shot." Triplett said he didn't remember how many shots were fired. "I saw the knife and panicked," Triplett said. "Did you intend to kill Mr. Finch?" Lauro asked. "No," Triplett replied.

⌘   ⌘   ⌘

During cross-examination, Bloom hammered away at inconsistencies in Triplett's testimony and repeatedly pointed out contradictions in his testimony. Bloom introduced evidence designed to show Triplett has a bad temper and resented Finch's relationship with his mother. Later, Triplett said the gun "went off accidentally." He also said he wasn't sure that Finch had a knife when he returned to the room and shot him. When Bloom asked why Triplett's mother would lie, Triplett said, "Maybe she's trying to seek revenge." He also said his mother might still be mourning Finch's death. "What she's doing is not right," Triplett said. Jurors are scheduled to begin deliberations today after receiving instructions from Judge George C. Keady Jr.

I could not get updates on what was happening to Haven. No press or cameras were allowed in the courtroom, and my mother never spoke a word about the proceedings. What happened in that courtroom? What did my mother say when she testified? When I finally did get information about what happened, all hope was lost.

Springfield Union
Friday, January 11, 1985
Murderer sentenced to life in prison
Triplett guilty of killing mom's fiancé
By HELAYNE LIGHTSTONE (Union Staff)

A Springfield man was sentenced to life in prison Thursday after he was found guilty of first-degree murder in the shooting death of his mother's fiancé. After about three hours of deliberation, a Hampden Superior Court jury found Haven Triplett, 21, guilty on a charge of first-degree murder stemming from the April 19 shooting death of Gregory Finch, 26. Triplett showed no signs of emotion when Judge George C. Keady Jr. sentenced him to a mandatory life term at Walpole State Prison with no chance of parole. The conviction will be automatically appealed. During the four-day trial, Triplett claimed he was acting in self-defense when he shot Finch after Finch brandished a knife during an argument. In closing arguments to the jury, however, Triplett's lawyer, Philip Lauro, conceded, "There was no self-defense" but argued the case warranted a conviction of manslaughter, not murder. Assistant Hampden District Attorney Francis Bloom argued that it was a case of "execution" and "deliberate, pre-meditated cold-blooded murder." He cited testimony from Triplett's mother, Mattie Triplett, the key prosecution witness. Mattie Triplett said the shooting occurred in a bedroom at her apartment at 650 Union Street after

Finch and her son had an argument. She said Finch flashed a knife, put it away, and Triplett left the room, loaded a gun, and came back and shot Finch. The first bullet struck Finch's face. When he was on the floor, face down and defenseless, Triplett shot him twice more, in the back of the head and in the shoulder, his mother said. "He had to make sure he snuffed this man's life out," Bloom told jurors during final arguments.

Throughout the trial, Finch's mother, grandmother and two sisters sat silently on a first-row bench behind the prosecutor's table. Finch's mother, Oralee Finch, called the verdict "just" but said, "It doesn't bring back my son." She said she sympathized with Mattie Triplett for testifying against her own son. "It must have been hard for her. I know. I'm a mother, she's a mother," Finch said. She said she and Mattie Triplett became "very close" when she was engaged to her son Gregory. Gregory Finch's grandmother Helen Gresham, and his two sisters, Angela Williams and Helen Finch, said they, too felt the verdict was just, and empathized with Mattie Triplett. "It must be hard for any mother to testify against her son while looking him in the eye. She just told the truth," Williams said.

I knew this information would forever change the relationship I had with my mother. The testimony she provided sent my brother Haven to prison for life. I would no longer be able to go snow shoveling with him, we would play no more games of Q-bert, and I could no longer learn from his wisdom or depend on him to protect me anymore. This was the point in my life when I began to distance myself from my mother. Whatever closeness we once had was now beginning to disintegrate. I had seen too much, been through too much, and watched my mother stand by idly when her children needed her most. Perhaps the fault is mine for expecting her to do more for her kids. After all, she wouldn't even protect *herself* from the same men who beat, manipulated, and threatened her children.

In the days to come, my mother's allegiance to Finch would be tested. She was Finch's sole beneficiary. Apparently, Finch's mom and the rest of his family did not like that she was going to receive the money from his life insurance policy. This made sense. It didn't seem right that the mother of the man who murdered their son and brother was going to be financially compensated. At the same time, Greg had signed my mother's name on the policy. There should have been no dispute. I thought back to the comment that Finch's sister made during the trial: "It must be hard for any mother to testify against her son while looking him in the eye. She just told the truth." I guess this empathy didn't really amount to much now that money was in the picture.

It is so strange how everyone bonds together in the face of tragedy, but as soon as money gets involved everyone is at each other's throats. I'm sure suddenly going from allies to adversaries with Finch's family must have been a shock for my mother. I wasn't surprised, though. I never liked or trusted any of them.

My mom received lots of emotional support from Finch's best friend, Al, to help her cope with Finch's death. He was there to drive her places and to make sure she had a shoulder to cry on. He kept her company so she wouldn't be alone. He was also there and took her side during the battle over Finch's life insurance money. As Al helped my mother through this difficult time, he began to develop feelings for her. He made it known that he wanted to have a relationship with my mother. In another extremely disturbing case of bad judgment, my mother began dating Al. She made this decision only two months after Finch was buried. This was the second time that her new boyfriend was the friend of the last man she dated. At this point it was beyond Finch to care, but if he was still alive and this had happened, I wonder if he would have been surprised that his friend Al was moving in on his woman. I would like to think not. After all, he had done the same to J.C. I had heard a man once say, "If she will do it for you, she will do it to you." I think this is what he was talking about.

I couldn't rationalize how my mother could make the decision to date Al. He wasn't going to be any different from the rest of the men she had dated. She had seen his tendencies as an alcoholic just like the rest of us had. She knew that Al was Greg's friend and that commonalities between the two existed. Had she missed that? My mother's decisions were so illogical that sometimes I just wasn't sure she was the one making them. It was like she was on autopilot with no one behind the wheel.

When the financial battle was over, my mother was victorious. She received seventeen thousand dollars from Finch's life insurance policy. She also had a new boyfriend, Finch's best friend, Al. She and Al decided to use the money to buy a home. History was repeating itself. They did no financial planning, we had the same automobile and the monthly payment to go with it, their combined salary was no different than Finch's and my mother's salaries, and, once again, my mother and her boyfriend decided to buy a home that they would not be able to afford long-term. They ended up buying a house up the hill in Forest Park. This is where I used to go play with my white friends, where my middle school was located, and where I went to try out for the Raiders. We were moving there. This house was even better than the house in the Acres. It had a woodstove, front and back yards, a garage, and an attic. On top of that, it-was a two-family unit, so my mother was now a landlord, and she already had tenants living on the first floor.

Our living conditions once again improved drastically, and I was appreciative. However, my conscience did not allow to me forget that the reason this change came about was because of Finch's death. Given a choice, I would have preferred to stay in the ghetto rather than swallow my pride and accept this post-humous handout from him. I did not have a choice in deciding where I was going to live, so I repressed my feelings and began to settle into my new environment. I knew better than to get too comfortable. I had ridden this merry-go-round seven months before in the Acres. It was no longer a question of *if* we would lose our home but a question of *when* we would lose it. I started marking Xs on my mental calendar to see just how long it would take before we had to move back to the ghetto.

My new neighborhood was on the good side of my dividing line theory. I immediately noticed how clean the streets were—there was no trash, no cigarette butts, and no candy wrappers. Even the few vacant lots I saw were free of debris. This helped me realize that every individual has ownership in his community. I know this does not sound like an epic realization, but it was for me. I grew up in and only knew about environments where the residents would freely throw garbage in the streets.

I soon came to find that Al was a little different from the other men my mother usually dated. It wasn't because he didn't drink alcohol; he was an alcoholic just like the rest. The difference was that he had a job, and he would get up every morning and go to work. I think he actually liked his job. I guess this qualified him to be called a functioning alcoholic. When he wasn't intoxicated, he was almost a decent guy. For the most part, we showed each other mutual respect, and he never tried to tell me what to do. We didn't have a relationship, just like with my mother's other boyfriends, but we were able to coexist without problems when Al wasn't drinking.

When Al drank, it appeared that he would consume twice the legal alcohol limit. I always knew when he was beyond intoxicated because he would get a wandering eye. One eye would be looking straight at you, and the other was off in La La Land. Another sign that he was way beyond intoxication was that he would become condescending and verbally annoying. If we were in the same room when he was drunk, he would start talking at me—not to me but at me. His favorite time to do this was when I was at the table studying. His favorite *talk at me* phrase was, "You think you smart, Mr. Moooreese?" He would just keep saying it over and over as he walked around the house making a fool of himself. I have to say it was quite funny.

Like most alcoholics, Al would slip in and out of a state of depression. When this happened, he would break into verse and start crudely singing a Harold Melvin and the Blue Notes favorite: "If you don't know me by now, you will never, never, never know me…" It was either that or he might start slurring an old Willy Nelson song: "You were always on my mind, you were always on my mind." I remember when I first told my wife this story, we both laughed out loud. She was able to relate because unfortunately her dad was an alcoholic. She told me her dad would sing the Billy Joel hit, "I don't care what you say anymore, this is my life…Go ahead with your own life, leave me alone." She dubbed these types of songs alcoholic anthems. She was so right.

Serena was five now. She was pretty independent, and she was tough. The environment she grew up in required her to be. This meant that she didn't let anyone push her around. If Serena was home when Al was intoxicated, he would repeatedly verbally harass her, but she would hold her own. Have you ever seen a drunken twenty-five-year-old man get outwitted by a five-year-old? It's the funniest thing you could ever see.

One time he crossed the line and took it too far. He started talking loudly at her and grabbed her arm to make her do something. That's when I stepped in to deal with him. He was out of control. I warned him that if he didn't stop acting stupid, I was going to subject him to my own form of restraint. I guess I was just wasting my breath because the alcohol didn't allow him to hear me. Needless to say, he kept annoying Serena. I found a piece of rope, wrestled him down onto my bed, and tied him up. I had him hog tied—I believe that's what it's called. I pinned him face down on the bed and pulled his arms behind his back. Then I wrapped the rope around both of his hands and forced him to bend both legs where his feet were at waist level. Then I stretched the rope from his hand and wrapped it around his feet and tied it off into a knot. I felt like I was at the rodeo. He struggled the whole time when I was tying him up and just kept saying, "You think you tough. You ain't tough, Mr. Mooooreese." After I had him securely tied, I left him lying face down on the bed. Before I left the room, I said, "I will untie you when you tell me that you will leave Serena alone."

He struggled for about half an hour then he finally got loose. The first thing he did was come into the kitchen, where I was studying, and endlessly ask, "Why you wanna tie me up? Huh? Why you wanna tie me up?" That's as far as I would take things with Al. Anything beyond that and I would have called the cops. I had already witnessed Haven's fate when he killed Finch, so I had absolutely no confidence that my mother would take my side if I had hurt Al.

Al's endless pestering didn't stop with Serena and me. If my mother was home when he was drunk, he would badger her by following her around the house, push her around, wrestle her down, and do whatever else he could to make her life miserable.

This occurred frequently. Many times the police arrived to deal with their domestic disputes. It was embarrassing because the calls were made from neighbors who could hear them arguing. I had seen my mother and Al fight, argue, and make up at least a dozen times. By now it was clear to me that my mother embraced volatile, abusive relationships, so I never intervened. I would have helped her throw Al out permanently, but I knew she would have never agreed to such a sensible idea. I always wanted to help her; she was my mother. But if I had, I knew she would have never kicked Al out for good.

One evening Al was physically abusing my mother, and she called for my help: "Reesie, help me!" This was the second time she called me to assist her with one of her boyfriends. The first time was when I was eight years old, and she asked me to help murder my father. I usually ignored her, but this time I replied, "If I help you, are you going to kick him out?" She never answered my question, and the fighting continued. Once I realized that she was not going to answer me, I said, "Okay, then he's your problem!" I picked up Serena, took her to my room, and closed the door so she didn't have to see the madness.

My room was at the opposite end of the house, and I could still hear them yelling. I'm sure the tenants downstairs heard them too. I sat on my bed with Serena on my lap with my hands covering her ears so she couldn't hear them. It sounded like objects were being thrown. I heard a loud thud, like someone had fallen out of a bed. I had to do something; this was getting way out of control. I decided to see if I could talk to them to stop them from fighting, so I told Serena to wait in my room. When I entered the living room, they were near the woodstove, wrestling. Al had my mother in a full nelson, and they both were facing away from me. I grabbed Al from the back to make him release my mother, who was still facing away from me. Then I placed myself between them.

I began to tell them to take it easy when my mother turned around. She had a wild animal look in her eyes, and she was holding a butcher's knife above her head. Just before she swung it down at me, I yelled, "Ma, put that knife down!" She didn't respond immediately. I think for an instant she thought I was Al. I knew I did not have enough time to get out of the way. I only had two choices and a split second to decide what to do. I could have tackled her and hurt her badly, or I could just stand there and get stabbed. I knew I didn't want to hurt my mom, so I braced myself for the impact of the knife. At the last second, I noticed that the look in her eyes changed. She realized that it was me she was going to stab, not Al. I remember seeing the color of her irises going from all black to brown, as if she was returning from a crazed hypnotic state. She lowered the butcher's knife then slowly walked to her bedroom without saying a word.

That was it for me. I had had enough! I had been studying math and English at the kitchen table an hour before, and now I was about to get stabbed with a butcher's knife. I made a choice that instead of getting stabbed, I would rather leave them to kill each other. My priority now was to make sure that Serena wasn't traumatized by the fighting, so I went back to my room and tended to her.

Sure enough, the fighting escalated, and they became even louder. By the time I came out of my room this time, the police were on the scene. I told Serena to wait in my bedroom again so I could find out what was going on. When I entered the living room, the police were talking to my mother, and the paramedics were examining Al. I noticed that he was bleeding. Blood was oozing from the left side of his chest where his heart was. My mother had stabbed him with that same butcher's knife she almost used on me. It looked like he was hurt pretty bad. I noticed that his demeanor with the paramedics fluctuated wildly. In one instance he was alert, walking around, talking loudly, and being belligerent. In the next instance he was slouching like he was going to pass out. During the times when he was alert, the paramedics tried to convince him to go with them to receive medical attention. He adamantly persisted that he didn't need their help. After some persuading, they were able to convince him to go with them.

The police continued talking with my mom to get her side of the story. I wasn't sure what was going to happen, but at the moment, it appeared that she might get taken to the police station for further questioning. That didn't happen, though. The police finished questioning her and left. I could only come up with one reasonable explanation why she did not get arrested. Al was profusely drunk and wreaked of alcohol. I smelled it, so I'm sure the cops smelled it. They probably figured that in his drunken stupor, he physically abused my mom, and he was stabbed when she decided to fight back. When I received information on Al's medical diagnosis, I realized that both Al and my mom were lucky that night. If my mother would have stabbed Al an inch deeper, she would have been charged with murder or attempted murder. This was how close the tip of the knife came in contact with his heart. Al was lucky because he was still alive. He was kept in the hospital overnight for observation.

Al came home from the hospital the next day. As expected, my mother allowed him to continue living with us. It just amazed me that years later, after being physically abused by several men and after the loss of a son, she was still doing the same thing. If not for her own safety and sanity, she should have kicked Al out for Serena's welfare.

I was fifteen now, and I was still too young to get a job, but I didn't let that stop me. I looked for one anyway and found one about a quarter mile from our house. I was walking by a Jewish deli, and I decided to go inside and ask the owner, Rick Rueben, if he needed help with anything. It must have been my lucky day because the busboy, who was also the dishwasher, was quitting in a week. They needed to replace him. The owner told me that he would pay me under the table. I knew this meant that he was going to pay me cash in order to avoid paying taxes. I guessed it was at least a little bit wrong to do this, but I was in a quandary. According to federal law, I was too young to work, so he couldn't claim me as an employee, and I really needed the money, so I took the job. My hours were 4:00 p.m. to 6:00 p.m. during the week and 9:00 a.m. to 2:00 p.m. on Saturday. The place seated about fifteen people, and it was always packed. My job was to bus the tables and then go into the back and wash the dishes. I didn't miss a day of work, I was never late, and I kept my mouth shut and did my job. After a few weeks I noticed that I started to have a little bit of money in my pocket. This was a change that I liked.

Rick and I had a very good employer-employee relationship. I always let him know I was extremely thankful that he had given me a job and trusted me as an employee. At the time, I couldn't figure out why Rick would hire me. We were different races and different religions. It didn't make sense. After a while I stopped trying to figure it out and let my experience at Reuben's Deli serve as a reminder that I should never judge people by their appearance, values, or beliefs.

Two years later I reached a major milestone: graduating from high school. My grandmother's spirit and words had carried me to this prestigious moment. I owed it all to her. There were no balloons, nobody gave me a new car, there was no college fund waiting for me, and my post-graduation opportunities were limited. I wasn't disappointed or discouraged by any of this, though. It didn't even bother me that I had no family members in the audience applauding when I walked across the stage to receive my diploma. In my mind, the only thing that mattered was that I accomplished my goal.

I had achieved a great milestone, but now the question was: what would I do next? Luckily, I had put a plan into motion six months earlier with my lifelong friend Douglas Greer.

We had signed up to enter the Air National Guard, and we were scheduled to leave for basic training a week after graduation.

They say "birds of a feather flock together," and that couldn't have been any truer in this case. Doug's life struggles were just as bad as mine. His mother became a drug addict while she was carrying him as a baby. She gave him up for adoption when he was born. He became a ward of the state until he was adopted. When we met each other, he had never met his birth parents.

His adoption to a new home came with many benefits. His new parents were really nice, humble people. He had his own bedroom, and he was fed well. Perhaps Doug was better off with his new life rather than the one he might have had growing up with a mother who was a drug addict. Only Doug knows.

Like me, he was surviving without much guidance, but somehow he was making the right choices. It seemed like both of us were impervious to the evils of our environment. On a personal note, there were always obstacles and misconceptions along my pathway. I felt like a rat in a maze, and I knew that every turn I took was critical. There was no turning back, and decisions had to be made in split seconds. There was poverty at the end of one corridor, riches at the end of another, sustained life at the end of the corridor on the right, death at the end of the corridor on the left, happiness down another corridor, and a corridor that led to lifelong despair. For me, being able to quickly make the right decision was crucial. I knew the decisions I would make were going to be final. The luxury of starting down one path and changing it later did not exist for me. Changing a life plan can cost time, money, and in some cases may require support from others. I had none of these resources, so I had to make sure I made the right decisions the first time.

Luckily I always had positive influences to help me make important decisions. My grandmother had told me that I needed to graduate. My brother Haven told me that drugs were bad, and Allan from the pizza shop told me that it was important to stay out of trouble and do the right thing. My mother even helped. She told me that it was not acceptable to steal by giving me some very memorable whippings. It would be Doug who was my positive influence six months before we graduated from high school. Because of him, I had a plan for my future. Doug's wisdom helped to vector me away the poverty, death, and lifelong despair corridors. I was now heading in the general direction of the riches, sustained life, and happiness corridors.

The critical moment occurred when Doug and I were walking home from school. Doug brought up the idea of going into the Air National Guard. I didn't know much about what he was talking about, so I just listened. He probably could see the look of skepticism on my face because the next words out of his mouth were, "If we stay here, what are we going to do after we graduate?" I said the answer before he even got all the words out of his mouth: "Nothing!" Today I know for sure that Doug helped me make the right choice to join the Air National Guard. I will forever be in his debt.

Our reason for going into the Air National Guard one week out of high school was simple logic. We both realized that this could be a way out of our environment and the beginning of something better.

Doug and I were scheduled to leave on a plane to Lackland, Texas. Our flight was leaving out of Bradley International Airport. Neither one of us had been on a plane before. You would think two teens who had faced the things we had wouldn't be afraid of too much, but we were afraid of the unknown: flying.

The plane was one of the biggest in operation at the time, a 767. It was huge. It had two rows of window seats on each side and four rows of middle seats. It was amazing. As we taxied the runway for takeoff, we both had our coats over our heads. I remember that I kept checking to make sure Doug was still hiding under his coat. If he wasn't, I would no longer be able to hide under my jacket. When I checked, he was still hiding. He was just as worried as I was about streaking through the sky at five hundred miles per hour on the huge aircraft. This was some beginning for two boys going into the Air National Guard, where flying on a plane needed to be second nature. We arrived in Lackland safe and sound. The flight was smooth all the way from Connecticut to Texas. We both expected it to be worse.

The military transformation that we were about to experience helped us both transcend the oppressive environment we called home. In a word, I would describe basic training as a "distraction." It made me forget about my broken family, I forgot that my background was laced with poverty, and I forgot about my ethnicity. None of that mattered anymore.

My squadron was the 23rd BMTS (basic military tactical squadron), and my flight (this is what a team of recruits is called) was Flight 188. The 23rd BMTS was my new home for the next six weeks, and the members of Flight 188 were my new family for the next six weeks. From the first day at basic, everyone in my group was treated equally badly. We were all insulted. We were all broken down to our rudimentary elements. Although things started out pretty bad, there were good aspects about my new home that I could not yet appreciate. There was structure, there was purpose, there were goals, and there was discipline. My new environment did not tolerate illiteracy, alcoholism, or physical abuse, like my mother had in her home. In my new environment, you would get respect once you earned it, and you would give respect when it was deserved. There was no tolerance for people who intimidated others into giving respect, like Finch had done. This was extremely liberating to see.

I knew we were in for a rude awakening on our trip to the base from the airport where we landed. There were about fifty of us all from different parts of the country. We were packed into a yellow school bus with padded green seats. The first sign of trouble was when a man in a military uniform stepped onto the bus. I think he was getting a ride to the base. The first thing he did was scan everyone on the bus. When he was finished, he looked down and shook his head from side to side as if to say, "What a pitiful group."

A glimmer of hope was restored when we arrived at the base. A very nice lady, let's call her Mama, stepped on the bus and in a nice, motherly way asked us if we were hot. She probably knew that many of us were not used to the Texas heat and humidity. She told us that if we had on long sleeves, it was okay to roll them up and that she was going to get us all bottles of water once we were processed. I was happy to be there then, especially if this was a sign of things to come.

She told us to line up single file and enter the processing building. She said we should go inside and sit down starting in the front row and fill the seats to the back of the room. She told us we would each get called to the front of the room to get processed in. This didn't go so well for me. My name was called, and I walked to the front counter, which was about twenty-five feet long with a military clerk every five or so feet. They were the processing clerks. I'm not sure what was bothering the first clerk. He was curt; he spoke sharply and frankly seemed pissed off. I wasn't sure what I had done to him, but I was glad I was moving to the next clerk. The next clerk was a woman who asked me my name and told me to sign a roster. She, too, was afflicted with the same pissed-off disease. When I began to sign the roster, I rested my left elbow on the counter. As soon as I did that, she lashed out at me. In a demanding, threatening tone, she snarled, "Get your elbow off my counter!" I jumped back and looked at the clerk, but she did not make eye contact. She just kept doing her job. Then I heard her say, "Sir, sign your name and move on." I finished signing my name as quickly as I could, being sure to keep my left elbow off the counter. I just wanted to get the hell away from her. I was thinking, *What a bitch!* I soon found that all the clerks were suffering from the same pissed-off disease. When I signed my last document, I was so glad I was done being processed. Once I was back outside, I returned to the bus. Mama greeted each of us with a bottle of cold water and asked us if the people in processing were mean. We all told her that they were really upset about something. She apologized to us and told us to get back on the bus, drink our water, and relax. What a relief. Things were going well again. Mama told us that it was time to go to our barracks. She said when we get to the barracks that we should line up in five single-file rows with our bags next to us. She told us that we could talk as we waited for our TI (training instructor) but that we just could not talk too loudly. The bus dropped us off, and Mama said goodbye. We lined up like she said and waited for our instructor. I found it strange that the entire barracks area was quiet and empty. The only thing that could be heard was the low hum of conversation from people in the group getting acquainted.

This was my first trip to Texas, so I had no idea how fast the sun sets. It disappeared so fast that it felt like someone flipped a light switch. As soon as that happened, I began to get bit by what felt like elephant-sized mosquitos that instantly caused welts to swell on my arms and legs. At the same instance, a swarm of what seemed like ten uniformed men with big-brimmed blue hats descended on our group. One of them was in my face. He was banging the big brim of his hat up against my forehead as he spit his alcohol-laced words: "Boy, don't you eyeball me! You look like a homo; you want to fuck me, boy? You better straighten up; stop slouching. Where you from?" I looked at him and said, "Massachusetts." He said, "Didn't I tell you not to eyeball me, boy? Do it again! Please do it again!" His verbal onslaught lasted for five minutes. Then, like the wind, he and all the other men except for one disappeared. We were about to learn lesson number one.

The sole TI in the front of the group had a real nasty scowl on his face. He was pissed off and agitated five times worse than the people at processing. He told us to pick up our bags then he told us to put them down. A scattered symphony of noise was heard as the bags hit the pavement. The TI got even more agitated as he looked at us and said, "Pure fuckin' geniuses!" He tried again. "Pick 'em up! Put 'em down!" Once again the scattered symphony of noise was heard as the bags hit the pavement. Completely disgusted, the TI said, "In the military, when we tell you to do something, you all do it at the same time." He tried again. "Pick 'em up! Put 'em down!" This time there was a solitary sound as the bags hit the ground. Lesson one was complete, and the transformation from civilian life to military life for me and my new family had begun. Mama had set us up real good.

That night, the training instructors made us line up by our beds and entertained and amused themselves at our expense. They made us dump all of our belongings on top of our beds then they took turns walking around the room to see who could inflict the worst humiliation. I had only brought a small bag with me. Inside my bag was a toothbrush, a change of underwear, a towel, and a large jar of cocoa butter for my dry skin. One of the TI's stopped by my bed, picked up the cocoa butter, and said, "What's this for?" I replied, "It's for my bad skin." With a scowl on his face, he looked directly at me and began to wipe some cocoa butter that got on his hand on my bed. Then he chuckled a bit, and as he shook his head up and down slowly, he said, "Yeah, rigghhht." My humiliation was nothing compared to what some of the other recruits went through, so I felt fortunate.

That night the TI's kept us up until midnight. At 4:00 a.m. we found out that there was a loudspeaker in our dorm room. First they played "Reveille" with the volume up full blast. This was followed by some lunatic yelling, "Git up! Git up! Git up! Git up!" All of this was happening while several TI's were in the room yelling, "I don't have all day. You better get dressed, boy! "Git movin'!" It was a nightmare. We all were rushed to get dressed and ended back in file in the same place where we first met our TI. It was physical conditioning (PC) time. It was 4:30 a.m., and we were made to do pushups, sit-ups, and run two miles. Most people couldn't do the pushups and sit-ups. Maybe it was because they made us do fifty each on the first day. When we jogged the two miles, we had to jog in formation. Some of the recruits fell out of file; they were yelled at and sent to the back of the pack. A few threw up, and those who were in decent shape made it through without a problem.

After we completed PC, we went to the chow hall to eat. We needed to be in single file while waiting for chow. Anyone who didn't line up properly was yelled at. We needed to be exactly twelve inches apart. I kept hearing, "Get in line! Form it up, boy!" Then I heard one of the instructors tell a recruit, "I said twelve inches, boy. Twelve inches! If you need to measure it, take out your johnson and lay it on the ground a hundred and ten times; that's twelve inches!" This was absolutely hilarious, but, trust me, at the time, nobody was laughing.

Once we had gotten our food, we had to stand at attention at our table until everyone arrived. The tables seated four people. Once the fourth person arrived, we had about three minutes to finish all of our food then we needed to go back outside and stand in formation. Getting outside was a problem. There was an area that we all had to pass on the way outside. Twenty TI's sat in this area. It was called "the snakepit." As you passed the area, one of the TI's would address you. You had to say, "Sir, yes, sir." Then he would taunt you and ask you questions from the air force study guide book that we all needed to memorize. If you couldn't answer his question, you might have to do pushups or jumping jacks. That wasn't the worst part of it. Your TI was most certainly at the table, and if you embarrassed him, he would give you a blood-curdling glare and deal with you later. You were going to pay.

The next day was haircut and uniform day. The humiliation continued. We were taken to the barber to get haircuts. Many of us still had our teen fashion hairstyles. When it was my time to get my hair cut, I sat in the barber chair, and the military barber asked me how I wanted it. Before I could respond, he began shaving my head clean using the closest setting possible on the clippers. As he was shaving my head, he said, "I will get it just like you want it."

One memorable event in the barber shop occurred when a recruit who had a hairstyle that I could best describe as an afro/rock-star mullet received his hair cut. The hair on the top of his head was standing straight up and was about ten inches high. His mullet had been grown out about twelve inches long. It reached the middle of his shoulder blades. Our TI told the barber to shave off all the hair on both sides of this recruit's head. Instantly the barber transformed his afro/rock-star mullet into a Mohawk mullet. Then the training instructor told the recruit to get out of his chair and run up and down the length of the barber shop. As he did, his mullet flapped in the wind behind him. The entire barbershop exploded with laughter. This time, even we recruits were allowed to laugh.

The days to come would prove challenging. I had seen a few recruits get "set back." They were moved from our group to a group that was just starting. This was a form of discipline for recruits who were not yet able to meet the minimum requirements of the training. I had seen recruits quit and go home. The mental and physical strain was just too much.

We were about to learn lesson number two. The TI's had us do training exercises that made absolutely no sense at the time. For example, they would take us on twenty-mile marches and make us carry our fifty-pound duffle bags when the sun was at its peak. We would sweat like pigs in the ninety-degree weather and get extremely exhausted. When the march was over, they would take us into a building that contained only chairs and a projector. There they would play the longest most boring films ever created. They were usually instructional videos on how to put on your dress blues or how to fill out military documents properly. Then they would turn all the lights out, let the film play, and leave the room. After five minutes we recruits would start to doze off. When you were somewhere between light and deep sleep, an instructor would show up by your side and yell, "Wake up! Sit up! Now! Now! Now!" He would literally scare the shit out of you. Imagine you are extremely sleepy and driving on the highway. You are in the slow lane dozing off and waking up repeatedly. You doze off for too long. Now think of that feeling you get when you hear the sound of your tires hit the warning track. Then multiply that by five. That's the feeling we would get when the TI startled us awake. Because of that feeling, I nicknamed this exercise the "sphincter muscle drill." You needed to have fast reflexes and control, or you might have an accident. After doing the sphincter muscle drill a few times, we caught on. Remember lesson one. The TI said, "In the military, when we tell you to do something, you all do it at the same time." It was about teamwork. We used the buddy system. Recruits sitting next to each other would take turns sleeping and looking out for the TI's. It worked beautifully. They got their point across.

It was time for lesson three. Another form of training that seemed to make absolutely no sense at the time was associated with going to the shaving clinic. Recruits had daily inspections from head to toe to make sure their uniforms were spotless. Everything had to be in place. Our gig line was checked. This is the alignment of the belt buckle to the zipper and the alignment of both the zipper and belt to the center line made by a shirt after it is buttoned. Our faces were inspected. Not one hair could be present. We had to be spotless. This meant that we had to shave with a razor every day. This is a black man's nightmare. Once cut, the curly facial hairs black men have would many times never be able to make it back outside the face. They would grow internally and create "shaving bumps." The medical name for this shaving problem is pseudo folliculitis barbae. Ninety percent of the black recruits and three percent of the white recruits had this problem. The solution for all recruits affected was to go to the shaving clinic. There they could get shaving tips on how to manage the problem.

I was uncomfortable with the social interactions that occurred from the first day I walked into the clinic. The shaving instructor was black. This seemed to make sense. Getting advice from someone who experienced the same problem worked for me. The problem came when he sat us all down in one room and began teaching us proper shaving techniques. Ninety-seven percent of the room was black, and three percent of the room was white. When the instructor was referring to the black recruits, he said "we" and was happy and dignified; when he was referring to the white recruits, he said "they" contemptuously. The other thing I noticed was that the instructor would happily answer questions from us black recruits, but he would appear bothered when the white recruits asked a question. I didn't like it at all. This went against everything I experienced, everything I had learned about how to treat people regardless of race. It didn't dawn on me until sometime after I was out of basic training that perhaps the extremely unbalanced racial composition of the shaving clinic was a perfect forum to let a few unlucky white recruits experience reverse racism. This was the only logical explanation that fit because in basic training recruits don't have time or opportunity to be prejudice. Everyone has to watch each other's back, just like in the sphincter muscle exercise. Once you are in the field and you get assigned to your military base, that's another story.

Lesson four: the front and back doors of our dorm were made of heavy steel, and they were locked at all times. The only way to get in the dorm was to be let in by the dorm guard. Every group had a dorm guard that was at post every day and every hour until lights out. The dorm guard duty rotated throughout the group. Each person was on duty four hours at a time. The rules for the dorm guard were simple. If you were on dorm guard duty, you needed to be at your post, no exceptions, and everyone who wanted to enter the dorm had to show ID. Seems simple enough, but there were some gray areas to the rules.

For example, the day I pulled dorm guard duty, I was at post from 6:00 a.m. to 10:00 a.m. This particular morning the group was planning to have a GI party. This was not your usual party. For this type of party, we traded the cake, balloons, and presents in for a large floor buffer, toothbrushes to clean the grout on the bathroom floor, mops, brooms, and chrome wax. After a normal party, everything is usually a big mess. After a GI party, everything in the dorm was spotless. On this day, the party was in full swing, and the dorm was starting to sparkle. Then it happened.

There were three loud knocks at the door, which echoed through the dorm. I looked out the small window of the door and saw that it was our TI. I said, "Sir, how can I help you, sir?" In an agitated manner with a scowl on his face, he looked at me and barked, "You better open this door, boy!" I said, "Sir, can I see your ID, sir?" It looked like flames were going to shoot out of his eyes when he snarled, "You starting to piss me off, boy. Open the door!" At this point I was totally confused and unsure of what to do. The dorm guard rule book said nothing about how to proceed if your TI shows up. I started to think that since it was my instructor, it would be okay to let him in. I almost unlocked the door, but at the last second I thought otherwise. Rules were rules. The rules of the dorm guard stated that "everyone" must show ID. I stood my ground. "Sir, please show your ID, sir." There was a smack on the glass. It was the sound of the TI's ID hitting the small glass window on the door. I unlatched the door and let him in immediately. He walked by me with a look of disgust and disdain without saying a word and went into his office. He didn't yell at me or make me do pushups, so it meant that I did the right thing. His message was loud and clear. Rules are rules. They apply to everyone. No exceptions.

Experiences that I had during basic training reshaped what I thought about myself. I could now see that I had true potential to accomplish anything. I had gone through a mental and physical metamorphosis. I had clarity and precision when it came to making snap decisions. I was in tiptop shape. I was ready for the world.

"Together we stand" implies that the others in the group have your best interest in mind. I now realize this: at times in life we are strongest when we depend on ourselves.

"Together we fall... Divided we stand."

Futility

"Don't ask for help; I will give it... Don't want my help; I will give it."

There was no family to greet me at the airport on my return home to civilian life. It wasn't expected but would have been nice. I had no girlfriend to meet me on my return. I did not have one at the time but that would have really been nice too. There was no one excited to see me. There was no one to tell me that they were proud I made it through basic training. At the time none of this made me unhappy. They were just observations that did not parallel what I had seen in the lives of other young adults.

Despite the observations I had made regarding my non- existent welcome home party, my return to civilian life was going well. I was happy to see that Al and my mother had not killed each other in my absence. I was relieved to see that my little sister, Serena, was healthy and was unharmed.

I was eighteen now. I had graduated from high school. I had completed military training in the air force. I was now a national guard member. To meet the terms of my enlistment, my obligation was to go to my home military base one weekend a month for training. I somehow seemed to be following the right path, but what was next? I knew that my first two priorities were to get a job and to apply for college admission.

Even though I had newfound confidence in myself, I was still apprehensive about meeting the educational and financial challenges of higher education. Since I wasn't 100-percent sure I could make it through four years at the University of Massachusetts, I chose to attend Springfield Technical Community College (STCC). The STCC campus ironically was directly across the street from my high school. Some of my classmates said that whoever was going to STCC after high school was going into the thirteenth grade. This never bothered me. I felt I was lucky to be able to attend college at all. Although I knew the courses were going to be easier and it was going to cost significantly less, I still was a little worried about being able to meet my GPA and financial obligations. Just like when I went to try out for the Raiders football team, I didn't let my shortcomings stop me from trying.

I applied to the computer maintenance degree program. My interest in this field was piqued from my seventh-grade science teacher, Mr. Deegon. Even though computers were not in widespread use yet, he was already a computer geek. One day in science class, he told us that fixing computers would be a lucrative job in the future. His words stuck with me. Five years later I followed through to earn a degree as a computer maintenance technician.

I didn't mind taking the bus to college and to my weekend military obligation, but this soon became inconvenient. Sometimes I would miss the bus, and when that happened in both cases I would have to walk long distances, or I would have to arrive late. That wasn't acceptable. I needed to be at college on time. I saved the money I received from my military stipend to purchase a car. A few weeks later I found a part-time job so that I could earn money to pay for gas and insurance. Within six months of being home, I purchased a car, I found a part-time job, and I had signed up to go to the local community college. My plan was in motion. I was going to get my associates degree in computer maintenance and find a job that would eventually lead to a career.

It was around this time that I received some good news about my brother Ervin. He was scheduled to be released from the group home detention center. I was ecstatic. It was going to be nice having my brother home. I was hoping that the voice of the court had spoken loud enough for him to listen. I was hoping that he had learned his lesson and was planning to stay out of trouble. He really needed to get focused on the present while thinking about his future.

Ervin was a good-looking young man who was shrouded with confidence. He never had a problem meeting ladies. Shortly after his return home, he started dating a very pretty woman named Terri. She had her own car, and she came from an educated family. Her father was a Massachusetts state representative. I was thrilled for Ervin. This was exactly what he needed: someone with a future, someone to keep him on the straight and narrow. I had high hopes that Terri would keep him out of trouble. Staying out of trouble was paramount for Ervin now because he was twenty-one. He had outgrown the group home detention center. His next step would be prison.

At this time in our lives I was hoping to build the relationship that Ervin and I did not have as children. I started to think that my hope might be reality when Ervin asked me if I wanted to go see Jeffrey Osborne in concert. In the past, he had never asked me to do anything with him unless it involved stealing. His offer came about because he and his girlfriend were going to go to the concert and they had two extra tickets. They gave one ticket to me and the other one to Ervin's friend.

The concert was being held in the Student Union Ballroom at the University of Massachusetts. This was an epic event for me. I had never been to the university nor had I seen a concert of this magnitude. I was in awe the entire time. I loved the music, the lightshow, and the fact that it was standing room only. This night was like a dream. I was with my big brother, he was with his lady, and there was no trouble. I couldn't ask for more.

Unfortunately, my pipedream didn't last long. About a month later I knew that Ervin was up to no good. I started noticing new stereo equipment in his room. There were four sets of speakers, about six amplifiers, two dual tape decks, an audio visual system, two turntables, and a sound mixer. I had no clue where this stuff came from, but it looked like he might have robbed a warehouse. I knew it would be fruitless to ask him how he "acquired" these items because he would just ignore me and change the subject. I was sure that it was all downhill from there, and there was nothing I could do to prevent it.

Two weeks later there were signs in our house that Ervin had perpetrated a robbery. I woke up one morning and saw that my white baseball glove inserts now had crusty maroon blotches all over them. It was dried blood! The first thought that crossed my mind was that someone was hurt pretty badly from the look of the gloves. The second thing I thought was that the group home had not rehabilitated Ervin at all. In fact, it seemed that his views and values had been skewed more toward criminal activity.

When I saw Ervin later that morning, he asked me if I needed any money. Then he pulled out a softball-size roll of cash from his pocket. I knew that the source of the money was affiliated with a crime. I wanted no part of it, so I told him that I didn't need any money. He told me to just take the money while handing me a twenty-dollar bill. I took it to make him happy. Deep down inside I didn't really want this money because I kept thinking about the person he probably assaulted to get it.

I think I was naïve to believe that all it would take was a pretty girl with a future to make Ervin change his ways. His behavioral DNA could not be changed. Traumatic events that he experienced as a child could not be decoded without professional help. I finally came to terms with the fact that Ervin was always going to have a close personal relationship with the justice system.

A few days had passed, and I no longer saw Ervin around the house. My best guess was that he was arrested and was in prison. This time his absence didn't bother me as much as it had before. I guess I was through worrying about Ervin all the time. I think I finally summed it up this way: everyone is responsible for their actions in life and must pay the consequences if those actions warrant it. If Ervin was in prison, I needed to accept this. After all, he alone would be the reason he was there.

I also realized that worrying about someone who is not concerned with his own welfare amounts to wasted emotion and unnecessary stress.

I had too many things to accomplish, too many obstacles to overcome, so I had to stay focused. If Ervin wanted to throw his life away, so be it. Unfortunately I could not follow through with the emotional detachment needed to follow through with the words. I wasn't sure I would ever be able to do that. Ervin was my brother, and I would always be concerned about him.

Two years had passed since Haven was sentenced to life in prison. For these two years, Haven and his lawyer worked to get an appeal heard by the Massachusetts Supreme Judicial Court. It was finally accepted. The primary basis of the appeal was the prosecutor's improper cross-examination, which pitted mother against son. After a review of the facts, the Massachusetts Supreme Court agreed to give Haven a new trial. All facts were presented and reviewed during this new trial, and in the end my brother's sentence was reduced to manslaughter. The appeal was an amazing success. It meant that Haven's new sentence was eighteen to twenty years and that he would be eligible for release from prison in about ten years.

Springfield Union
Tuesday, July 14, 1987
Man admits reduced charge of manslaughter
By CYNTHIA SIMISON (Union Staff)

A Springfield man whose conviction for first degree murder in the shooting death of his mother's fiancé three years ago was overturned by the State Supreme Judicial Court pleaded guilty yesterday to a reduced charge of manslaughter. Haven Triplett, now 24, was sentenced by Judge William W. Simons in Hampden County Superior Court to an 18- to 20-year state prison term as a result of a plea bargaining agreement presented by prosecution and defense lawyers. Triplett admitted that he fired the shot that killed 26-year-old Gregory Finch in April of 1984 in the apartment he shared with his mother and Finch at 650 Union Street. He told the judge during his plea hearing that the shot had been fired "during a struggle between me and my mother. She tried to take the gun and it discharged." Triplett had been serving a mandatory life sentence to state prison until the state's highest court overturned his conviction last November. The court ruled that evidence of questionable behavior by the defendant should not have been admitted during his trial in January 1985 before Judge George C. Keady Jr. The justices also said that Triplett, who testified in his own defense, should not have been forced during cross examination to comment on his mother's truthfulness as a witness because it violated his right to a fair trial. During yesterday's plea hearing, Assistant District Attorney Francis Bloom, who had prosecuted the case at trial, read to the judge a statement given to police by Triplett's mother, Mattie Triplett, who witnessed the shooting. She told police that her son and Finch were arguing over money which Haven Triplett had won in a craps game and which Finch believed he should share with his mother. Finch told Haven Triplett to leave the home and not to return, according to the statement. Finch then pulled a knife out of his back pocket and threatened the other man, after which Haven Triplett went to a bedroom and loaded a pistol, the woman told police. The mother said she attempted to grab her son to restrain him but that he pulled past her and went into the bedroom where Finch was shot once, according to the statement read by Bloom. Bloom said the woman also told police that her son then fired two more shots into Finch's head as he lay on the floor. Testimony at the trial by mother and son had conflicted with Haven Triplett testifying that he had shot Finch in self-defense because he feared for his and his mother's lives. Attorney William Bennett a new attorney for Triplett told Simons during the plea hearing that his client did not agree with the circumstances of the shooting as outlined by Bloom in the reading of Mattie Triplett's statement. But Bennett said that Haven Triplett would admit to having fired the shot to the head, which resulted in Finch's death.

The following documents started the process to get Haven's sentence reduced to manslaughter and explain the summary of argument for his appeal.

SUPREME JUDICIAL COURT
COMMONWEALTH OF MASSACHUSETTS

HAMPDEN COUNTY   S.J.C. NO. 4009

COMMONWEALTH OF MASSACHUSETTS,
Appellee

Vs.

HAVEN TRIPLETT,
Appellant.

APPEAL FROM THE JUDGMENT OF THE SUPERIOR COURT

BRIEF AND ARGUMENT
FOR APPELLANT

JOHN M. THOMPSON, ESQ.
145 State Street, Suite 602
Springfield, MA 01103
(413) 781-4342 1785

SUMMARY OF ARGUMENT

The prosecutor's tactic of persistently questioning Defendant Triplett directly and indirectly on his mother's truthfulness, credibility and motivations violated his right to a fair jury trial and to have the credibility of the key prosecution witness' testimony evaluated solely by the jury (6)...morning of January 9, 1985. One of the prosecutor's major cross examination themes was that Haven Triplett's testimony directly contradicted Mattie Triplett's; this was established quickly on the subject of whether Finch had ever struck Mr. Triplett's mother:

Q Did you hear your mother yesterday say he never struck her, did you hear her say that?
A Yes.
Q You disagree with that?
A I'm not going to call my mother a liar.
Q I didn't ask you that. What I'm asking you, you would disagree with that?
You're saying in fact on at least two occasions you saw Gregory slap your mother?
A Yes, I did.

App. l07. Mr. Triplett's response—"I'm not going to call my mother a liar"—clearly indicates the dilemma this questioning tactic placed him in.

(**12) [*567] "It is a fundamental principle that a witness cannot be asked to assess the credibility of his testimony or that of other witnesses."

In this case, the credibility of the mother and her son was the critical issue before the jury. The jurors had to determine whether to accept the version given by the mother or that given by her son. The questioning by the prosecutor was designed both to discredit the defendant by pointing out the inconsistencies between his testimony and that of his mother and to try to make the defendant say that his mother was a liar. Such a tactic is impermissible.

The fundamental principle that is mentioned in the previous citing has now become case law:

A witness may not express an opinion about the credibility of another witness See Commonwealth v. Triplett. 398 Mass. 561. 567. 500 N.E.2d 262, 265 (1986).

I was ecstatic when I heard the news of Haven's appeal. I started to think that my hope of rebuilding my family might still be possible. I visualized my utopia. Haven would get released from prison, Ervin would realize that his existence was valued, my mother would stop dating alcoholic bums and find a real man that she could build a future with, and Serena would get good grades in middle school. I knew I had a long way to go to make it all reality. I just didn't realize how far.

I've always thought that deep down inside my mother meant well when she did things for other people; however, she would overextend her hospitality. In the process of giving help, she would always neglect her children and herself. We were always her third priority. Her boyfriends were first, and her friends were second. She always allowed her friends to turn our already struggling household into a food kitchen and harbor home. It always started with one of her *friends* who was down and out, needing a place to stay for a *few days*. The *few days* would eventually turn into a *few weeks*, and the *few weeks* would turn into a *few months*. By then it was as if they were a new family member. I don't know why my mother never gave her *friends* a deadline to leave when they moved in. It felt like she was more concerned with the welfare of these people than her own family. Every last one of them was unemployed. Not a surprise. This was the primary reason they needed a place to stay. I never saw any of them looking in the newspaper to find a job, and I never saw any of them pounding the pavement to see where help was wanted. I mean, really, I had found a job when I was sixteen by walking less than a mile and inquiring within.

The place I checked didn't even have a help wanted sign in the window. If I could find a job, they could too.

Their presence in our home was a major problem. I could see it, and I could feel it. We had more mouths to feed, more bodies to warm, and we used more electricity and water. The thing we did not have was more money to pay for these things.

The first *friend* my mother let stay with us was a thirty-year-old gentleman who looked more like he was fifty. I was never formally introduced to him, so I didn't know his real name. He had gray hair, a deep voice, and initially seemed a bit nervous around me for some reason. My mother told him he could sleep on the couch in the living room, where the only television in the house was located. From that point on, nobody could watch TV until he woke up. This was more than inconvenient for my other family members. However, I had an enormous amount of studying to do for my community college courses, so it wasn't an issue for me.

His nervousness around me didn't last long as he started to settle in and claim ownership of his domain in the living room. His comfort level was extremely apparent as he would now freely grab the remote and change the TV station. It no longer mattered if there was someone else in the living room.

His behavior mimicked J.C.'s when it came to his domestic entitlement. I would always see him eating out of a bowl or off of a plate, but I never saw him once washing dishes. Like J.C., he was on the couch when I left for classes, and he was on the couch when I returned from work.

When he wanted to impress my mother, he would tell her fantastic stories about serving in Ronald Regan's cabinet. He would tell her how he worked in the office next to Ronnie. Then he would let her know that he was related to J. Paul Getty, only that people called him J. Paul Ghetto.

His stories were funny, and inside I was laughing, but I couldn't get absorbed by them. I couldn't forget that this guy was eating food that should have been for me and my little sister. I couldn't forget that he was staying warm and living in my mother's home for free. He had it made, and he knew my mother would let him get away with freeloading as long as he wanted. His new entitlement really became clear when he brought his girlfriend to his *temporary* residence to ask if she could stay the night. He was brazen enough to ask, and my mother was foolish enough to allow it. I was astounded! Once I saw this, I realized that nothing was sacred. There were no boundaries, and everything was allowed in my mother's home.

From this point he never asked again if his girlfriend could stay over. He just took it upon himself to decide that it was not a problem and allowed her to stay over any time he wanted. This was outrageous enough. It got worse when he started bringing two plates of food from the kitchen to the living room: one for himself and the other for his girlfriend.

I saw it all from the kitchen table with my face buried in books. I was writing book reports for English, I was reading stories for my literature class, and I was solving math problems. I was taking three college courses during the day, I had two part-time jobs, and Mr. J. Paul Ghetto and his girlfriend were on the couch twenty-four/seven. They watched TV and ate the entire day, and my mother didn't say a word. This lasted about four months, and then he and his girlfriend finally left. My guess is that our accommodations were no longer up to their standards, and he found something better.

The next charity case my mother gave shelter to was a family of four: Ronald, Ivy, Jojo, and Iyana. Ronald and Ivy were boyfriend and girlfriend, and Ivy was Jojo and Iyana's mother. For the second time, our couch transformed into a bed for *friends* in need.

Now it was Ronald and Ivy who were sleeping where Mr. J. Paul Ghetto slept, and Jojo and Iyana were sleeping in Serena's room with her. This situation was just like Mr. Ghetto's. It was supposed to be a temporary option that would last until Ronald and Ivy could find a place to live. I couldn't help thinking, *Where does my mother find these people?*

Like Mr. Ghetto, everyone initially was on their best behavior and recognized that they were guests in my mother's home. In a few short days, things changed drastically. The refrigerator was raided on a constant

125

basis for whatever scraps were available. Ronald and Ivy were eligible to work and had no physical limitations, but neither of them was looking for a job. I guess if I were them and my mother allowed me free reign in her home, I probably wouldn't have looked for work either.

After a few weeks of living with the new semi-permanent guests, I learned that Ivy had a drug habit. She was addicted to crack cocaine. I discovered this one day when I came home from work. I noticed that someone was on the couch wrapped in three blankets. I could only see the top of their head sticking out of the blankets. It was Ivy. From the movement of the covers I could tell that she was shivering. The house was at a comfortable temperature, so I knew she wasn't shaking because it was cold. I went in the living room to take a closer look and to make sure she was okay. She just kept shivering and never moved a muscle or made a sound. I wasn't sure what was going on, but this circumstance seemed vaguely familiar. It reminded me of my father's girlfriend Yvonne. She, too, was always cold and was either wrapped in blankets or had the heat in the house much too high. I decided that I would not ask any questions about Ivy's condition once I observed my mother, who was in the adjoining room, showing no concern for her. Two questions I wanted to ask my mother were why she didn't have a problem with my little sister seeing this, and how she was going to explain it to her. But I never did.

Things got even worse a few days later when I came home from work and Ivy, who was now feeling much better, asked me if I liked the coat that Jojo was wearing. Then she asked me if I liked the dress Iyana was wearing. I can still hear her today: "Don't they look nice?" It didn't dawn on me until a week or so later why my opinion was important to her. Ivy had gone in my room and stole my Sears credit card out of my wallet, and then she used it to get her kids a new wardrobe. When I received my credit card statement in the mail a week later, I put all the pieces together. My opinion was important to Ivy because I had purchased her children's clothes.

I didn't even get angry or upset at Ivy. I was defeated by all the chaos in our house and probably figured that it wouldn't do any good anyway.

If I would have pressed charges, my mother probably would have gotten mad at me, and Jojo and Iyana would have probably gone into foster care. My only action was to look her straight in the eye and say, "I know what you did." When I did that, she started to apologize profusely. I half-way accepted her apology and from that day forward I did not speak or interact with her in any way. Six months later, Ivy and her family left my mother's home and did not return.

I don't know why my mother always befriended alcoholics and drug addicts. In their presence, there is always drama. They say things and do things that lie outside the normal standards of acceptable social behavior. Even though I didn't classify my mother as an alcoholic or drug addict, I did see her exhibit the same destructive behaviors.

This brings my mother's *friend* Clarence to mind. Clarence had no redeeming characteristics at all, yet my mother constantly invited him to our house and considered him a friend. Most of the day, Clarence was in a pissy drunk stupor. When he would visit, he would just sit around the living room with my mother and Al and communicate with them through a series of indistinguishable slurs. As he did this, he would laugh continuously. Other times he would just sit in a chair in our living room with his head down as if he were taking a nap.

One night when I was studying at the kitchen table I saw Clarence slowly staggering off-balance through the kitchen. He was headed in the direction of our bathroom. When I looked up to see him, the only thought I had was that I would never have a person like him in my house as a guest. But it wasn't my house, and there was nothing I could do, so I returned to my studies.

Clarence never made it to the bathroom. I heard a sound that reminded me of storm rain pelting an awning. When I looked up again, Clarence was standing near the stove with his head down like he was sleeping while standing up. He had his pants unzipped and he was urinating on our linoleum kitchen floor. I thought, *What in the fuck is going on!* This was way out of hand. When I told my mother what was happening, she had no reaction. She just told Al to help Clarence get to the bathroom, and she started mopping the kitchen floor. At that moment I thought about a scene in *The Planet of the Apes*, one of my favorite movies. I pictured me in the role of Charlton Heston, screaming, "It's a mad house! A mad house!" After the kitchen accident I thought, *Okay, Clarence crossed the line this time. My mother is going to sever her friendship with him.* She had to. Imagine if Serena had seen this despicable act. It didn't happen, though. To my disbelief, she stayed friends with Clarence. My only thought at this point was that he needed to do something more detestable. I thought if he had a bowel movement on the kitchen floor, she might then dissolve her friendship with him.

I was struggling through college. The days went by extremely fast. My classes were not exceptionally difficult, but I had no time to study or go to the library. I had two part-time jobs that I had to keep in order to pay for my automobile. I didn't think about the hardships and obstacles too much; I just did what needed to be done. The spirit of my grandmother was still carrying me through life. Her words were still echoing in my head: "Forget about what the rest of those kids are doing; you get your work done!" I thought to myself as long as I was meeting my GI Bill reimbursement requirements of a C grade or higher, I had nothing to complain about. I was making progress toward my future.

It had been six months since the couch in our living room was used as a bed. The pipeline of useless *friends* who needed a place to stay *for a little while* had dried up for now. I embraced this minor reprieve and used the time wisely. I was able to concentrate a little better without having to worry about someone shaking on the couch from crack withdrawals or urinating on the kitchen floor in front of me.

My mother and Al had not had a big blowout argument since the last time. Things seemed to be going pretty good. This was just a misconception on my part, though. A few days later the truth came to light.

It was Saturday afternoon, and Serena and I were watching television. I hadn't seen my mother all day, and Al was at work doing overtime. There was a knock at the backdoor. When I answered the door, I didn't recognize any of the people standing in the inside hallway. There were four men. The one in front was wearing a badge. He asked me if my parents were home, and I said no. Then he explained to me that he was the sheriff and that he was here to secure the home. He showed me a court order and told me that the deadline for my mother to pay the mortgage passed yesterday. Then he told me that my sister and I had to leave the house now. I certainly did not expect a visit like this from the sheriff, but I wasn't fazed. Hardship and I were good friends.

I asked the sheriff if I could get my little sister a coat. He told me that I could but that I had to hurry up because he had a crew that was going to pack up all our belongings and place them on the curb. He told me if we didn't pick up our property before trash day, the sanitation department was going to haul it to the dump. I grabbed a coat for Serena, and we left the house.

We were homeless. I grabbed Serena's hand, and we started walking down the street. I didn't know where to go or what to do, but I wasn't worried. I was familiar with life's adversities. I knew I would figure something out.

I started thinking about why and how this happened. I had no idea that the mortgage was behind. If I had known, I could have helped my mother and Al pay it. I started putting a timeline of events together in my head. It occurred to me that our house was in jeopardy of foreclosure while my mother was allowing people to freeload off of her. What had happened to the old saying "Take care of home first"? This thought was bad enough; however, I thought more about the timeline of events and started to get angry. It was evident to me that my mother knew the house was in jeopardy of foreclosure. She had to know the exact date the sheriff would arrive. Why did she leave Serena and me to deal with this alone?

These were the thoughts that crossed my mind as my little sister and I walked away from the only place we knew as home. We walked about two blocks, and luckily I noticed a car that looked like the one my mother owned. I looked closer and noticed that it in fact was my mother's car and that she was sitting in the driver's seat. She looked like she was in a trance. Her head was laid back on the headrest, and she was staring at the roof of the car.

I always tried to be respectful to my mother and other adults because my grandmother taught me that it was the polite thing to do. This time, though, I forgot all of my home training and raised my voice at her. The extent of her neglect this time was just too much. She should not have done this to Serena. If it would have just been me, I wouldn't have been so angry. When Serena and I reached the car, we got in the backseat, and I let her know what was on my mind. I said, "Ma, why are you sitting here? You knew they were coming! Did you think they were going to leave just because you weren't home? Why did you leave Serena and me to deal with this alone?" She never responded. I don't see how she could anyway. She knew there was no excuse for her actions and continued to stare at the roof of the car. After I unloaded my angry tirade, I shut my mouth and sat back in my seat.

I thought it was ironic that we were kicked out of our home, and now *we* were the *friends* who needed a place to stay. There was a small problem, though. The people whom my mother once helped were nowhere to be found. Most of my life I had seen my mother overextend herself for people whom I knew would never return the favor even if they could.

Poor money management, bad planning, and bad decision making, resulted in the loss of our home for the second time. I felt bad for Serena. I didn't like the fact that she had to go through this again; she deserved better. I wanted to ask my mother if she had ever considered that her choices directly affected her daughter. I didn't really need to ask because I had seen evidence over the last nine months that she had not. The good thing is that Serena had me. I would die before I let anything happen to her. I would do whatever was necessary to make sure she had shelter. If this meant quitting school, so be it. Fortunately, it didn't come down to that because my mother found Serena and me temporary shelter.

My mother took us to her friend Ms. Gladys's home. She informed Ms. Gladys about the foreclosure then they talked for a while. When the conversation concluded, she told me that Serena and I were going to be staying with Ms. Gladys for a while. I knew my mother and Al would have to find another place to stay because Ms. Gladys's apartment only had enough bedrooms for herself and her three children. Serena and I would have to sleep in the living room on the couch. How ironic. Now we were the *friends* in someone's home using the couch as a bedroom.

Neither Serena nor I had a change of clothes because the sheriff made us leave so abruptly. This made me think about how we were going to get our belongings that would be placed on the curb. I didn't have a place to bring the items, so I had to let my mother handle that. A few days later, my mother told me that she was able to retrieve most of our household items that were put on the street. She took me to a place that she had found for temporary storage so that I could get my clothes.

The entire time while I was living at Ms. Gladys's house, I felt like an intruder, a stranger. Ms. Gladys did not provide the same level of freedom in her home that my mother had when her *friends* lived with us. I was not free to go into the kitchen to get a plate of food or bowl of cereal. Ms. Gladys never verbally expressed this as a rule, but through her actions I got the message. I think she decided to handle things this way to spare my feelings.

What I noticed was that the refrigerator and cupboards were practically bare anytime I looked in them for something to eat. However, in the early evening when it was time for Ms. Gladys to cook, she would miraculously have all the items she needed to make dinner. Then all the food would disappear immediately after her children made their plates.

I was under the impression that my mother had an agreement with Ms. Gladys. I thought she was going to provide a place for Serena and me to sleep *and* eat. This apparently was not the case based on how food magically appeared and disappeared. The agreement must have been that Ms. Gladys would only provide shelter, but I was never told. It was uncomfortable living under these conditions, and I wanted to leave, but I had nowhere else to go. In order to eat, I used money that I had saved from working. I didn't have to worry about Serena because my mother would pick her up every day to take care of her.

It was clear to me that Ms. Gladys's children were her only priority. I can't blame her for doing what she did. In fact, I applaud her. She put family first. If my mother had done the same, we probably wouldn't have lost our home.

It took about a month for my mother and Al to find us a permanent residence. Our new place was one street away from our old apartment on Union Street—less than half a mile from where Finch was killed. It was in a single home that had two floors. We moved into the first floor, and the landlord lived on the second floor. After four years and a poorly managed seventeen-thousand-dollar investment, we ended up right back where we had started. We had made absolutely no progress.

Fortunately, my personal growth did not mirror the progress my mother and Al were making. My progress was just the opposite. I had reached another milestone. I had earned my associates degree in computer maintenance from the community college. There were still no balloons and no new car. Maybe next time.

About this time I started getting bits and pieces of information about Ervin. Mainly what I understood was that he had gotten into some real trouble that had landed him in prison for six years. I didn't know exactly what he had done, but I knew he was in prison because I had talked to him a few times when he called collect. I was still concerned about his welfare, but I was powerless to help him, and I accepted this. I decided that I should focus my energy on what I needed to do to achieve a better life and a better future.

I was at a crossroad now and needed to decide what I would do next for my future. I thought about continuing my education at a university, but I could not figure out how I would pay for my classes. I could afford the community college because I only had to pay for commuting to school. My GI Bill benefits covered the tuition. If I enrolled at the university, I would need to pay for housing and a meal plan, which was not covered by my GI Bill benefits.

I wasn't fortunate enough to get an academic scholarship like my friend Tim, who was an honor roll student. I wasn't a super athlete, so I couldn't get an athletic scholarship. I wasn't able to get government benefits that Doug received as an adopted child. Financial aid also was not an option. I was unable to get my mother's tax records, which were needed to complete the financial aid packet. Every time I asked for them, she told me she would get them for me, but she never did. I later found out that my mother had no records to give me because she hadn't properly filed her taxes for the last few years. I never got all the details, but if I had to guess, I would say that she was probably getting audited and was working with the IRS to clear up some issues.

With no opportunity to attend college, I decided that I would start working to earn my living. I promised myself that I would try to get a bachelor's degree at another time. I told my friends Doug and Tim that I had tried everything and looked at every option to attend the university but came up empty. They knew my life, they knew my situation, so they understood and told me not to give up. I told them that giving up was not in my DNA.

I went back to STCC and used the co-op job placement service that they offered. It made finding a job much easier since the job database was only for students from the college. Luck was on my side. A few weeks was all it took, and I landed a job. I was twenty now, and it was time to move out of my mother's household and earn my living. The only reason I had stayed so long was to earn my degree and expand my future employment options. I was glad I tolerated the madness in her home. It was worth it.

My new job was going to be working as a computer maintenance technician. I had made Mr. Deegon's suggestion of becoming a computer maintenance technician a reality. My duties were replacing and reformatting computer hard drives, installing the DOS operating system on new computers, picking up and delivering repaired systems, and replacing computer mother boards for IBM PCs and MacIntosh systems. Replacing the Mac mother boards was my favorite thing to do because there was some danger involved with the procedure. The Mac systems had flyback transformers, which were part of the CRT display. They needed to be discharged before the mother boards could be changed. If they were not discharged properly there was a risk of getting a hefty eye-opening electrical shock. I found myself sweating every time I changed one.

My new residence was located next to a hotel that had been converted into apartments for low- and no-income tenants. It was known to be a place that harbored drug dealers, prostitutes, and thieves. It was all I could afford. I was starting off great. I lived in an efficiency apartment. It was a fifteen-by-fifteen room with a small kitchen. My bathroom was external to the apartment. It was a ten-foot walk from my front door down a common hallway. I wasn't completely thrilled with the place, but I figured that I wouldn't be there long, so I could tolerate it temporarily.

Before I left my mother's home, the engine on my car sprung an oil leak and then died. With little savings, I could only afford to buy a '69 Dodge Duster with a slant V6. The car was almost an antique. It wasn't anything to look at, but it ran well and took me where I needed to go. I went to work every day, paid my rent, and stayed out of trouble. I had a few minor issues with some of the residents at the hotel, but I never let things get out of hand. I knew better. I had too many other things going on in my life to let them be a distraction.

Next to the hotel was the city welfare office. I noticed that the cars that arrived at the welfare office were often late model. They had a coat of shiny new paint and many had shiny new rims. This confused me and simultaneously made me angry. I was working hard every day, driving a beat-up automobile, and living check to check to survive. How could someone on welfare afford this type of car? Perhaps welfare supplements were now paying more than my employer? Not likely. None of this made sense. I grew up on welfare. We lived in one of the worst projects in New Haven, and my mother couldn't afford a car. She had to take the bus.

Perhaps things had changed. Maybe the government had implemented a supplemental automobile credit? That couldn't be it either. Maybe it was now permissible to use food stamps for automobile purchases? Not likely either. It really got under my skin. I thought about it for a while and figured out the loophole people used to circumvent the welfare system.

Here's how it works. Two unmarried people move in together. This makes it impossible for the government to establish a connection between the two people. The residence they move into must be rented by the person who receives assistance. The next step requires the person who is not on welfare to get a full-time job. Now the unmarried couple living together can receive food stamps to pay for groceries and get reduced rent from the section 8 program while benefitting from the income of a full-time salary. Presto! Now there is enough money left to pay for a late-model car, nice clothes, and entertainment.

Knowing everything I did about welfare benefits, I could have probably found a way to scam the government, too, but I couldn't. This went against everything I learned, everything I believed. My life wasn't easy, my life wasn't great, but it didn't matter. I had decided that I would live my life as honestly as possible. Anything less would dishonor my grandmother.

I lived about two miles from my mother's apartment. When I could, I would visit with the primary purpose of seeing my sister. On one visit, I was approached by the landlord, who let me know that the rent had not been paid in a while. He asked me to speak to my mother to find out why. This puzzled me. He lived just upstairs; why did he need *me* to speak to my mother about the rent? Perhaps he felt comfortable approaching me with the issue because even though we had our problems with each other when I had lived with my mother, we both tried to remain respectful.

I approached my mother to find out what was going on. She told me that things had been difficult, and she hadn't been able to pay. I told my mother that if she thought it might help, I could move back home and pay her rent for my bedroom. I figured that I was paying rent anyway; why not pay it to her so she could pay her rent? I already knew that my mother allowed lots of craziness in her home, so I wasn't exactly thrilled about moving back; however, she was my sister's caretaker, and I could see that they were about to get thrown out of their home. I had to move back so I could make sure my Serena had a roof over her head.

When I moved back in with my mother, I found out things were worse than I had imagined. The gas had been turned off because she hadn't paid the bill. She was using the oven from the electric stove to heat the entire house. I had no idea how long she had been doing this. I could only imagine how much the electric bill was going to be. There was no way she was going to be able to pay it. I just knew that the electric service was soon going to get terminated.

Things didn't add up. Both Al and my mother worked. There should have been more than enough money to pay bills. I didn't bother to find out why they were struggling. I knew my mother would not tell me. After all, she has always kept information from me—you know, small things, such as the arrival of the sheriff to evict us out of our last home!

I speculated on several reasons why conditions in the house were so bad. I thought that maybe my mother's wages were getting garnished by the IRS or by the banks that owned the houses she had tried to buy. If I was correct, her income would be significantly reduced. This would explain the nonpayment of rent and inability to purchase oil for heat. These were the only reasonable explanations I could think of; however, knowing my mother, I was sure there were plenty of ridiculous reasons as well.

In order to make sure Serena wasn't subjected to these hardships too long, I returned to the mad house and tried to help. I was pretty good at managing finances, so I told my mother to let me help her with the bills. She agreed and gave me the pertinent information that I needed to manage the budget. I'm sure she didn't reveal everything to me, but even with missing information, I was able to help get the rent current and the gas turned back on within about a month.

I had kept in contact with Doug and Tim while they were pursuing their degrees at UMass. I visited anytime I could. I would drive up to the university to meet up with them after they had completed all their classes for the day. Most of the time, we would go to the gym to play basketball. Sometimes when I would visit on the weekends, we would just hang out.

Doug and Tim were my looking glass into university life. They told me what it was like going to the university and never missed an opportunity to ask me when I was going to enroll. They knew my financial situation, and they knew why I wasn't enrolled already, but it was good that they kept after me. Their inquiries made me even more motivated to find a solution. Again, I told them quitting is not in my DNA.

While I was visiting them, I was introduced to a girl who was attending the university. We showed mutual interest in each other and eventually started dating. Anytime I visited Doug and Tim, I would always go by and see her too. After a few months of dating, she began coming to my mother's house to see me. She never said a word about how poor I was, although I'm sure she noticed.

We usually got along pretty well, but one day everything was going wrong. We had argued for the better part of the day. I was angry, and she was upset. After a while I couldn't take it anymore. I was exhausted and didn't want to deal with the arguing anymore. I left her in my room and took a walk. I was about a mile away from my house when I finally started to feel better and decided to head back home. Suddenly, a man appeared in front of me and put the barrel of a nickel-plated nine-millimeter handgun an inch from the center of my forehead. I heard him say, "If you move, I will blow your head off!" At that moment everything slowed down to a snail's pace as various thoughts crossed my mind. The first thought and maybe the most foolish was that I should take the gun from him and stick it up his ass! My next thought was that this idiot must have a seeing problem. I wasn't wearing the latest fashion and I didn't have gold chains around my neck or jewelry on my fingers. If this was a stickup, he wouldn't be getting any valuables.

I remember getting more and more aggravated the whole time this gun was in my face. The longer he held it there, the more pissed I got. I had told my friends Tim and Doug that giving up was not in my DNA; apparently fear wasn't either. I only felt anger, and my blood was boiling. More thoughts ran through my head. It was broad daylight. We are on the main road in town. People were walking around, and they saw him. They would be able to identify my killer. Time was restored back to regular speed in my mind when I heard the fuckin' punk say, "Get on the ground, lay on your stomach, and put your hands behind your back!"

I felt the muzzle of a gun being pressed at the back of my head. Time slowed down again, and the only thought that crossed my mind was, *This is it—time to die.* At that moment I felt handcuffs tighten on my wrists and the man, whom I assumed was an undercover officer, got on his walkie-talkie and said, "I got him right here." I had no clue what he was talking about. I hadn't done anything. I didn't even feel right working "under the table." I always tried to "do the right thing," so what the hell was he talking about?

My mind wandered, and I thought it would have been nice if the undercover had identified himself. I almost made a move that would have gotten one of us killed—most likely me—and it would have been for nothing.

About thirty seconds later, a dark-blue Crown Victoria arrived at our location, and the officer told me to get up. He assisted me into the back of the undercover patrol car. There were three undercover detectives in the vehicle. The one in the back next to me looked like he weighed about three hundred pounds. I could tell that he had not attempted a pushup in fifteen years. The officer in the driver's seat began driving down the main road in the direction of my neighborhood. Thoroughly annoyed, I demanded answers from the police. I directed my questions to no one in particular. "Why'd you arrest me? What am I being arrested for?" The detectives just ignored me. In an aggravated tone, I told them that I hadn't done anything. "You got the wrong guy!" None of the detectives responded.

After a few blocks, the detective who was driving pulled the Crown Vic over and parked near a pharmacy. The officer on the passenger's side got out of the car and pulled me out of my seat. He brought me over to three men who were handcuffed and lined up against the pharmacy wall. He asked me if I recognized any of the handcuffed men. I told him that I did not know any of the men in the lineup. Then he asked each of them if they recognized me. They all stated that they did not know me. The officer put me back in the car, and we started moving again. I started repeating the words, "You got the wrong guy" over and over again. Finally Mr. Pound Cake lost his patience and said, "Shut your mouth!"

When we arrived at the police station, I was taken to a holding room. It was a twenty-square-foot room with a solid oak door that was almost six inches thick. One of the detectives removed my handcuffs and told me to go inside and wait. Fifteen minutes later, two officers opened the door, and they instructed me to take off all my clothes. After making sure I was not concealing anything—*anywhere*—they allowed me to put my clothes back on. Then they left the room. Ten minutes later, two more detectives opened the door to the holding room. The officer who opened the door was the one who was driving the unmarked Crown Vic.

He said, "Is that him? Is that the guy you made the buy from?" The other officer shook his head to indicate no. They closed the door and left. Five minutes later the officer who was driving the Crown Vic opened the door. He told me that I wasn't the guy they were looking for, and then he asked me if I wanted a ride back home.

I was furious, but I controlled my temper and said, "Yes, I want a ride back home." I mean, really, I wasn't going to walk five miles back home when I should not have been at the police station in the first place. When I came out of the room, the undercover officer who had the nickel-plated nine-millimeter aimed at my head was outside sitting at a desk that was surrounded by six other police officers. When they saw me, they looked in my direction and began to laugh. I felt my blood pressure boil. I had been falsely detained and almost killed by the undercover officer who had not properly identified himself. I had been inconvenienced and humiliated. Now I was being disrespected and mocked. All of this was piled on top of a life riddled with poverty and family problems. I saw all black momentarily. If I would have had access to a weapon at that moment, it would have certainly been my last day on this earth. Without hesitation, I would have tried to kill everyone in the room.

When we got in the police car, Mr. Pound Cake was in the backseat with me again. His first words were, "You were right; we did have the wrong guy. Sorry 'bout that." Maybe he thought I would respond with, "Oh, that's quite alright, old chap," but I didn't say a word. I was still fuming mad about the whole ordeal. As we approached my street, I told them to let me out at the corner. I didn't let the fact that I was poor change how I wanted to be viewed by my friends and neighbors. I wasn't a criminal, and I did not want to look like one.

I entered my house to find my girlfriend worried sick about me. She hadn't heard from me for at least two hours. When she saw me, she gave me a big hug and said she was sorry that we had an argument. Before I sat down to tell her what had happened, I thought to myself, *What a unique way to get over an argument.*

My computer maintenance job lasted for about a year, and then I was laid off. The economy had taken a turn for the worse with the coming of the Gulf War. Many companies were reducing head count to prepare for rough times that were to come. My national guard obligation had been fulfilled one year before the war started, so there was no possibility of my getting activated.

I had mixed feelings about this. On one hand, I felt that it was my patriotic duty to enlist full time so that I could do my part for my country. On the other hand, I kind of felt that the six years I had already served absolved me of the responsibility of re-enlisting. I still felt turmoil from my self-imposed obligation to serve. At some point I made a choice. I decided that I would just consider myself lucky to have missed the war and continue with my civilian struggles. In the end, I did not feel 100-percent comfortable with my decision.

I had been laid off just before the start of the University of Massachusetts fall semester. Instead of viewing my layoff as a setback, I viewed it as an opportunity. My philosophy on life is that with every ending comes a new beginning. I started to think that this might be my chance to start attending classes at U Mass. I still had the financial issue to contend with, but I knew I would figure something out. By this time, I wasn't worried about leaving Serena and my mom anymore. The money I had paid for my room had helped to bring the rent current and allowed my mom to put oil in the tank. They were all set now, so I felt comfortable leaving.

I could only think of one option that would allow me to enroll at UMass. It was to use the open line of credit that was available on my Visa card. I figured this could at least get me started, and I would have three months to figure out how I could enroll the following semester. I had to think about tackling this problem a semester at a time, otherwise I probably would have never made an attempt to enroll.

I went to the bursar's office and arranged to have my entire semester charged to my credit card. This included housing and the cheapest meal plan available. I remember the expression on the cashier's face. It told me three things: the first was that people didn't do this much, the second was that she somehow could relate to my struggle, and the third was that she was proud that I decided to try to further my education at all costs.

Doug and Tim had told me which residence hall was the best, so I arranged my housing there. I was in! I already had an associate's degree in computer maintenance, and I knew a fair amount about electronics. My obvious choice for a major was electrical engineering. I had heard horror stories from many different people about the difficulty of the classes and the demand they put on an individual, but I did not let that stop me.

I registered for my courses: Calculus 1, Chemistry 1, and Introduction to Computer Architecture. I told my advisor that I was going to sign up for two more courses since students were allowed to take as many classes as they wanted to during a semester. I figured this would be a way to get the biggest benefit out of the semester. My advisor told me that three courses would keep me plenty busy and didn't recommend that I take any more. I didn't agree with him. I was ready to go all out; however, I decided to comply with his suggestion.

I think my first calculus class brought me back to reality. Even today I remember the words the professor spoke as he entered the class. It was almost a threat, and it was done with a sneer. His exact words spoken in broken English, with a thick Russian accent, were: "My name is Cornelius Pillen. This is Calculus One. This semester I am going to torture you until you know this material inside and out."

His words scared the hell out of me, so I dropped the class and enrolled into a different Calculus 1 course the next day. The first day of the new Calculus 1 class was much better. The professor started out by reassuringly stating, "We don't want to rush things. Today is our first day; let's start slow and try an easy problem." That was music to my ears. He put the first problem on the blackboard in front of the class. I recognized the problem and believed I could even figure it out—I was thrilled!

Then he said, "Let's take our time and expand upon this problem." I knew he had been putting on an act and that I was in trouble when he rolled up his shirt sleeves. I started to get really concerned when I noticed that three of the four sides of the room were blackboards. The remaining side of the room was a wall of windows. My concern turned to panic as he worked the problem. By the time he had finished expanding the "easy problem," he had filled up all three blackboards. I thought back to how Mama, the lady who greeted us at the air force base, had set me up. This professor must have been her cousin! He set me up to think that we were going to coast through this course at a reasonable pace, only to crush me in the end. Fortunately, while he was in the middle of expanding the problem, I figured the game out.

I had heard rumors that the lower-level engineering classes were used to "weed out" people who were not fully committed to doing the work necessary to earn an engineering degree. This process was a tool the school used to prevent graduating mediocre engineers. Once I remembered this, I stopped trying to keep up with the professor's analysis of the problem and stopped taking notes. I was taking a risk, but I figured there was no way he could teach this way for the entire semester. If he did, no one would pass.

There were a total of thirty-five people in attendance for that class. Counting me, there were *fifteen* in the next class. The professor had successfully weeded out twenty people. I knew exactly what those twenty people felt like because the same thing happened to me. I was one of the students who were "weeded out" of the first calculus course I registered to take.

After three months of brain-twisting chemistry, mind-numbing Pascal software, and some "easy" calculus problems, I had passed all three courses. I managed to get fair grades like I always had. I had earned three Cs. For many students these grades would have been devastating, especially for someone like my friend Tim, who always earned A's and an occasional B. For me, these Cs were a statement of my unknown potential and a testament that I could handle higher education. I was ecstatic. I realized that achieving a bachelor's degree *was* a reality.

During the semester, I had worked a part-time job to pay down the charges I applied to my credit card. My effort wasn't enough. I still owed too much and didn't have a large enough open line of credit to continue. I knew the dream was over. There was no more money. I had also failed in getting my mother's tax returns so that I could apply for financial aid. I had asked her for them the entire semester.

In regard to financial aid, something I had seen during my semester at UMass really confused me. My dorm had a basketball court on the east side of the building that was across the street from the financial aid office. My friends and I played ball on this court almost every day. When we did, I couldn't help noticing the steady procession of visitors that entered to apply for aid. I was obviously jealous of these people. I felt like many of them were only applying for financial aid in order to save their parents money. This was prudent; however, my need for financial aid was much more critical. If I didn't get it, I could not go to school. Period!

My jealousy merged with confusion after I saw a family of four arrive at the financial aid office in a brand-new model Mercedes Benz. I watched from the basketball court as a young male college student emerged from the Mercedes with a financial aid form. I could only think that the financial aid process was seriously flawed as I watched him walk toward the office. I knew I couldn't really blame the student and his family for utilizing financial aid options that were available for everyone. I knew I probably couldn't even blame the financial aid process; however, I let my judgment and emotions get clouded that day. It was no one's fault that I was dealing with an unfortunate circumstance that was preventing me from getting financial aid, but I was still angry the rest of the day.

I pleaded and tried to negotiate with the cashier's office to let me pay for my enrollment in installments, but they wouldn't let me. I did everything I could, but it wasn't good enough. I was sunk. It was over. I told Tim and Doug that I tried everything I could think of to financially support my educational aspirations but had failed. I needed to go back to work to earn my living. I also let them know that I was going to get my bachelor's degree if it was the last thing I did so to expect my return. I still made subsequent visits to the school to visit Doug and Tim. While I was there, I always made an effort to go see the electrical engineering department advisor. My visits with him were strictly to keep abreast of financial aid funds or programs. I kept hoping that an opportunity to get financial aid would come along that did not require tax information.

I moved back in with my mother and started applying for jobs, but the country was still in an economic downturn because of the Gulf War. It was difficult for anyone who was looking for employment. After about eight months of sending resumes to employers in Massachusetts and Connecticut, filling out countless applications, getting several phone screens, and making unsolicited inquiries to companies where I wanted to work, I finally ended up finding a low-paying electronic technician job. It was at a company in Connecticut named Power Systems. It wasn't ideal, but the state of the economy was one that highlighted and emphasized the saying "beggars can't be choosers."

The primary product produced at Power Systems was high-voltage copier power supplies. I was hired to troubleshoot the supplies that did not work. Like with the Mac flyback transformer, there was risk of getting an eye-opening shock when repairing the supplies. Most of the electronic technicians (techs) repaired the supplies that operated at fifteen thousand volts with low current. Getting shocked with this voltage was enough to make anyone spew a series of expletives and immediately remember how careful they needed to be when troubleshooting. At least two to three people would get shocked each day.

There were about thirty-six semienclosed work stations where techs would troubleshoot the supplies. When we were sitting down, we could not see each other because of the height of the work station walls. Most techs would get shocked because they had made the mistake of bringing a low-potential point too close to a high-voltage point on the power supply. This would cause the high voltage to arc through the air to the lower potential, which could be a finger, an arm, etc. Every time this happened, a sound similar to an electrostatic discharge could be heard. The difference was that the volume of the sound was amplified by ten. Every time we heard this sound, all the techs in the area would stand up to locate its origin and find out who the victim was. As we stood up, we would always follow up by saying, "Good morning!" This "greeting" was specifically for the person who had gotten shocked and simply meant we knew they were awake now. It was easy to know who just got "zapped," as we called it. It was the tech in the area who was still sitting down spewing expletives. No one ever seriously got hurt, so it was a way of keeping the job fun.

There were many benefits to my job, like being able to save enough money to buy a better car. I went from the '69 Dodge Duster to a '78 Caprice Classic. It wasn't anything to look at, but the car ran great and had power everything: doors, locks, steering, etc. It had amazing shocks and an incredible suspension system. I didn't feel potholes or bumps anymore. It also had a power sunroof. My favorite features of the car were the bench seats and the sunroof. The sunroof had a small leak near the passenger door that I never got repaired. I called this leak my "honey, get close" feature. Anytime I had a date and it rained, the girl would have to move closer to me out of the way of the leak. I would always act annoyed about the leak, but in my mind I was really saying, *That's it...a little closer, a little closer.*

Having a new car was great, but the biggest benefit of my job was that my duties supported my future goal of getting a bachelor's degree in electrical engineering. I hadn't forgotten or given up. As a matter of fact, during one of my visits to the school, the electrical engineering advisor at UMass gave me some information that would have been extremely beneficial a year earlier.

He and I had a discussion around my issue of not being able to get my mother's taxes to apply for financial aid. Without a pause he said, "In the appropriate section on the financial aid form, mark down that your parents are deceased." Hearing him say that was shocking! I thought he was crazy and viewed his suggestion as bad advice. I knew what he was proposing was morally wrong on the highest level. He was telling me to lie on an official document! This had never even crossed my mind. I thought back to the inequity that I felt as I watched the college student get out of the Mercedes to apply for financial aid. I thought about all the educational opportunities I had missed because I hadn't been able to apply. I began to rationalize his suggestion. I would only be telling a partial lie because my father *was* deceased. I started to think that maybe my advisor was on to something. It seemed obvious to me that I was not the first person in this type of dilemma who he had given this advice to. Perhaps his advice to tell a partial lie was what my situation called for. Maybe he was right. It was too late for me to find out, though, because I was back in the work force earning a living. Quitting my job to go back to school would have been risky and did not seem like the smartest option for me at the time.

Six years had passed since Ervin went to prison. I got word that he would be returning home soon. I had forgotten a lot of things that had happened in the past between us when we were younger, and I was excited that he was coming home. We were both in our twenties now. I anticipated that our relationship would be different.

I had been so busy during the time that Ervin was in prison that I had never taken time to go see him. This meant that we hadn't seen each other in six years. I wasn't sure what to expect when I saw him. He arrived at my mother's apartment with a closely shaved head. He was wearing a trench coat, and he had grown a twelve-inch-long beard that was groomed so that it ended at a point. He looked like a crazy, bald-headed gnome. When I saw him, I said, "Wow!" Then I started laughing at him. He smirked some, and then he smiled. It was nice having my brother home.

Now that Ervin was home, I started planning my own personal family reunion in my head. In two more years my brother Haven would be eligible for release from prison. I thought that maybe my broken, dysfunctional family might get a second chance to rebuild on more solid ground. We were all older and wiser now. Perhaps we could see the error in our ways and help each other rebound from a once hopeless future. I again vowed that I would do everything in my power to make us a family again, despite our turbulent past.

My first order of business was to help Ervin get a job. I knew he was volatile and easily drawn to trouble. If he had too much idle time or could not earn money, I knew he would end up back in prison. I had to help him because I knew it would be next to impossible for him to get a job with his new prison record.

I had been working at Power Systems for four years. I knew the company was hiring, so I developed a background story for Ervin to memorize. He was going to use the made-up profile if I could get him an interview. I knew that there was a chance that I might get fired for going through with this plan, but I had to take the risk. I had no choice. This was the only way to keep my brother out of prison.

While I was working my connections to get Ervin a job, he was reintroducing himself into society. After six years in prison, I'm sure it was necessary. While I was at work, I assumed he was trying to re-establish contacts with some of his friends. I wasn't naïve, though. I had a notion that he was probably plotting a robbery or some type of unlawful act. The clock was ticking.

I soon came to find that he was the same old Ervin. He would disappear for days at a time then show up out of nowhere. He did this for the first three weeks after he was released from prison then he settled down and I saw him at home on a more frequent basis. Now that Ervin was settling in, I thought this might be a good opportunity to reach him. I told him that I didn't want him to get into any more trouble. I let him know that if he needed anything, he should let me know first. When I was done talking to him, I knew it hadn't done any good. He just looked off in the distance and said, "I ain't trying to hear that." That wasn't the response I had hoped for. I wasn't done yet. I knew at the right time, I would try to reach him again.

A week later Power Systems called Ervin in for an interview. I felt like this job might be the lifeline that could keep Ervin out of prison. If he stuck to our plan and used the made-up profile we created, I knew he would get hired for two reasons: Power Systems did not do background checks, and I had submitted Ervin's application for one of the easiest jobs at the company. If he was hired, he would be working as a burn-in room technician. He would be responsible for connecting and disconnecting repaired power supplies in a temperature-controlled burn-in room. In the burn-in room, the power supplies were cycled on and off for a specified time in order to check their functionality.

It worked! Ervin was hired, and he was going to start on the following Monday. The job didn't pay much, but for now it was better than nothing, and it would keep Ervin off the streets.

My efforts to help Ervin stay out of prison were plausible, but deep down inside I knew it was only a matter of time before he went back. After all, most people who get out of prison have only been rehabilitated to get better at whatever they went to prison for initially. Ervin wasn't going to be any different; however, I just kept hoping I was wrong.

One incident that I witnessed confirmed my fear that Ervin's return to prison was imminent. ATMs had come into widespread use while Ervin had been in prison, so he had never seen one. One day Ervin and I were driving through town. I believe we were headed to the park to play basketball. I drove past a bank whose front was made of all glass. As we passed by, Ervin could see a woman counting her cash disbursement from the ATM. It looked like she had taken out about four hundred dollars. To Ervin, it seemed like she was just standing inside a building counting money. As we passed the glass window of the bank, I heard Ervin say, "Is she stupid? Don't you know I will fuck her up?"

If someone else had been in my car that day, they would have been shocked to hear Ervin's detestable statement. I wasn't, though. I had grown up in the same household as him, so nothing he could do or say at this point would surprise me. I knew for sure that Ervin would have absolutely followed through with his assertion if he had been walking near the bank and was not a passenger in my car. The only thing I could think at this point was that Monday morning couldn't arrive soon enough. The plan was for us to commute to work together. We lived in the same house, and we would be working the same shift. This worked out well for Ervin since he didn't have his own car.

I was extremely busy on Monday and did not see Ervin at all on his first day at work. On the way home I asked him how his first day went, and he said, "Everything was alright." Coming from Ervin, this meant that his first day had been fantastic. This restored my hopes that he might stay out of trouble.

Ervin was going to work on a steady basis. I started dreaming about starting a business that he and I could run. I believed that together he and I could do great things. The possibilities would really be endless when Haven joined us. We would be unstoppable. Like the Mafioso say, "Fahgetabout it." I couldn't wait until we all united. Then Ervin gave me a little scare and almost ruined my dream. After a few months of living with my mother, one Friday night he disappeared like he always had. He didn't move his belongings out; he just took what he needed and moved in with a woman he had met. She lived about ten miles from my mother's house. My dreams were restored when he made contract with me on Sunday night and told me where to pick him up for work. Her residence was in an ideal location. It was on the route that I would naturally take to get to work. This meant that I could pick Ervin up without going out of my way. The first few times I arrived to pick him up, he was ready to go. Every time he came downstairs from his girlfriend's second-floor apartment ready to work, I felt a twinge of hope for him.

It had been six months now, and Ervin hadn't been in any real trouble since his release from prison. He did get into one physical altercation close to where we worked, but for Ervin to only have one incident in six months was a success story.

Archie, one of the manager's at Power Systems, who was also a friend of mine, set up a basketball game against a group of employees from another company in the area. Archie recruited eight players. Ervin and I were two of the players. He scheduled the game to be played after work at a court that was just down the street from Power Systems. The game was competitive. There was some bumping and shoving and some friendly trash talking—that's how it is in a street ball game.

Apparently a player from the other company became irritated with Ervin. I can't recall why, but the man yelled at Ervin, and then he squared off in a confrontational stance. This man was about six feet tall, weighed about 250 pounds, and was solid muscle. Ervin was six feet tall, 170 pounds, and was thinly built. As soon as the guy squared off, Ervin hit him with a whirlwind uppercut punch without saying a word. It was the kind of punch that starts with your fist and arm in the front of your body, and then your entire arm goes through an upward rotation motion and then a downward rotation motion behind your body until your arm and fist end up back in front of your body, ready to land a devastating uppercut. This is exactly how Ervin hit the man, and then he just stood there and waited for him to make the next move. After Ervin landed the punch, I stepped in between them to break up the fight. When I did, Ervin yelled, "You can't keep saving these people!"

Ervin's punch had split the man's chin. From the look of the gash, I could tell the man was going to need some type of medical care. He backed down from the fight and left the court cradling his chin. My guess was that he was headed to get stitches. This was just his luck of the draw. He sure picked the wrong guy to mess with that day. The game resumed.

The next time I went to pick up Ervin to go to work, he wasn't waiting for me ready to go. He poked his head out of the second-floor window of his girlfriend's apartment and told me that he wasn't going. I was confused and said, "What? What do you mean you're not going?" He repeated himself: "I'm not going today." I paused for a moment to suppress the words that went through my head and replied, "Okay." As I drove to work alone, I was furious. I had put my reputation and my job on the line for him, and that was all he could say: "I'm not going today." He didn't say, "I'm sick," "I hurt my foot," or "Tell my boss I will be out today." All he said was, "I'm not going today." What a crock of bullshit! I knew Ervin was really telling me that he was quitting the job. His choice to quit meant that his protective hedge was gone. He was now free to get involved with as much wrongdoing as he could find. I knew there was nothing I could do to make him change his mind about going to work because he was his own man.

Even though I had received Ervin's message loud and clear the first time told me that "I'm not going today," crap, I still stopped by his girlfriend's apartment the next two days to see if he had changed his mind. As expected, he told me he wasn't. After the third attempt to pick him up, I finally stopped wasting my time. I knew this was the beginning of the end, and things were about to take a turn for the worse.

I had watched both Ervin and my mother continuously make self-defeating decisions that worked against their own success. My observations of what they valued and what they wanted helped me develop the following philosophy: people are happy with their choices and life if they have not made a course correction over a period of time. This is especially true when they have family and friends who are willing to help them change for the better. For a long time it had been foolish of me to think that my efforts and influence alone could make someone decide to change. This does not work because change is a desire that starts from within.

For us to truly be effective and make a difference in life, we should invest time and effort helping those who want and appreciate our help.

"Don't ask for help; I will give it...
Don't want my help; I will give it."

Destiny

"Follow a course of self-destruction and you may succeed... Follow a course of self-fulfillment and you may succeed."

I t was Friday night, and I was just leaving work. As I was driving home, I thought about the last time I had seen Ervin. I remembered that it was about a week ago in a Blockbuster video rental store. He was there with his girlfriend, and they were renting movies. He appeared to be doing well from what I could tell, but something just wasn't right. I couldn't place my finger on it, so I just ignored the strange vibe I was sensing. When he saw me, he smiled. We shook hands and chatted briefly before he left.

Just before my commute home was over, I decided that I would go by his girlfriend's place in the morning to see if he wanted to go play basketball. Domino four was about to fall.

My plan to visit him the next day quickly changed once I arrived home from work that night. I walked in the house, and it looked like a tornado had passed through each room. I went into my bedroom to find that all the clothes in my closet had been taken out and had been thrown on my bed. The drawers from my dresser had been taken out, and the contents had been dumped on the floor. My lamp had been knocked over. It looked like someone had been searching for something.

My mother solemnly told me that the police stormed the apartment looking for Ervin and that she did not know why. We both knew why, though: Ervin was in trouble again. I told her that I would drive to his girlfriend's apartment to find out what was going on. When I arrived at his girlfriend's place, I noticed that the front door was open and that there were two detective-style Crown Victorias in front of the apartment. When I reached the front door, I saw a man sitting on the arm of a sofa and another man standing near the door entrance. When they saw me, the man who was standing near the door entrance grabbed my arm and asked me who I was. Instead of answering his question, I told him that I was there to see my brother. The man sitting down asked me when I last saw him. I could surmise that these men were detectives who were driving the Crown Vics that were outside. I told the detective that I last saw Ervin about a week before.

Then the detective who was sitting on the arm of the sofa held a metal stereo amplifier in front of me and asked me if it was mine. I replied, "No." He insisted that I take a closer look and said, "Just take it and look at it." I told him I didn't need to because I didn't own an amplifier. The other detective asked me my name so he could call it into the station on his walkie-talkie to make sure I didn't have any warrants.

While we were waiting for dispatch to respond, he asked me if I had ever been in trouble. I told him that the only thing that might show up on my record is a warrant from the game and fishing department for fishing without a license. When I told them that, they both started laughing. A minute later the station confirmed that I did have a warrant in my name for fishing without a license.

My warrant was a result of not paying a fine of fifty dollars when the game warden caught me and some friends fishing illegally. We were dumb, risk-taking high school students who figured we could fish in a private lake without having a license—we wouldn't get caught. We did get caught, though, and two of us, me and another person in the group, received fines. We both ripped up our fines and cursed the warden.

The detective with the metal amplifier said that he needed me to really be sure that it wasn't mine. I assured him again that it wasn't. Then he asserted, "Just touch it!" I adamantly said, "No, it's not mine." The next words I heard from the other detective were, "You are under arrest for the warrant we have on file." I didn't say a word. I surrendered peacefully and was taken to jail by another officer who arrived on the scene. My car was taken to the police station impound. This was the same police station that I had been taken to when I was picked up for suspicion of selling drugs. This time, though, I didn't get put in a big room with a thick wood door.

Two different officers processed me. They made me give them everything out of my pockets, along with my shoes and my belt. Then the officer behind the counter asked me if I wanted to make a phone call to have someone come and pay my bail. I asked him how much it was. He didn't know because this wasn't something people commonly went to jail for, so he had to look it up. The answer to my question was funny for some reason because the officer at the security desk started laughing out loud. Instead of telling me the answer to "how much?" he notified the other officer that bail for fishing without a license is a thousand dollars. Then he told me that I should have stolen a car because the bail for stealing a car is thirty-five dollars! They both enjoyed a laugh at my expense as I stood there bewildered and stunned. When they were done laughing, I told them that I would not need my phone call. I didn't know anyone with a thousand dollars; a phone call was useless.

That night in jail was quite entertaining. I was put in a four-by-six-foot cell that had a thick plastic sheet in front of the bars. My guess was that this was to prevent the prisoners from hurting themselves, or maybe it was to prevent prisoners from spitting on the guards as they walked by. Regardless of what it was for, it reminded me of a movie that I had seen a few years back, *Silence of the Lambs*. The main character in this movie was put in the same type of cell because he was a vicious, dangerous killer. I guess I fit the bill—I was dangerous for fishing without a license.

My cell accommodations consisted of a steel twin-size bed, a matching steel sink, and a steel toilet with a quarter roll of toilet paper. That was it. I tried to sleep, but the programming on my sleep-number bed wasn't working, so I sat up most of the night.

There were about twenty other cells that were adjacent to mine that were occupied with temporary guests like me. Comedy hour started around 2:30 a.m. This is when the most vocal person in lockup that night—let's call him Loudmouth—started to annoy and provoke the guard on duty. The direction from which his voice came indicated that his cell was about three cells away from mine. I could tell that Loudmouth had been arrested on a DUI charge because the words that came out of his mouth were slurred and unintelligible. He reminded me of my mother's friend Clarence.

The first stance Loudmouth took in order to annoy the guard on duty was as a victim. He told the guard that he was going to die if he didn't get his heart pills. "My chest hurts…I need my pills! I need my heart medication!" He said this three or four times until the guard told him to shut up.

He next tried to represent himself as if he were in a court of law. He asked the guard if he was going to be liable if he died. "Are you willing to accept responsibility if I die? Are you the one I should sue for withholding my medicine? Are you?" He said this three or four times until the guard yelled, "Shut up!"

That was it. No more mister nice guy. He started yelling profanities at the guard and challenged him to a fight. "Let me out of here and I will beat your ass! Come on, tough guy!" The guard didn't respond this time. I was glad Loudmouth was there because the night would have been pretty boring without him.

At about 4:00 a.m., an officer unlocked my cell and took me to get my arrest photos—you know the photos that they always show on TV with the criminal facing left then facing right and looking straight ahead. He also fingerprinted me then returned me to my cell. After I was fingerprinted, I put everything together. I was arrested for the fishing without a license warrant because I didn't touch the metal amplifier that the detective tried to hand me. He was trying to get my fingerprints, which were not on file. Perhaps I should have touched the amplifier. If I had, perhaps I would not have had to spend the night in lockup. But then I also would not have had the opportunity to tune into the Loudmouth comedy show. The last thing I would have missed was the chance to feel like Hannibal Lector, a dangerous criminal. The rest of the night was uneventful and went by extremely slowly. When I was released at 9:00 a.m. the next morning, I asked the guard at the main desk where I could retrieve my vehicle. He told me it was in the police impound. Fortunately I was able to get my car without any trouble and headed home. As I drove home, I began thinking about Ervin. What had he done? Why were the police looking for him? I also thought about my girlfriend. It occurred to me that I had been missing since yesterday afternoon. I imagined that she was going to either be mad at me or worried sick.

When I entered my mother's apartment, I went into my bedroom to find my girlfriend waiting. She jumped off the bed and gave me a big hug. In a very worried, concerned tone, she asked me, "Are you okay?" I replied yes, then she asked, "Are you in any trouble?" The question confused me because there was no way she could have already known that I had been arrested the day before. I responded by telling her that I was not in any trouble but that I had been arrested. I began to tell her about how the detectives tried to get my fingerprints when I had gone to see Ervin. She interrupted me and told me that the news updates had been associating my name with a horrible crime.

She frantically told me that news reporters were announcing that the police were looking for me in connection with the rape and murder of an elderly woman. I was shocked, confused, and at a loss for words. I said, "What? Are you kidding me?" At that moment the telephone rang. It was my Aunt Elaine. Now she, too, was asking me if I was okay. Before I could respond, she said, "Did you do what they said you did on TV?" I told her, "I didn't do a thing." She then asked to speak with my mother. After I gave the phone to my mother, I went back into my bedroom with my girlfriend. Then I saw it for the first time. WWLP, Channel 22, broadcasted the following: "Police are on a manhunt for Maurice Triplett, wanted for the rape and murder of seventy-nine-year-old Alice Kelly."

What the hell was going on? It only took a few more seconds after hearing this news update for me to put it all together. The police weren't looking for me. They were looking for Ervin! This is why the detectives were at Ervin's girlfriend's house. This is why I was arrested. But why the hell were they saying my name? My whole world came crashing down. Too much was happening at once. I was being misrepresented as a rapist and murderer on network TV, an elderly woman was killed by a despicable act of violence, and my flesh-and-blood brother was the primary suspect of the crime.

My girlfriend and I were hypnotized by every news report. We could not move. It was so bad that in between the broadcasts we didn't even speak to each other. We watched again and again as Channel 22 reported that I was a rapist and murderer. It happened three more times within a thirty-minute period. One of us came up with the idea to check the other television stations to see what they were reporting. Surprisingly, the other networks were only stating that "police are in search of a man who is wanted" for the crime. They did not mention the name of any suspect. At that moment my girlfriend and I snapped out of our trances and called Channel 22. My girlfriend frantically told the person that the station was reporting the wrong name and that the information should be checked.

The people at Channel 22 did not acknowledge our state of panic and lackadaisically assured my girlfriend that they would look into the problem. After we hung up the phone, I believe the staff member completely ignored our notification. The next two consecutive updates that were aired still reported my name. We called back, and this time I asked for the general manager. I was informed that the GM was unavailable. I told the person with whom I was speaking that "the broadcasts need to stop right now, and your station needs to issue an apology." The person on the other end of the phone apathetically replied, "We will look into it, sir."

The next news update used my name again. We called them back one last time and repeated that they had the wrong name. The person from the TV station replied in a rude tone, "We are looking into it; if that's not good enough, sue us." We had tried everything we could think of to get Channel 22 from reporting erroneous information. The only thing we managed was to get indignant responses. We were completely frustrated and defeated after dealing with the staff at Channel 22. We knew we were at the end of our rope and that nothing else could be done right then. We briefly discussed that we would look into suing the station at a later date, as they had suggested.

Later that day, all of the stations, including Channel 22, finally had the correct name of the suspect. They were now announcing that Ervin Triplett was connected with the crime. Channel 22 issued a single, half-hearted retraction of earlier statements connecting me to the crime. The retraction was delivered in a way to make them seem like an innocent participant in the mishap. I could tell that this was intentionally done to make watchers infer that the mistake was not their fault. I still remember the reporter's face and the words he used. "Authorities are looking for Ervin Triplett for the rape and murder of seventy-nine-year-old Alice Kelly. Earlier today," he paused for effect, "we had reported another name." This bull crap retraction, if you can even call it that, only made me angrier with the station. They would have been better off not making it at all. After hearing it, I knew that I was going to go out of my way to make them pay for their arrogance, incompetence, and lack of accountability.

I continued to scan the stations to confirm that they were all using the correct name of the suspect. Now that they all had the name correct, the focus was now on a nationwide manhunt for Ervin. I was reliving this experience for the second time. Nine years earlier, the same TV stations and same police force were on a manhunt for my brother Haven. For the second time, one person was dead, one of my brothers was on the run from the police, and I was at home watching it on the news. As I thought, *How could this be happening again?* I also thought about the script of my life. It was versed in throes of misfortune. Every page of my manuscript was filled with tragedy, crime, and poverty. I began to think about the next chapter. I pictured my little sister sitting on her bed feeling sad and feeling a loss. She was watching a news update of the police on a nationwide manhunt after me. This *had* to be my destiny. I couldn't see it any other way. My brothers had given me two well-drawn-out blueprints of murder. My mother had allowed me to preview many instances of attempted murder. My turn was coming—it was only a matter of time.

When I returned to work on Monday, I expected a flood of questions from the people who came to know Ervin, but this never happened. Most of them simply said that they were sorry that Ervin got into trouble, and some said nothing at all. I was thankful that my work employees didn't ask too many questions and that I did not have to go into detail about what had happened.

I was nervous when I was told that the human resources manager wanted to see me. I had lied to get Ervin a job, and we both had falsified information on documents. I knew it was time to pay for the consequences of my actions. When I entered his office, he let me know that he heard about what happened and that I should not expect anyone to treat me any differently. Without making me address the specifics of what I had done to get Ervin a job, he indicated that he would have done the same thing. His empathy for what I had done was clear when he looked me straight in the eye and said, "I have a brother just like that, and I would have done whatever I could to help him too." His reassurance put me at ease. I was relieved to know that I wasn't going to lose my job.

Over the next few months I was going to learn the truth about Ervin as the news media began to publicly dissect his life.

What I learned from the newspaper articles that I read and the reports that I watched on the news confirmed what I had always known. Ervin was a one-man crime wave, a true menace to society.

Sunday Republican
Sunday, September 13, 1992
Slaying suspect a symbol of system's failure
By JACK FLYNN

First arrest came early

...Even before Triplett was jailed for his first adult offense, he had compiled a juvenile record that one court official described as "horrendous" during a sentencing hearing. While Triplett's juvenile offenses are not public, Lauro recalls that he was one of the youngest defendants ever held at the state's detention center in Westfield...

For all but 10 months during the past 10 years, Triplett has been locked up in one jail after another—either serving time for his 1983 conviction for breaking into a home in the Forest Park section or for parole violations he committed after his release from prison. Triplett's first arrests as an adult came less than a month after he turned 17, the threshold for the adult correctional system. He was charged with breaking into two homes in Forest Park section, including one where a prayer meeting was underway. After Triplett pled guilty to one count, Judge Porada—citing Triplett's lengthy juvenile record—sentenced him to a fifteen-year term at Concord State Prison, leaving him eligible for parole in 18 months. "If you don't change your ways and stop this nonsense," Porada said, "then you are going to end up in jail a good part of your life. I hope you don't take it as a lecture, just that I really care about someone like you...and I just see your life going down the drain," the judge said. Triplett's first parole, issued on Jan. 3 1985, came after two years and lasted exactly one month. No records are available on why Triplett was sent back to prison. Triplett's next parole came in August 1986; he lasted three months before being arrested twice in one week—first, on an illegal firearms charge after a fight outside the After Five Lounge; and then again after allegedly stealing a car and leading six police cruisers on a chase through downtown Springfield before ramming an unmarked cruiser.

This information helped me understand the voids of time when he was missing from home. Now I knew exactly where he was. The more I learned, the more I felt cheated. I had stayed up all those nights worrying about Ervin's safe return home when he himself was the one jeopardizing his own safety.

My feelings of being cheated were now coupled with the anger, disappointment, and sadness that I felt as I sat on my bed. It felt like I was watching Ervin's final act of unspeakable horror unfold. I was forced to admit to myself that my brother was a monster. He had to be. He had killed an innocent elderly woman. What kind of person does it take to do that?

As I thought back and put the timeline of the crime together, I realized that he had murdered Alice Kelly the day before I saw him at Blockbuster Video. I could not have imagined in my wildest dreams that the strange vibe I had sensed that night was associated with murder.

It took the police about two months to apprehend Ervin. They didn't have to work hard, though; he was already in jail in another city for attempted auto theft.

Sunday Republican
Sunday, September 13, 1992
Slaying suspect a symbol of system's failure
By JACK FLYNN

As Triplett stood handcuffed in a Springfield courtroom last week, a Hampden County prosecutor accused him of killing a 79-year-old woman last month, only weeks after he had been charged with two other crimes: breaking into a woman's apartment in Westfield and assaulting an elderly woman in Springfield. When police began their manhunt for Triplett on the murder charge, they found him locked up in East Granby, Conn., where he was being held on $5,000 bail after allegedly trying to steal a car. Police also consider Triplett a suspect in the unsolved murder of a male flight attendant in June in a downtown Springfield hotel.

One of the *Sunday Republican* articles about Ervin, written by Jack Flynn, was titled, "Slaying suspect a symbol of system's failure." Jack was more right than he could know. The penal system had failed Ervin, Ervin's case worker, Tyrone, had failed, and I had failed. We all failed. Our failure of not rehabilitating Ervin became our failure to save Alice Kelly's life.

I believe we all tried to help Ervin, but it was not enough. I did everything in my power to help him, but my conscience has never been satisfied with my effort. It wasn't until I heard the details of the cold, callous, senseless crime that my feelings of failure to help my brother turned to feelings of numbness.

Springfield Union
Friday, February 5, 1993

Triplett pleads guilty to first degree murder
By BRIAN MELLEY

> On Sept. 6, Triplett confessed to murdering Kelly... He said he awoke the morning of the murder in his mother's 166 Quincy street house and was on his way to the basketball courts at Forest Park when he passed Kelly's apartment in the elderly housing complex. He noticed that Kelly's back door was open so he walked in. The 5-foot-tall, 90 pound woman was doing something at the sink when she turned and saw Triplett. "I panicked," he said in his confession. "I lunged forward and grabbed her by the neck. The woman hit me on the side of my head... She couldn't say anything because I was squeezing her throat. I used both hands. We fell by the front door, which was closed. I was scared. In a matter of minutes it was all over. The woman wasn't moving at all and I just sat there for a while." In his confession, Triplett said he raped Kelly after she was dead to cover up the crime. But an autopsy showed that he raped her before strangling her and he admitted that in court... "I then picked her up and took her to the bathroom... I just wanted to get rid of her. I dropped her face down in the tub."

This started a metamorphosis within me that allowed me to distance myself from the man I knew and loved as my brother. It was now clear to me that Ervin did not value his own life, so it made no sense for me to value it. He had made his decision and decided his own fate. I needed to accept that.

Dissolving any connection with Ervin became even easier when it occurred to me that the lady he had murdered was close to my grandmother's age. I thought about a billion things when I made this connection. I felt terrible for the men and women who lost a mom, the men and women who lost a sister, and all the children who lost an aunt and grandmother. What if this were my grandmother? How would I feel? What would I be prepared to do to the person who did this to her? This realization and moment of clarity allowed me to purge all the caring, love, and concern I had for Ervin. It was like the depiction of a spirit leaving a body.

As more information about the case was released, I was sure Ervin would end up dead because it was reported that Alice Kelly's son was a correctional officer. This meant he had ties and could be influential behind the walls of the prison system. I was sure if he could find a way to retaliate for the death of his mom without being associated with the incident, he would arrange it. If Ervin did end up dead, I would have to accept his fate because he had unjustifiably taken an innocent life for no reason.

Unlike Haven's trial, Ervin's trial was not closed to the public. Coverage of the trial was broadcast on TV for all to see. I watched as court officers escorted Ervin to the witness stand. He was wearing a University of Michigan coat with his hands cuffed behind his back. His hair was braided past his shoulders, and each braid was terminated with red, white, and blue twist ties. He didn't look like he was in court at all. He looked peaceful, serene, and content as if he were taking a walk in the park. I concentrated on the look on his face and realized that he really just did not care about anything. The image of my brother that I saw on the television that day is burnt into my mind forever.

When Ervin was halfway across the courtroom, it happened. The courtroom exploded into mad chaos. The son of Alice Kelly charged toward Ervin. I watched as Ervin, who was handcuffed, turned in the direction of the charging man while trying to keep his balance. The court officers surrounded Ervin and blocked the Kelly son from reaching him to retaliate for the unspeakable things done to his mom. Several female relatives in the Kelly family were screaming and crying as the Kelly son was restrained by court officers.

I sat on my bed and watched with a broken spirit as my brother tried to fend for his safety. I couldn't turn the station off—I had to watch. I know I didn't want to see Ervin hurt, but at the same time I didn't want to help protect him either. He had to pay for what he did; it was his day of reckoning.

The trial proceedings disappeared from my TV as the station took a commercial break. I'm sure this was done so that the court officers and judge could bring order back to the courtroom. When coverage of the court case resumed, the Kelly family members were all sitting back down, and Ervin was sitting on the witness stand. He was there because there was no need to go through the jury selection process. There was no reason to review evidence, and it was not necessary to cross-examine witnesses. Ervin had told his lawyer that he wanted to confess and enter a guilty plea to the charge of first-degree murder.

Springfield Union
Friday, February 5, 1993

Triplett pleads guilty to first degree murder
By BRIAN MELLEY

The jail khakis Ervin Triplett Jr. wore when he confessed to murdering 79-year-old Alice Kelly to police officers were penned with these words: "I'm gone for natural life." Yesterday he got his wish by taking the rare step of pleading guilty to first-degree murder in the first known case of its kind in Western Massachusetts. He was sentenced to life in Cedar Junction Prison without parole. The mandatory sentence was not enough for numerous Kelly family members who hailed their deceased mother and grandmother, called Triplett a coward and criticized the justice system that had let him walk free without bail on another charge 12 days before the murder. Some suggested cruel punishment like Alice Kelly's last minutes. Sharon A. Kelly, a daughter-in-law, suggested castration and lynching. When Paul Kelly ended his tearful remembrance of his grandmother by yelling, "Rot in hell, you bastard," Triplett replied, "I will see you there." Then the courtroom erupted. A number of Kelly family members rushed toward Triplett but were held back by court officers... Judge Moriarity called for order. "One more outburst like that and you're all out of here. I can sympathize with your feelings, but I cannot tolerate that kind of behavior." ...Defense lawyer Terry Scott Nagel said Triplett told him from the beginning that he wanted to plead guilty. He agreed to be returned here from Connecticut, and he told Nagel not to file any motion to bar his confession from evidence. "I've represented defendants in a dozen murder cases, and each presents a unique challenge," Nagel said outside court. "In this one I had the defendant order me not to put on a defense. That is so unusual." Tests by psychologists and psychiatrists determined that Triplett was sane and competent to stand trial, Nagel said. Because he had no evidence for an insanity defense, Nagel had no choice but to honor Triplett's wish. District Attorney William M. Bennett said his office researched the law to see if a first-degree murder plea is acceptable. He said he found no prior cases in this part of the state, but at least one in the Boston area. Lawyers who passed through the courthouse during the day said they had never heard of anyone pleading guilty to first-degree murder. If anything, people charged with first-degree murder plead guilty, at the most, to second-degree murder, which also carries a life sentence, but offers a parole hearing in 15 years. If not, they take the case to trial where there is a chance of acquittal and an automatic appeal if they are convicted...

Triplett stood up in his University of Michigan coat and listened to the sentence... He moved his head side to side to each word as the judge said his prison sentence..."for the rest of your natural life."

It finally became clear to me that Ervin had always wanted his destiny to be life in prison. On this day he was getting his wish.

As I watched him on the stand confessing to capital murder, I knew this would be the last time I would see him. I knew I would not be able to bring myself to visit him in prison and try to have a normal conversation. After all, I am not sure what I would say to a person who deliberately throws his life away.

After some soul searching, I closed this chapter of my life. I thought back as far as I could and realized that I did not have one pleasant memory of the man I once called my brother. It has been twenty years since I have seen or spoken with Ervin.

Death, tragedy, and personal loss were all old friends to me. My experience with this trio made it easier for me to accept Ervin's loss. I knew that I now had to accept that my dream of reuniting my family would never materialize. I knew I would now have to settle for much less. This made me change my objective from reuniting my entire family to helping my little sister prepare for her future. I knew if I didn't intervene as an influential figure in Serena's life that she would probably end up dealing with the same hardships as my mother.

My plan was to assist Serena with her middle school and high school studies whenever I could. I was also going to start a college fund for her so she would have a better chance of attending college than I had. It was evident that when the time came, neither her mother nor father was going to be able to help her with the financial burden of college. I knew I was her only hope outside of grants and scholarships, and time was running out—she was already in ninth grade.

Serena stood a good chance of getting a scholarship because she excelled in school. Every marking period her report card had nothing but As and Bs, and she consistently made the honor roll. She had nothing but redeemable personality traits. She was respectful to adults, she was focused in school, and she wasn't promiscuous like some of the girls I remember when I was in middle school. I am not sure exactly where Serena acquired her commendable characteristics. I believe I helped some, but I know I can't take full credit.

On a daily basis I would tell Serena, "Whatever you do in life, don't be like your mother." I wasn't proud that I had to say this to her, but my mother didn't leave me a choice in the matter. She was not being a good role model. Her priorities were scrambled. She let others drag her down financially, she chose the people she dated carelessly, and, worst of all, the ranking of her family and own well-being was placed last in the hierarchy of importance. I could not sit idly by and let Serena think that the way my mother chose to live her life was her only option in life. If I had learned anything from my grandmother, it was that the voice of guidance can sometimes have more influence than an environment.

I didn't forget that Channel 22 had unjustly labeled me as a rapist and murderer. Was this done deliberately? I initially didn't think it was, and I probably would not have taken any further actions if not for two things. The first is that Channel 22 kept making the error even after my girlfriend and I had called to inform them that they had the wrong name. The second is that someone on the staff flippantly replied, "We are looking into it. If that's not good enough, sue us!" This response made me feel that the station was being malicious and reckless. They were the only station making the error, and as far as I was concerned they had not done anything to correct it.

I never found out exactly how the error was made, but I had my theory. Here is what I think happened: I came home from work and found that my bedroom was ransacked by the police. I went to check on Ervin after my mother told me that he was the one they were looking for. My arrival to Ervin's girlfriend's house was followed by my arrest for fishing without a license. The primary reason I was arrested was so the detectives could get my fingerprints. At the exact same time Ervin was thirty minutes away in Hartford, Connecticut, locked up for attempted auto theft. All that was known at the time of Channel 22's report was that a man named Triplett was being sought by police. My guess is that the confidential source used by Channel 22 somehow received my arrest paperwork. I believe that attention was only given to my last name and the fact that I was arrested in Springfield, where the Kelly murder occurred. The confidential source had failed to read the charges for my arrest and then erroneously reported my name to the Channel 22 news staff. In a heated rush to be the first network to break the news about the murderer's capture, Channel 22 incorrectly released my name as the suspect.

To follow through with Channel 22's recommendation to sue them, I contacted a lawyer and explained the details of my case. The lawyer agreed to represent me on a contingency basis. My girlfriend and I met with him once a week to begin building a file. He told us up front that cases like these usually end up without a monetary award because the affected party usually can not substantiate *damages*. He explained that professionals who deal with the public have a reputation that can be *damaged*. For example, if I were a doctor, I could claim that clients no longer wanted to use my services because of the broadcast. I could show *damages* in the form of a reduction in clientele. If I were a business own-er, I could claim that since the day of the broadcast, people no longer bought my products. I could establish *damages* in the form of a reduction in sales.

This concept of damages seemed to leave the common person with-out recourse. When he explained this to us, I thought about dropping the case until we talked a bit more. He asked me if I had ever been in trouble for anything, and I told him that I had been arrested for fishing without a license. He told me that if that was the only thing on my record that we could probably establish damage to my reputation by what peo-ple in my community might now think about me. He convinced me that all the work I had put into keeping myself out of trouble for my entire life was maliciously undermined by Channel 22. He said this should be worth something. I thought about what he said and realized that he was right. Channel 22 *was* malicious and careless about what they reported, and it was also hard work staying out of trouble in the neighborhoods where I lived. This new perspective helped me decide to continue with the lawsuit.

For six months my girlfriend and I worked with my lawyer to build a case against Channel 22. Collecting evidence of the malicious broadcast was easy since it was all public. The difficult part of building the case came when I had to meet with Channel 22's legal staff for depositions. I was grilled about different aspects of what their lawyers kept calling "the mistake." I thought how pompous it was to call something that occurred continuously for three hours a mistake.

I had been prepared to expect the worst by my lawyer, so I was able to answer the repetitive and insulting questions with little agitation. When depositions were over, my lawyer told me that I had done great and that he had a good feeling about the trial.

On the day of the trial I was leery of retaliation from the Kelly fam-ily, especially after seeing the altercation at Ervin's trial. I know if the shoe was on the other foot and someone in my family was viciously mur-dered that the targets for my reprisal would include brothers, sisters, aunts, uncles, and the family pet. I knew my safety might be in jeopardy between the time I parked my car until the time I entered the main court. However, the environment that I came from did not allow the emotion of fear to be an excuse. I knew I had to go through with the trial. My girlfriend and I entered the courthouse without incident and went to meet my lawyer. As I was walking down the corridor, a gentleman walked up to me, extended his arm for a handshake, and said, "Hi, I'm Terry Nagel. I defended your brother Ervin. He's wasted goods. I wanted to put on a defense, but he wouldn't let me. Good luck today." And he was gone. Wow, it was absolutely mind-blowing to hear it from the horse's mouth. For a brief moment, Ervin's lawyer made me think about why my brother had made the choice to forego a defense. I quickly realized that I would never figure that out, so I gave up thinking about it and focused back on my own case.

We continued down the corridor to meet with my lawyer, who informed us that Channel 22 had made a settlement offer of ten thousand dollars. He followed up by telling me that the choice to accept or deny the offer was totally up to me. My first thought was to reject the offer because after my deposition and lawyer's fees were deducted, I would be left with only three thousand dollars. I found it strange that I had taken this position with a cash offer on the table. To someone from my humble background, three thousand dollars was a truckload of money; however, I knew exactly why I felt the way I did. I was going to need much more than that to help Serena get through college. On a selfish note, I wanted to punish the television giant for being smug with me and for minimizing what they had done.

After my girlfriend and I discussed it, I told my lawyer that we preferred to let the jury hear the case and let them decide whether we should prevail. The trial lasted for about an hour. Both my attorney and the defense attorney asked me and my girlfriend questions about the *mistake* that Channel 22 had made. Once both attorneys rested, the judge took over. He informed the jury that they needed to answer five questions listed on a form that was given to the jury foreman. The judge told the jury that the answer to each question had to be a unanimous decision, and then they went into deliberations. The jury was out for a little more than half an hour before we were called back into the courtroom to hear the judge read the verdict.

The first four questions on the form were related to whether the jury felt that Channel 22 was responsible and at fault for airing the broadcast with the incorrect information. The judge reported that the jury answered them in favor of the plaintiff. The last question asked for the dollar amount award that the jury felt that the plaintiff should receive based on damages. The judge reported that the jury had entered an amount of zero dollars—ZERO dollars! The verdict was zero dollars because I did not have a reputation to damage in the eyes of the justice system. Had the jury truly put themselves in my shoes? Did they realize that if they let a broadcast giant like Channel 22 remain unaccountable, they would continue to develop reports based on unverified information? Did they think about the same thing happening to them?

I was disappointed with the jury's decision not because there was no cash award but because the verdict minimized the worth of the common blue-collar worker's reputation. This experience made me realize that if I was ever on a jury deciding a case like this, I was going to hold the corporate giant responsible, regardless of whether the plaintiff was a doctor or a common citizen.

There was a rumor floating around my mother's job that there would be layoffs because Digital Equipment hadn't stayed competitive in the new computer age. My mother had worked there for seventeen years. Her longevity at Digital would prove to be profitable. DEC was offering an early retirement plan dubbed "the golden handshake." The people who chose to take the golden handshake would receive one thousand dollars for every year of service in addition to six months' severance and a payout for unused vacation. For a while my mother debated whether she should take the early retirement package. She probably was thinking, *What will I do next? Will I be able to find another job?* After weighing the pros and cons, she decided to take the package. After taxes, she ended up getting twenty-four thousand dollars.

My mother was in shock and had no idea what to do with the enormous check. For starters, she didn't have a checking account. Either she or one of her so-called *friends* had written bad checks from an account that was in her name. This act of fraud had landed her in Chex Systems. Chex Systems is a national database that banks use to monitor people who maliciously write bad checks. If you end up in this system, no bank in America will grant you checking account privileges.

My mother was in a dilemma. Against my better judgment, I stepped in to help her out. My reason for doing this was selfish. I was motivated to help because I knew Serena was going to benefit from this money. Also, if I didn't help, I thought my mother might do something foolish like ask one of her *friends* to put the money in their account. When the thought first crossed my mind, I winced as I visualized her not getting a dime of it back.

I offered to let my mother keep her severance in my savings account. I had no savings anyway, so it was just like the money was in a separate account. Before we made the deposit, I made her agree to some ground rules. I was forced to do this because my mother was not good with budgets or money management. On top of this I anticipated being blamed if the money was spent too quickly. Our agreement was as follows: I would only make withdrawals out of my savings account when she gave me permission, she was going to pay off all her old debts, and she was going to get a part-time job in order to replenish any money that was spent. This was going to be a fresh start for her. Once she agreed to the terms, we went to the bank and made the deposit.

My mother asked me to handle the task of paying off her old debts. I did the research to find out who she owed and how much. Once I was done paying her creditors, she had about eighteen thousand dollars left.

I calculated that this money would only last about a year with her every-day living expenses and reminded her to find a part-time job as soon as possible. She needed to keep her severance replenished until she found a full-time job.

Around this time, my mother added some new *friends* to her inner circle, Ralphina and Lorenzo. Ralphina was a nice lady who never said an ill word to me, but something wasn't quite right with her. It was like she was a few fries short of a Happy Meal. I just couldn't pinpoint what was missing. Lorenzo was like my mother's friend Clarence. He was another pissy drunk alcoholic who slurred his words as he spoke them.

My mother, Lorenzo, and Ralphina were together every day now that my mother was retired, and neither Ralphina nor Lorenzo worked. When I would return home from work, they were always sitting in the living room. They were three of a kind, like peas in a pod. I had kept a close watch on my mother's part-time job search, which appeared to be slim to none. It was evident to me that she hadn't looked because every day for months she and Ralphina were in front of the television going crazy when one of them beat Tetris level five. Out of respect, I didn't say too much about her laidback effort. The one thing I did do was warn her again that her money would not last. My warning fell upon deaf ears.

In the days to follow, I noticed that Al wasn't around anymore. I hadn't seen her kick him out, but he was no longer living with us. Questions began to cross my mind. Did he do something worse than what he usually had done to my mother? *Could* he do something worse? Why hadn't she kicked him out before? Maybe the thousands of dollars that were in my savings account had liberated her from feeling like she needed the financial "crutch" that Al provided? I had no answers to these questions, but Al was for sure kicked out for good. I saw it with my own eyes and still couldn't believe it. I thought, *Finally! She figured out the error of her ways—no more alcoholic bums!* I was happy and thought my mother was turning her life around, but I was wrong. My mother's new independence and confidence had nothing to do with deciding to make the right changes in her life. Her new attitude was really a smug demeanor supported by eighteen thousand dollars that she had in my savings account. I found this out when she spit some of her newfound venom at me. It happened after I made one last plea for her to get a part-time job to supplement her cash funds.

It happened one day when I came home from work. As usual, the national Tetris championship was in full swing. As I walked by, I said, "Ma, you really need to get a job…you can't keep playing Tetris and expect your money to last forever." She replied, "I have money. I don't need a job!" I said, "Okay, remember you said that, and when all your money is gone, don't say I didn't warn you." That's when she said, "It's time for you to go. You need to get out my house!" Wow! Imagine that. I was worried about her welfare, hadn't laid a hand on her, didn't call her a bad name, had not urinated on her kitchen floor, or taken advantage of her friendship, yet I was the *only* one (besides Al) that she had ever told to get out of her house. The only reason I was still living with her in the first place was to help her out with the rent, so moving out wasn't a problem. I told her I would be out by the end of the week and that I would give her a bank check in the amount of the remaining golden handshake funds. I knew she was going to squander the money and that she would have none left in a matter of months, but that was her problem now.

Moving out of my mother's apartment was going to be beneficial and was going to result in a lifestyle upgrade for me. My credit was decent, I had a pretty good job, and my girlfriend, who just graduated from the University of Massachusetts, was planning to move in with me. With two incomes, finding a decent place was going to be a breeze.

We found a place in a huge, three-story home. The living room and den both had shiny hardwood floors. There was a stacked washer and dryer in the kitchen and a modern stove and refrigerator. We were also given one parking space near the garage in the back of the home. I was ecstatic. This place was much better than my first apartment near the welfare office.

The home was located on the dividing line of respectable and corrupt neighborhoods. How ironic. I was living on the invisible line that the city board member had drawn on the map of Springfield. If I walked a quarter mile to the right, I would be in the middle of gang activity and low-income housing. If I walked a quarter mile to the left, I would be near a private boarding school for girls and a gated condo complex. From there, I could see the Springfield skyline. This contrast in neighborhoods actually worked out great for me. When I wanted to see my friends and get a Soul food or Spanish food dinner, I would exit my driveway and turn right. When I wanted to go downtown to the mall, visit the Museum of Art and Sciences, or go to the library, I would exit my driveway and turn left. I had the best of both worlds.

After finding this place, I was glad that my mother had kicked me out. My only regret about moving was that I wasn't going to see Serena every day. When I was moving my last box out of my mother's apartment, I told Serena that if she needed anything to give me a call. I also told her that every chance I had, I would visit to see how she was doing.

Around this same time my brother Haven contacted me to tell me that he was now eligible for parole. He told me that in the next few days he would be meeting with the parole board to see if he could get release approval. The first time he met with them they had set a date and approved his release. This was fantastic news.

A few days after his scheduled release, Haven contacted me to let me know that the parole board did not grant his release as promised. He was furious that he had been lied to and felt that he was being manipulated. He summarized how he felt about the parole board process. His exact words were, "This is bullshit!" I knew exactly how he felt.

I thought I knew what might be going on, so I shared my thoughts with him. It seemed to me that the parole board was now acting like the professors who taught the first year of engineering school. The only difference was that instead of trying to weed out students, they were using games and manipulation to weed out inmates who were not ready for release. My belief was that they would give an inmate false hope of an approved release to determine mental stability and emotional control. What better way to do this than by playing a few mind games that might result in uncontrolled acts of anger?

When Haven and I would speak on the phone, I would tell him to just be patient with the process. He had already done ten years in prison and was so close to getting out that at this time more than ever he had to walk on eggshells. I told him to just hang in there and let him know that I already had a place set up for him in my apartment.

In the back of my mind I was still contemplating my return to college. My problem was that I just didn't know how I would ever make it happen. It felt like I was trapped. If I quit my job and gave up my apartment to go back to college, I wouldn't be able to survive. If I kept my apartment and job, I could survive but I couldn't go back to college. Despite my quandary, I knew that I had to find a way to continue my education. My grandmother and my instincts told me that education was the key to progress, and that is exactly what I wanted. For now, I was just doing what was necessary to prepare myself for the moment when opportunity came knocking.

A big part of my plan was to try to save as much money as I could. I convinced my girlfriend to support this strategy. We agreed that we would stay focused on our goals and would not live beyond our means. Where I'm from, living beyond your means is called living "ghetto fabulous." This disease is rampant throughout poverty-stricken ghettos, and you can see it for miles around. It usually starts attacking the wallet and brain at the age of sixteen and gets progressively worse. Symptoms begin with erratic, thoughtless brain signals. The carrier starts to believe it is a good idea to purchase a brand-new forty-thousand-dollar car while living in a state-funded apartment. Studies have concluded that the ghetto fabulous microorganisms thrive heavily and mass produce in businesses like Rent-to-Own operations. In these environments, the disease usually enters stage two. During this stage the carrier realizes the appliance they've always wanted could be in their living room in a matter of days. All it takes is the simple stroke of a pen on an ill-advised contract. As it stands today, the only known cure for this disease is a swift smack to the back of the head. I could not tell you why I never caught this disease. Perhaps it was the 10 cc inoculation of knowledge that my grandmother gave to me. In any case, we were both aware of this highly contagious epidemic and tried to avoid getting infected at all costs.

It had been about three months since my mother kicked me out of her house. I didn't harbor any hard feelings against her, so I decided to stop by to see how she and my sister were doing. This is when I first met Richard Murchison, or Murch, as he was known in the streets.

My mother sure knew how to pick them. This guy was a shady-looking character who always had a smirk on his face that looked like he had just swindled you out of your last five dollars. He always looked like he was on his way somewhere and never looked relaxed. When my mother introduced him to me, my only thought was that I wouldn't trust this guy with a bag full of pennies.

I was surprised to find out that he wasn't an alcoholic. I wasn't naïve, though, because with my mother's circle of friends and boyfriends, the balance of nature always applied. They always had at least one major character flaw. The word on the street was that Murch had been in prison and that at one time in his life he made his livelihood as a pimp. When I learned this, only two thoughts crossed my mind: *Another perfect choice* and *I have to get Serena out of that house.* There was nothing I could do about the choices my mother made, but I could do something about getting Serena out of that environment.

I told Serena that I wanted her to come live with me, but for some reason she declined my offer. I didn't ask her to explain why she didn't want to move; I just let it be. I let her know that if she ever changed her mind the option would always be available.

This time it turned out that my mother was going to go the extra mile with Murch. She was planning to marry him. I could not figure out what she was thinking. Perhaps I should have asked myself if she was thinking at all. Maybe it was just me being too critical. I'm sure there are several women who are waiting for an ex-convict pimp to come into their lives.

I couldn't bring myself to go to their wedding because I didn't want to give them the impression that they had my support. Plus, I was never invited. I can't remember how I received details of their wedding, but someone told me that they had a small ceremony at the local church located down the street from my mother's apartment. She was no longer Mattie Triplett; she was now Mattie Murchison. Her new name had a good ring to it, but even I knew that a successful marriage needed much more than a good name. From what I knew about them both, a long, happy marriage was not in the cards they were holding. Mooch, as I called him, didn't have a job, and he had no aspirations to get one. He, too, was dead weight, just like the rest of my mother's ill-chosen suitors.

I tried to keep from thinking about how their wedding was funded, but I knew. I was sure my mother had to foot the bill from her golden handshake funds. I tried to keep from thinking that the only reason Mooch was marrying my mother was because he heard she had come into some money. I didn't let it bother me too much because even if it were true, I wasn't planning to intervene. I guess I just accepted the fact that my mother was doing what made her happy. Who was I to get in the way?

After my mother was married, my visits to her apartment became less frequent. I hadn't checked in for a while, but I figured everything was fine since I had not heard from Serena. My assumption was proven wrong in the worst way when I finally decided to stop by to see how Serena was doing.

It was around 5:00 p.m. in the middle of the week, and I had just finished my shift at work. On my commute back home I started thinking about my sister, so I went by my mother's to visit her. I knocked on the door when I arrived. Serena answered the door and let me in. I gave her a big hug and we went into the living room to talk. I started catching up with her to see how things were going in school. She told me that everything was going fine and that she had made the honor roll once again this quarter. I was happy to see that, despite her environment, she was still able to focus and persevere. It told me a lot about her character. In the middle of our conversation, I asked her to hold her thoughts while I went to use the bathroom.

As I walked through the kitchen to get to the bathroom, I noticed that there were two steaks cooking on the stove and two empty sponge cake molds on dessert plates sitting on the table. They were the kind used to make strawberry shortcake. They were only missing the strawberries and whip cream. I figured my mother was making dinner...but steak and strawberry shortcake? That was never the main course when I lived there. I guessed things had really improved since the last time I had visited.

When I returned from the bathroom, my mother was in the kitchen putting the steaks on two different plates and completing the fixings for the strawberry shortcakes. As she was doing this, we spoke to each other briefly then she took the food and disappeared back into her bedroom. Now it made sense. She had made a special treat for her husband. Clearly, this was a sign that they were getting along well. They had to be because I noticed the happy demeanor in which my mother fixed the plates. Mooch wouldn't have been my choice for husband of the year, but if he was making my mother happy and if she wasn't getting physically abused, who was I to judge?

When I returned to the living room to finish talking with Serena, she looked at me somberly and said, "I'm hungry, and there's no food in the house." At first when she said it, I thought I didn't hear her clearly because I just saw our mother making steak and strawberry shortcake. I turned my ear to her to make sure I heard her correctly this time and said, "What?" She said it again: "I'm hungry, and there's no food in the house." Something didn't add up. I decided to go check the refrigerator and the pantry to see if there was anything that I could put together for her, but she was right: there was nothing.

Instantly my temperature doubled. I could feel sweat beads on my forehead. It felt like my blood was pumping through my veins and arteries three times faster than normal. If I were Bill Bixby, I would have turned into the Incredible Hulk on the spot. I was so mad that I felt like killing everybody!

You had to be kidding me! My mother was in her bedroom with her mooching husband eating one of the best meals I'd ever seen her make, and my little sister was sitting outside the door to her room hungry! Arrrggghhh! I felt that I was going to lose it and go crazy, but the one sane brain cell I had left overpowered my thought process. Somehow I was able to keep my emotions under control. Short of executing everyone in the house, I decided that the best course of action would be to keep my mouth shut and take Serena with me to get her something to eat.

I found myself a little upset with Serena too. Why hadn't she called me to let me know that this was occurring? I thought about it and realized that Serena did not want to ask me for *anything*. She would rather deal with the problems on her own. The more I thought about it, the more it made sense. That was the code in our family. Deal with your own problems—handle it yourself. She was cut from the same cloth as the rest of us, and she was following suit. It wasn't her fault that we all taught her exactly the wrong thing to do. Once I realized this, I kicked myself a bit for getting upset with her.

I had a long talk with her as I took her to buy her dinner. My goal was to try to modify her thinking about asking for help. She needed to know that it was acceptable to ask for help and that she didn't have to feel guilty or weak for getting support to solve a problem. I let her know that what she had been taught was flawed and self-defeating behavior.

I left my mother's apartment that day with my emotions in a knot. Her despicable display of neglect made me feel like cutting her out of my life for good, but I wanted to think about it a bit more. It had been a long day. I was exhausted, and I needed to rest, so I went home and quickly fell asleep on my couch.

A few hours later, I was awakened by the telephone. It was my friend Archie. He said, "You watchin' it?" I told him I didn't know what he was talking about. He followed up by telling me that O.J. Simpson was in his white Ford Bronco being followed by police down a California highway. The exhilarating yet shocking news woke me up out of my groggy state. I said, "No way!" Then I turned the TV to CNN and watched with the world. As I viewed the slow-moving Ford Bronco, I thought, *Finally, something good to watch on TV, something I can relate to.* When I heard the details of what had happened, the thought that crossed my mind was that this story and I were old friends. There were two people dead, it was being televised and broadcast on TV, several families were affected by a tragedy, and, in the end, everyone was going to lose.

Two months was all it took, and Mr. Murchison was ready to take his name back and leave my mother. I found this out when I stopped by to visit and check on Serena. Two months must have been the time he needed to manipulate my mother into spending her nest egg. The money was gone, so now it was time for him to leave and find another victim. It seemed logical to me that an ex-pimp would follow this principle.

Mooch's speedy exit made my mother turn back to her friends Ralphina and Lorenzo and her daily challenge of trying to topple Tetris level 5. Once again my mother had ended up exactly where she had started almost one year ago. She was barely making ends meet, debts were piling up, and she and her friends were wasting time doing a bunch of nothing on a daily basis.

If not for the fact that my little sister lived with my mother, I probably would have stopped visiting a long time ago. I was mentally exhausted and did not want to see, hear, or be around stupidity anymore. I had been tolerant long enough. I told Serena that, going forward, I was only going to visit a few times a year. I told her that if she needed anything she was going to have to call me and ask for it. That day, I left my mother's apartment with no plans of returning for a while. It was time for me to focus on more positive things.

It was April 1994, and Haven called to tell me that he had met with the parole board once again and they granted his release. They had done this a few times before, so I could tell that Haven had no confidence that they would follow through this time. He told me that his best guess was that he would be released some day in July. I told him that when he found out the exact date to give me a call and I would be there to pick him up.

I spent the next three months devising ways to supplement my salary. I was hoping that I would be able to double or triple my money so that I could go back to school someday. It was all a dream, but I had to try something.

In my search to find an investment opportunity, I met two young entrepreneurs. They were trying to do the same thing I was—paving a way to a better life. We noticed that in our town, many of the local clubs had been shut down for one reason or another. This left our city lacking any quality entertainment. We viewed this as an opportunity and decided to pool our money to promote entertainment venues. We talked about hosting concerts, holding dance parties at nightclubs, and renting banquet halls to have comedy shows.

We started out with small venues at first to get a feel for what people wanted. Once we felt that we understood the market, we upgraded the size and notoriety of the headliners at our venues. We aired radio advertisements, walked the city late at night to distribute flyers, and had free ticket giveaways to promote our events. It was hard work, but we did it all. We lost money or broke even on four of five promotions. The fifth promotion yielded an insignificant return on investment in comparison to the promotional work we did. Obviously this was not the outcome we wanted, but as far as *I* was concerned, it wasn't all for nothing.

From working as an entertainment promoter, I learned the ins and outs of running a business, I learned how to negotiate, I learned the hard lessons of making a bad deal, I learned why contracts were necessary, and I learned why it was important to have good business partners. These were valuable intangible benefits that I probably would not have learned any other way. The final benefit, which I categorize as an invaluable experience, was meeting the entertainers we hired to perform. At the time when I met them, they were struggling comedians; now they are Hollywood stars.

One of the comedy shows that we promoted hosted two small-time comedians. One of them was named Fred Ricks, and the other was JB Smoove. This particular comedy show was a blast. It was standing room only, and the audience could not stop laughing. It was a really good night. My partners and I each made one hundred dollars after all the expenses were paid. It wasn't much, but at least we didn't lose money.

The bonus for me this night was that I had to pick up Fred Ricks from a hotel and bring him to the show. He was planning to stay the night instead of taking the ride back to his home in New York City. I remember our ride back to the comedy show. Fred was explaining to me that even though he was still taking small shows like the one he was doing that night, he was working on something that would get him a Hollywood deal. I remember thinking that he was just talking, even though he sounded sincere. But years later in the year 2000, I saw him debut in a movie directed by John Singleton entitled *Shaft*. In 2001 Fred again emerged on the Hollywood scene. This time he starred in *Baby Boy* – another movie directed by John Singleton. Fred was serious the night he told me that he was working on something. My brief interaction with him that night makes me feel like I was a very small part of his success story. It is a thrill to know that I had a personal moment with someone who made it in Hollywood.

JB Smoove was the other comedian who performed that night. He also became a Hollywood comedian/actor. In his breakout role, he starred as a character named Leon on Larry David's TV comedy "Curb Your Enthusiasm." Then he followed his debut by co-starring on a TV One comedy, "The Real Househusbands of Hollywood." Both shows are hilarious, and JB Smoove is still funnier than ever. Every time I watch the show and see him, I relive the comedy show my partners and I promoted. I again feel like I, in some way, served a purpose in helping him to achieve his success.

In a different comedy show that we promoted, we hosted Fred Ricks again, but this time he told us that we could add Tracy Morgan to the venue. He personally knew Tracy and was going to bring him as the main host. Even though we had littered the town to let everyone know that Tracy Morgan was coming, the crowd that night was sparse. The show still ended up being a big hit because Tracy had everyone in the small crowd falling out of their chairs. It was so bad that most of the time it was hard to hear his routine over the gut-busting laughter. Years later, Tracy Morgan would host "Saturday Night Live" and star on a hit TV show entitled "30 Rock." I was absolutely positive that it was my handshake and brief conversation with Tracy after the comedy show that helped him achieve all his success.

After months of nightclub parties and comedy shows, I somehow had not become rich. In fact, I ended up losing money in the end. My plan to make the money I needed to go back to school didn't pan out, but I could not complain. My personal interaction with Fred, JB, and Tracy was beyond the value of any money I would have made.

It was late July, and I anticipated a call from Haven. The call never came. Instead, I came home from work one day and he was sitting on the couch in my living room talking to my girlfriend. What a fantastic surprise! I remember the day like it was yesterday. He was sitting on my couch wearing tan khakis and a t-shirt. He looked calm and relaxed but also looked like he was on guard waiting for an inevitable attack. I understood. He had just come from a dangerous place that housed dangerous people. He himself was dangerous, so his demeanor made sense.

After we greeted each other, I asked him how he was able to get to my apartment. He told me that he took the bus. He said, "I couldn't wait to get away from there. It cost me every dime I had, but it was worth it!" I felt an internal calm and a sense of recovery. It felt like a new beginning with my big brother back home. It was time for Haven to reclaim the remaining years of his life.

When I first saw Haven's discharge paperwork, I thought about its symbolic representation. It did not represent innocence or guilt; it represented "life, liberty and the pursuit of happiness." This paperwork meant that Haven would be free to walk in the park; it meant that he would be free to live; it meant that he had options and choices that prison did not provide; and, last but not least, Haven was not going to die in prison. I can only imagine the true magnitude of the exhilaration Haven felt when he realized this.

The Commonwealth of Massachusetts
Department of Correction
CERTIFICATE OF DISCHARGE

Know all men by these presents

It having been made to appear to the Commissioner of Correction that

Haven Triplett .... No. W-41046 ....

A prisoner sentenced to .... MCI – Cedar Junction ....

Is entitled to have the term of his imprisonment reduced by a deduction from the maximum term of said sentence for good behavior.

Now, therefore in accordance with the law so made and provided in chapter 127 Of the General laws (Ter.Ed.) and Acts in amendment thereto it is ordered the Commissioner of Correction that the said prisoner be, and is hereby discharged from Further Imprisonment on the.......20th........day of ....July 1994

Larry F. DuBois

_____

Commissioner of Correction

Commissioner of Correction:

The above-named prisoner was discharged from imprisonment in accordance With the above order of the Commissioner of Correction on this ....15th........day of ....July 1994

Williams Coalter

_____

Superintendent

FORM 111.

I wasn't sure what Haven's plans were now that he had his life back. At the moment it didn't really matter. All I knew was that I needed to be there for him in his time of need. I converted my dining room into a place for him to sleep because my girlfriend and I only had a one-bedroom apartment. Unfortunately this did not give him the privacy that he needed or that I wanted to provide, but it was the best I could do. For the first few days after his release from prison, I just tried to leave him alone so he could adjust to his new surroundings and his new freedom. I thought he might appreciate the gesture.

For the first week it seemed as though we had all gotten along well, but that was only my perception. My girlfriend had issues with my brother that she was keeping to herself. All along I think she felt uneasy about having my brother live with us, but she never mentioned it to me. I think she felt this way because she came from a middle-class family and a protected environment. She had never been in a situation where she had to share living quarters with an ex-convict. Even still, she tried to tolerate the situation. She knew the story of my life, and she knew I had to be there for my brother. If she had been a barrier and prevented me from helping Haven, she knew that she and I would have problems.

She silently dealt with her issue with Haven for as long as she could. When she couldn't stand it anymore, she approached me and explained her problem. She told me that she was uncomfortable talking with Haven because of the harsh manner in which he spoke. She explained that his questions were not really questions but more like demands. For example, instead of asking her if she could give him a ride somewhere, he would say, "I need you to drop me off downtown." As she explained, I deduced that part of the issue was that she did not want to say no to him because she felt obligated to me. She felt that she had to comply so that I wouldn't get upset with her, but this couldn't have been further from the truth. I probably should have clarified this up front. To resolve her concerns, I arranged a sit down to discuss the problem. During our discussion, I mediated and tried to explain her problem to Haven. From what I could see, Haven did not appear that receptive to the change he was being asked to make. During our conversation, I began to see why my girlfriend felt the way she did. At the same time, I realized that this was probably the least abrasive Haven could be after being out of prison for only a little more than a week. I knew it was going to take Haven some time to adjust to society, but I did not have the time to give him under the current circumstances.

After several hours of trying to resolve the issue, I realized that the only solution was to ask Haven to leave. I wasn't planning to kick him out on the street; I would never have done that. I knew that Haven had been trying to rebuild his relationship with our mother and that she had offered him a place to live if he needed one. At the end of two short weeks, I asked Haven to go live with her. I felt horrible for the next few days. I had waited all this time for my brother to come home only to kick him out of my house. I was not going to win brother of the year, that was for sure.

A few days later he moved his items to my mother's apartment and began living there. Fortunately, there were no hard feelings between us, and we kept in touch. Haven later told me that he was glad things worked out the way they had. He told me that moving in with our mother had given him the opportunity to rebuild a relationship with her. I was happy to see that something positive came out of our temporary dissention.

Al and Murch were both old news by now. My mother's friend Lorenzo viewed this as an opportunity. He began to think that maybe he might be able to establish a relationship with my mother. His only competition for my mother's attention was her friend Ralphina and Tetris level five.

Lorenzo wasn't shy about letting me know how fond he was of my mother. On the rare occasions when I would visit, if he was there, he would stand close to me and lean in like he was going to tell me something private. As he swayed back and forth like he was trying to catch his balance, he would slur the following words through his alcohol-laced breath: "I love your mother...your mother's a beautiful woman...I love your mother." I don't have a clue why he felt I needed to know this. Maybe he thought if he slurred it properly that I would put in a good word for him? This for sure was not going to happen. Apparently, he didn't need my help anyway. Three months later, when Haven and I spoke, I was disturbed to hear that Lorenzo had successfully wooed our mother into a relationship. This news made me appreciate having my own apartment. I was glad that I did not have to see or socialize with another one of my mother's unemployed, useless, alcoholic boyfriends.

About a week later, my girlfriend and I were awaken at 4:00 a.m. by a knock on our bedroom window. We must not have heard the knocks on the door as we slept. Domino five was about to fall. I pulled the curtain back to see Haven standing outside my window. I knew he had not come by at this hour of the morning to give me good news. I signaled Haven to go to the front door. As I walked down the hallway to go open it, I thought to myself, *What happened now?* I did not want the answer to my own question because nothing would have prepared me for what was coming next. When I opened the door for Haven, I noticed that my mother was with him. My mother had a somber look on her face, and she would not look me in the eye. Once they were inside, she said, "I have some bad news. Haven, you tell him."

Haven looked at me and said, "Maurice, Serena is dead." I stood there for a minute waiting for them to tell me that this was a joke, but neither of them spoke. I looked at my mother's face then at Haven's face, and I said, "Stop playing! This is not funny!" But my mother confirmed it. "I'm sorry; Serena is dead. The coroner from Mercy Hospital called to tell me that she was in a car accident."

My eyes started to well up with tears, and I gave my mother a real big, tight hug. Then everything went black. I found myself on my bed with my face in the pillow crying and my girlfriend trying to console me. I had just lost my best friend. She was only sixteen. There were so many things that she didn't get a chance to do. One more year and she would have graduated from high school. I had so many plans for her. It wasn't fair.

When I was finally able to collect myself, I went back into my living room, and my mother and Haven were gone. I called the hospital to try to get some details on what happened. When the coroner got on the phone, I asked him if I could come down and see Serena. I needed to see for myself that this was real. That's when he told me, "It's probably not a good idea." He didn't understand. I needed to see my sister. I kept pressing to see her, and he kept fending me off. He respectfully kept telling me that I should not come see her. I just couldn't get through the night without making sure it was her. This wouldn't be real until I saw her with my own eyes. I didn't give in and kept begging him to allow me to come see her. Finally, as compassionately as he could, he said, "You probably won't be able to identify her because there is not much left. Her body was burned beyond recognition in a car fire. This is why I highly advise against coming to see her." That's when I realized that out of respect he had been trying to keep me from hearing the horrific circumstances of my sister's death. My heart sank, my head dropped to my chest, and I finally gave up. The coroner was right; I didn't want to see Serena the way he had described her. I remember feeling like my life was over too. I was numb. I wanted answers. I started getting horrific images of my sister squirming to get out of the car. I should have been there for her. I let her down. I was supposed to protect her forever. I had not kept my promise.

After talking to the coroner, the only information I had was that there was a car accident, but I still had no details. How did my little sister die? A day later I received a call from a girl who was in the car with Serena. She was calling from her hospital bed, where she was suffering from a broken hip as result of the accident. She told me that she and Serena were in the backseat of a vehicle that was being driven by her boyfriend when he swerved out of the way of another car and crashed into a telephone pole. The rear right passenger side of the car collided into the pole. This was where Serena was sitting, and it was also where the gas nozzle receptacle was located. The impact caused the car to burst into flames. A frantic effort was made by the girl's boyfriend and the other male passenger to get Serena out of the car, but the fire was too hot. In their attempt to free Serena from the burning car, one of the boys ended up with third-degree burns on his hands. She said that neither speed nor alcohol contributed to the accident. Once she finished telling me the story of how my sister died, she told me that she had retained a lawyer and was suing Honda, the manufacturer of the car they were driving. She told me that the basis of her lawsuit was a known safety issue that caused the car to burst into flames. I thanked Serena's friend for telling me what happened and hung up the phone. My dream of reuniting my family had just been obliterated. First I lost my grandfather, then Ervin, and now my little sister. My days started and ended with waiting for the next tragedy.

Serena's wake was held at my mother's church. There was no casket, there would be no funeral, and there would be no headstone. I was not able to get any mementos from Serena's bedroom because my mother allowed Serena's friends to take most of her personal items. The one and only precious thing that I was able to get was her ashes. My mother had her cremated and asked me if I wanted her ashes. I felt fortunate to have a precious reminder of the little girl who I used to play with while she sat on a bean bag in our living room, a reminder of the little girl I used to walk to Headstart every day. I was more than happy to take her ashes that fateful day, and I still have them.

I really didn't care about much after my sister died. I blamed my mother for her death; I hated everybody and everything. I broke up with my girlfriend and moved to my own apartment. For months, I had dreams that Serena was still alive only to wake up to the horrible reality that she was dead. I became a recluse and cut myself off from everyone else so that I could mourn. I stopped seeing my friends and mostly stayed in my apartment when my workday was over. My emotions fluctuated from sadness to anger and from disappointment to guilt. I was not good at discussing feelings and emotions, so I needed to be alone during this time. This was crucial in order for me to administer self-therapy. This is what I needed to do, and I didn't care whether or not other people understood.

When I finally emerged from isolation three months later, I decided to seek out a lawyer in order to initiate a lawsuit like Serena's friend had done. The lawyer told me that the ignition of flames on impact is a known problem with Honda automobiles and that he was going to lead an all-out assault on them to make them pay compensation for my sister's death. I would have thought that the lawyer's contempt for Honda would have made me feel better, but it didn't. Still, I had to do something. I knew the lawsuit wasn't going to bring Serena back, but I felt powerless and figured that doing something would be better than losing her for nothing. I let my mother and Haven know that I had put this action in motion and that I would keep them apprised of any progress.

When I next spoke with Haven, he caught me up on his progress of reintegrating into society. He told me that he had started looking into post-release educational programs and benefits for ex-convicts. One of the programs he found was going to enable him to attend American International College (AIC). He was now going to be able to work toward a bachelor's degree. I was glad that Haven was planning to take the constructive educational route to better himself. He was excited and ready for the challenge. I told him that if there was anything I could do to assist him, he just needed to let me know.

As Haven worked toward bigger and better things, we started having lengthy phone discussions. We talked about the newly blooming relationship between our mother and Lorenzo. The whole thing bewildered him. He could not understand why our mother would even consider this guy as a companion. He was an alcoholic, didn't have a job, and was uneducated. This was par for the course as far as what I had seen in the last ten years while Haven was incarcerated. I tried to let him know what to expect as "normal" while he was living with our mom. He hadn't seen all the drama that I had or felt the pain that I had as a result of my mother's bad decisions. I knew that Haven had a long road ahead of him to understand my mother's unexplainable self-imposed harm.

Haven had spent ten years in prison with murderers, rapists, and the like. He faced every challenge without fear, and I had never seen him waver. For the first time in my life I saw him visibly shaken when he stopped by my apartment three months later. He was extremely distraught when he told me that he heard a rumor that Lorenzo had AIDS. He broke out into a cold sweat as he spoke about the possibility that our mom might now have AIDS as well. He looked to me for ideas on what we should do. I told him that I understood his concern and his stress more than he could imagine. I had spent the last ten years going through similar emotions and was a wreck most of the time when Ervin or our mom did something detrimental to their own welfare. I explained that the only way I was able to keep from having a nervous breakdown was by taking a step back to view the result of each situation. I noticed that I was always the only person stressed out and worried every time Ervin or our mom decided to throw their lives away. It was killing me every time it happened. I finally couldn't take it anymore and stopped worrying.

I empathized with the fact that he couldn't turn off his feelings and concern for our mom like a light switch, but I suggested that he at least try to keep his concern or involvement in perspective. This was the best advice I could give him. I had been through too much to be overly concerned about her welfare, especially when she wasn't.

A couple of months later I was contacted by my lawyer. He called to let me know that he had received a settlement offer of ten thousand dollars from Honda. I was happy to hear this news, but at the same time I felt like the offer was a smack in the face. Was my little sister's life only worth ten thousand dollars? As I talked with my lawyer, my heart and brain were in an emotional wrestling match. My brain would first say, "Be happy that your sister didn't die in vain" then my heart would reply, "This little monetary award won't bring her back, so what's the point?" This internal struggle continued while I was on the phone with my lawyer, so much that I probably didn't hear half of what he was saying. The one thing I did hear him say was that I needed to come to his office and sign a document that would relinquish all compensation from the lawsuit to my mother.

I told the lawyer that I did not want to sign the document because my mother makes bad choices with money and would spend it foolishly. Plus, I was the one who had initiated the lawsuit, so the money should be given to me. He told me that the issue was out of his hands. The justice system identifies the mother of a child as the closest next of kin over any siblings. It didn't matter who initiated the lawsuit. I told him that I understood but that I still was not going to sign the document and asked him to find an alternative option.

A week later I received a letter from my lawyer's office that stated that the settlement funds had been dispensed to my mother. My lawyer had found a way to proceed without my signature. I was furious! Giving the money to my mother was a big mistake. I was absolutely confident that it was going to be squandered.

The next time I talked to Haven I found out how right I was. He told me that our mother used the money to buy Lorenzo a truck. I was angry, stunned and speechless. What the hell was my mother thinking? This time her actions hurt me to my soul. That money represented the lifeblood of my little sister, and she had frivolously used it to buy her alcoholic boyfriend a truck! I was done with her. This was the straw that finally broke the camel's back.

That day, eighteen years ago, was the last time I had anything to do with my mother.

Each of us has our own destiny, and we always know when we have reached it. What makes each destiny unique are the obstacles that must be overcome to reach it and the desired destiny itself. For some, destiny is success; for others, destiny is failure.

"Follow a course of self-destruction and you may succeed… Follow a course of self-fulfillment and you may succeed."

Ten Years Later

I was thirty-one now. My education and training made me a terrific candidate as an electronic technician; however, there were no high-tech companies left in Springfield. This started my migration toward the Boston area, where there were many more viable employment opportunities. After a short round of interviews, I acquired a decent job. I was hired as an electronic technician at a small start-up company on the outskirts of Boston. I leased the most reasonable apartment that I could and made my move to the Boston area.

All along I could picture what I wanted in life. I wanted my own family: a beautiful wife, children, and a healthy, prosperous household—one where each family member learned from one another. I labeled my utopia "my continuous pathway to happiness."

I knew that my first step toward this destiny was to make sure that I shed all the baggage I had accumulated during the first twenty years of my life. I didn't fool myself. I knew that if I wanted a chance in a stable relationship, I needed to transcend my past. I knew that if I was ever going to be successful as a husband, I would have to do research to establish my own ideas on what it meant to be part of a healthy family. I began to reinvent myself through many hours of self-therapy. During this time I lived in isolation for almost two years. I focused on improving my social skills and ideas about anger and violence. I also enrolled in a part-time engineering program at Northeastern University. It was a six-year program designed for business professionals who wanted to continue their education. Northeastern was the only school in the area that offered this program. They must have known it, too, because the program was expensive. I was lucky that my job had tuition reimbursement; otherwise, I would not have been able to afford it.

Life was a struggle, but nothing could compare to where I came from, so I just forged ahead.

My daily routine was enmeshed with my aspirations to graduate from Northeastern. My day started at 6:30 a.m. with a thirty-minute commute to work. After an eight-hour workday, I had to commute forty minutes into Metro Boston during drive time. I would not wish this on my worst enemy. The drive was a fifteen-minute commute without traffic. My course load was two classes per night. The first started around 7:00 p.m., and the last one ended at 10:00 p.m. My commute back home was thirty minutes. Each night I received homework from both classes that was due the next day, so I stayed up as long as I could to complete it. I usually would not get to bed until after 1:00 a.m. By the time my head hit the pillow, I was already asleep. My weekends were spent trying to catch up on the homework that I was unable to do during the week. This meant that I had to be at the university library from 8:00 a.m. to 6:00 p.m. on Saturdays and Sundays. On top of all of this, the work was extremely difficult. I was struggling just to get by. I needed a C in order for my job to provide tuition reimbursement and to stay off of academic probation.

I managed this schedule for about two weeks before I started to second guess whether I was going to be able to sustain it for six years. I remember reaching a critical crossroad where I had to make a decision on whether to continue the almost unbearable schedule. The moment of truth occurred one day when I left work and was driving to school. I pulled into a gas station and parked my car off to the side away from the gas pumps. I did not need gas. I just needed to think. I had to make sure what I was doing made sense. I sat there for twenty minutes thinking about the road ahead. I thought about working my way up the company ladder instead of trying to get a degree. I thought about failing out of school after investing significant time and effort. I thought about how much out-of-pocket money I would need to pay. It all seemed too much to bear.

As I sat there in the gas station, I made myself a promise that, after that day, I would make a commitment to either attend school or to work my way up the chain at my company. I would no longer second guess my decision. Here is how I decided what to do. I had two options available when I was ready to leave the gas station. I could turn left toward work and home or I could turn right toward school, and I would have my decision. I remember almost letting the steering wheel go while drifting into oncoming traffic. I have no idea how the car turned, but it did, and I was headed toward school. The only thing I could think of was that the spirit of my grandmother, who had passed away about a year earlier, turned my steering wheel toward school that day.

Before I knew it, two years had passed, and I was still achieving grades that kept me out of academic probation. I was getting closer to achieving a bachelor's degree. My motivation came in many different forms.

The voices of my UMass engineering friends that echoed in my head were motivation. After one semester at UMass I could not afford to go back. I had told many of my friends that I wasn't going to give up; I was going to get my electrical engineering degree if it was the last thing I did. Most of them said, "Everybody says that, but they never get their degree. You won't either." Hearing these words motivated me even more.

The fact that I only had one shot to get my degree also motivated me. I knew that I couldn't afford to repeat courses, so failure was not an option. I was also motivated because I felt like I would be letting myself and my grandmother down if I didn't get my degree.

After a while neither the commute nor the long days and nonexistent weekends were an issue. I was in a groove now. I was on track to complete my education, and my job was stable. At this point, I had already lived alone for three years and had reinvented myself. I could feel the change and growth from within and felt that I was now capable of having a normal relationship. The list of requirements that I had for the woman whom I wanted to meet seemed basic: a nonsmoker, no children, and she had to like everything I liked. I wasn't asking for *much.*

Because of my age and the fact that I wanted to start a family soon, I knew I didn't have a lot of time to invest in the wrong woman. To expedite the process and improve on my probability of making a love connection, I joined a dating service. The dating service rep told me that I was guaranteed to meet professional women who met my specific criteria. Of the six or seven women I was paired with, none of them was what I was looking for. I sure was picky.

After twenty-five hundred dollars and a year of dating, I pretty much just gave up on the dating service and explored other avenues. I tried the club scene and went on a few party boat cruises. Again, I did not find what I was looking for. I relaxed my criteria. Children were okay now but being a nonsmoker was not negotiable. I met a few women who almost fit the bill, but the serious relationship I was looking for did not follow. The chase for the right companion tired me out. I was defeated. It was time to let destiny take over.

Once I stopped the feverish search for the lady of my dreams, I thought of a few adequate proverbs that fit my situation: *You are trying too hard* and *You will meet the right one when you stop looking.* I soon found that the person who came up with those sayings was correct because shortly after I threw in the towel, I met the woman who would become my wife.

It was Thanksgiving night 1999. In the nontraditional sense, most families come together on this day, prepare a feast, and enjoy each other's company. For several different reasons this was not my favorite holiday. Every year it reminded me of three generations of tragedy that I had experienced within a ten-year period of my life. My father had died from AIDS. All of his brothers and sisters—my aunts and uncles—were due to drugs or violence. My brother Ervin was doing life in prison for rape and murder. My little sister had died in an automobile car fire. I had disowned my mother for her final act of disrespect to my little sister. My oldest brother, Haven, and I were still trying to reestablish our relationship and make up for the ten years we had lost when he was incarcerated. And my grandmother and grandfather had passed away from natural causes. This was my world, this was my life, so I didn't feel pity for myself. I lived through the happiness of others who celebrated this day. It felt like I had an extended family as I visited different family friends in my town.

Unfortunately my friend Tim, whose parents had divorced a few years earlier, was in a similar situation. Although his journey to a broken family was a bit different, he, too, was not going to be with his family on that Thanksgiving. Tim had grown up in one of the most perfect families I had ever seen. As a child, I remember that his mother and father was the perfect couple. They were raising four boys whose ages differed by only a few years. The eldest son was in college, and his siblings, including Tim, were doing well in school. Tim's father had a stable job, and he was working his way up into the ranks of leadership. His mother was the perfect housewife who also doubled as a mom to many of the kids in the community, including me. They lived in a very nice apartment just on the outskirts of the ghetto. Everyone in our community was envious. But that was no more. Once Tim and his siblings became adults and moved out of their once-perfect household, his parents had an ugly divorce. The fallout was unrepairable damage that divided his family down the middle.

I had talked to Tim earlier in the day to see if he wanted to hang out and maybe go to a nightclub in Springfield later that night. He said that he would be thrilled to join me and was glad that I had asked. When I picked him up that night, we sat in my car for a while trying to decide where we should go. We had our choice of two nightclubs. One was in downtown Springfield, and the other was uptown. We decided we would try the downtown club. When we arrived downtown, a sign was posted on the door of the club stating that it would be closed until further notice. Our only option was to go to the other club.

All along I knew I did not want to go to this club. I knew the type of people who typically were there. This is part of the reason we chose to go downtown in the first place. Many of them were just living day to day and had no real aspirations for a better life. Some I knew personally and wished to have nothing to do with. But I wasn't the rude type. If I had run into someone that I knew, I would pretend to be happy to see them while thinking, *What a waste.* Another reason I really didn't want to go to this club was that they were hosting an urban poetry night, better known as spoken word. These venues attracted speakers who used suggestion and clever poetic metaphors to entice an audience. Listeners would have to interpret a hidden message in the poetically spoken verses. The hairstyles and clothes many of these poets wore reminded me of the fashion from the psychedelic era. I had nothing against the people or the art; however, it just wasn't my thing. Regardless of how I felt, we still had to go there. It was the only open club in the city. I wasn't thrilled.

By the time I left the club, I had met a beautiful, pleasant, and intelligent woman, the type of woman I had always dreamed about meeting. She was independent, had her own apartment, and was working on completing her master's degree. Her ambition was thrilling and had me exhilarated, but the best part about meeting her was that she was fine and she was single!

I hadn't met a woman in a nightclub in a while, so I did not have any clever pick-up lines to dazzle her with. It was like I was on a baseball team and the field was rained out: I had no game! Fortunately, I didn't need it that night. When I approached her, I quickly found out that she wasn't looking for the fast-talker, Rico Suave type. She seemed to enjoy open, honest communication. I was a master at that.

I introduced myself, she told me her name was Gina, and then we talked continuously for about forty minutes. It was one of the most stress-free, natural-flowing conversations I'd had in a long time. I wasn't struggling to find words or trying to impress her, and we didn't have any uncomfortable silences. During our conversation, we found that we had so much in common. We discovered that we had both been employees at the same company, we both knew one of the key people who worked in the human resources department there, we were both struggling students, we both lived alone, we were both nonsmokers, and we both had no kids. I knew I would need to wait to see if she fit my last criteria: liking everything that I liked.

How ironic. I met the lady who would become my wife in a nightclub that I arrogantly did want to go to – in a place where I just knew I was better than everyone. I almost missed out on the opportunity I had been waiting for, but instead I got lucky and learned a lesson in humility. That night after my friend Tim and I left the nightclub, I told him that she was the woman for me.

Now I had something else besides school that I had to invest time in—Gina. I had no problem doing that because I could just tell she was a catch. The vibe she gave off was extremely positive, and she was investing in herself. I loved it.

There were two problems that I had to resolve with regards to building a relationship with Gina. The first was that she lived in Connecticut, which was an hour and a half away from Boston. The second was that she had no idea who I really was. I knew there was no short-term solution to the distance problem, but I really liked her, so I knew I would just have to tolerate it. I felt the only solution for letting her know who I was would be to tell her my story. There was a chance that I might lose her, but I felt that I wanted her to have all the information about me upfront so she could make an informed decision. After all, she might have wanted to meet someone who was religious; I wasn't. She might have wanted to meet someone who had a close-knit family; my family was broken.

A week after we met, I wrote her a letter that was basically a condensed summary of the first few chapters of this book. I figured that she would either head for the hills if my crazy life story was too much to handle, or she would stick around to find out more. I was hoping her decision would be the latter. A few days after she received my letter, I was pleased to find out that not only was she planning on staying to find out more but that she actually appreciated the fact that I had opened up to her so early. I was glad to hear that. After a few months of dating and daily long-distance phone conversations, Gina and I decided to be exclusive; we were a couple. I was in a relationship that I had hoped for with the lady I had dreamed about. If I had to mark a point in time when I felt the Triplett curse was broken, this was it.

On the weekends she would come up to Boston to visit me. Between the loads of incredibly difficult homework that I had, I somehow was able to make time for us as a couple. We went out to eat, visited the Museum of Science, went shopping, visited Harvard and MIT, went to Downtown Crossing and China Town, took boat cruises, people watched at Faneuil Hall, and so many other things. When we finished doing the town, the seven thousand dollars that I had worked so hard to save in my bank account was gone. This was the most money I ever had in my entire life, and it pretty much disintegrated. I have no regrets, though, because it went toward a good investment. I still joke with my mother-in-law about the money I spent wooing her daughter. During phone conversations, I ask her about the seven thousand dollars that she owes me, and we both have a good laugh.

I was on the verge of completing the greatest goal I had ever achieved. My classes were extremely challenging, but I was still getting by. My relationship with Gina was still fantastic. I didn't need to wait any longer to know she was the lady I was going to spend the rest of my life with, so I proposed. Things didn't go that great, though.

Without Gina knowing, I called my future in-laws to get their blessing to wed their daughter. My future father-in-law, a mechanical engineer, proudly gave me his approval. He liked me because I was an aspiring electrical engineer and knew that I was on the right track for a bright future. The discussion with my future mother-in-law was a bit different. We, too, had a great relationship, but now that I was asking to take her daughter away, her protective instinct was unveiled during our conversation. "You *are* going to take care of my daughter, *aren't you?*" "Yes, I will." "You won't hurt my daughter, will you?" "No, I won't." I knew that she was only questioning my integrity because she was worried about her daughter's future. I tried to reassure her that I would do everything I could to fill every day of Gina's life with love and happiness. Once I did that, she gave me her blessing. I said thank you and let my future in-laws know that I was going to propose that weekend.

I organized everything. Gina was coming to visit me in two days. I already had the ring, and I had made reservations at the Top of the Hub, a classy restaurant in a skyscraper that boasted a bill of about two hundred dollars per couple. I had done some masterful planning and was ready for the execution. The next day I started to get a cold. That night, I loaded up on Nyquil and hoped that I would feel better with a good night's rest. In the morning I felt worse. My nose was runny, my head was clogged and fuzzy, and my entire body was weak. I didn't lose hope, though. It was only 8:00 a.m., and Gina wouldn't be in Boston until 4:00 p.m. Perhaps I would be better by then. Even if I wasn't, that would just be too bad for me; the show must go on. Everything was in place, and nothing was going to stop me from proposing.

When Gina arrived that night, she suggested that we stay in when she saw that I was still sick. She clearly did not know what I had in store or she would have never suggested something so absurd. I told her that I would be fine and that I wanted us to stick with our plans to go out to eat. She reluctantly agreed after I forced the issue.

We arrived at the restaurant, parked the car in the basement garage, and took the elevator to the fifty-second floor, where the restaurant was located. When the elevator opened, we were pleasantly greeted by the maître'd. We were seated. From our table we had a magnificent, absolutely breathtaking view of the Boston skyline. Once I saw that, I knew I was the man! I was awesome! As I was giving myself a pat on the back, I became dizzy, and the cold sweats kicked up a notch. It was clear that being fifty-two floors up was not helping my condition. Once the water and menus were brought to the table, that's when I noticed that I had a few small problems. Between my runny nose and foggy thinking, I had completely forgotten the engagement ring. I had also forgotten my wallet! Now the cold sweats really kicked in.

As I assessed the situation, I thought, *I'm in a high-class restaurant planning to eat an exquisite meal with no money and planning to propose without a ring.* For crying out loud! I didn't panic, though. I played it cool as I felt my rugged life training kick in. I had been in tough spots before, so I was confident that I could get out of this dilemma. I gently grabbed my girlfriend's hand and said, "You know I've been sick with a cold, right?" She acknowledged yes. Then I said, "We have a small problem. I was dizzy and forgot to bring my wallet." Her eyes opened up in disbelief as I put my hand up and said, "Wait, wait, wait, I think I have a plan. I'm going to go to the men's room, and I want you to follow and go to the ladies' room. When you come out of the bathroom, meet me at the elevator, and we can slip out unnoticed." My girlfriend was a trooper; she agreed to do it! The plan quickly fell apart as the maître'd noticed us leaving. He chased us to the elevator and exclaimed, "Is everything alright? What can we do to fix your problem?" I was too embarrassed to tell the truth, so I just said, "Everything is fine." As we stood there desperately waiting for the elevator, the maître'd kept asking questions. The more he asked, the more embarrassed I became. Finally, the elevator arrived, and I escaped from having my dignity damaged any further. By the time this ordeal was over, it was late at night, and many restaurants in Boston were closed. We were still hungry so we looked for another place to eat. All I can tell you is this: we were the best-dressed couple in the pizza shop that night as we ate our pepperoni, mushroom, and green pepper slices and drank grape soda. So much for my masterful planning and being the man; I felt more like a loser.

The next day I felt better and made up a new plan on how I would propose. I made up a story and told Gina that since our dinner didn't go well, I wanted to go dancing at one of our favorite nightclubs. I suggested that we go shopping for some nice, dressy outfits. Of course she was all in for that. I took her to Downtown Crossing, a ten-square-mile area in Boston that had about one thousand retail stores. Gina was in heaven.

We spent the entire day at Downtown Crossing then went home and relaxed for a while. My plan was to have us both get dressed up real nice to go dancing. Then I was going to take her to the Harbor Hotel and propose under the stars on the harbor deck next to the water at midnight. This time my plan was executed flawlessly. I still remember the look in Gina's eyes as I dropped to one knee and asked her hand in marriage. That moment was priceless and one I will never forget.

After all I had been through, finally my life was headed in a positive direction. With Gina by my side, I knew better days were ahead. We were married in Jamaica two years later. Gina's entire family (and now my family) was all there. My new bride and the wedding were both absolutely beautiful. I don't mean what I am about to say in the religious sense, but I was reborn that day. I had a new start.

When the wedding was over, I was still Maurice Triplett, and my new lovely bride was still Gina Ferguson. She would have taken my last name, but I refused to give it to her. There was no significance in that name. It was cloaked in treachery, drama, and death, and it did not belong to anyone I would want to call family. Gina knew all this because while we were engaged, I explained to her why I did not want to pass the name Triplett down to her or any children that we might have.

I explained it this way. My biological father's last name was Morgan. At the time when we were married, my mother's last name was Murchison. My brother had legally changed his last name to Williams (which was my mother's maiden name). The man who carried the Triplett name was not a part of my life and did not want to be. In fact, I think he hated me because, as a love child, I was a reminder of the wretchedness he was subjected to when my mother stepped outside of her marriage. The last thing I told Gina was that the Triplett family tree and its rotten apples were getting chopped down by me. I was it: the last of the Mohicans! The end of the line! The lineage of Triplett, of which I was from, would die with me.

I was married now and had one more year of school left. With Gina moving in with me, I had to find a nicer place to live. I thought my place was fine, but apparently *someone* didn't think so. I knew this was part of the "collective bargaining" agreement that came with marriage, so we started apartment hunting. This is when we met the wonderful person that would be our landlord for the next year. Her name was Carole Hannigan. I'm sure she never realized how she helped me through my final phase of overcoming my past. Her smile and pleasant personality were exactly what I needed to complete my transformation.

I remember our first phone conversation. I called about the apartment she posted for rent in the newspaper. We were both direct with each other without being disrespectful. It was almost as if we had already known each other and had established a comfort level that allowed us to communicate in this fashion. She told me that she owned a three-family home. The third floor was empty, but it was not for rent; she lived on the second floor, and she was renting out the first floor. She told us that she was not in a rush to rent the place out; however, if she found the right tenants, she might consider it. I read in between the lines and understood exactly what she was saying, and I liked her that much more. What I heard her say was, "If you show up to my place and you have the look and feel of being dishonest, deceitful, and disrespectful, I'm not going to rent to you—period!" I was fine with that and appreciated her being honest and upfront without being arrogant. Gina and I scheduled a time for her to show us her apartment.

As we drove down the street that the home was on, Gina said, "Oh, I hope it's that one; it's the best house on the street." As we approached the home she was referring to, we found that it *was* Carole's home. My wife and Carole had the same taste. It was then that I knew everything was going to work out just fine. We went inside to meet our prospective landlord. Carole's entire demeanor was simple and complex all in one. I could tell that she could be the sweetest person that you could ever meet, but at the same time she was no one's doormat. Rub her the wrong way and you would regret it. The look in her eyes told me that she had seen and been through hard times and knew how to handle herself in any situation. She was like me. I liked her from the day we first shook hands. She gave us a tour of the first-floor apartment. It was a well-kept, very clean place. Gina loved it.

She called us a few days later to tell us that we qualified for the apartment and that we could move in as soon as we wanted. We must have passed her internal personality and ethics assessment and qualified as good people. As her tenants, Gina and I became very close with her. She told me that I could come to her apartment and use her computer anytime. She had an aboveground swimming pool in her backyard that she said I could use anytime I wanted. She trusted me with her grill and allowed me to use her outdoor patio furniture that she kept locked in the garage. Her trust in me helped to view myself as a good person. Through her kindness, I felt exonerated for the dishonest things that I had done in the past in order to survive.

The special relationship Gina and I had with Carole grew more and more as time passed. We did nice things for each other for no reason at all. During the winter when it snowed, Carole and I would try to each be the first outside so we could clean off each other's cars and shovel the walkway. Carole also had a small vegetable garden and a green thumb. Every year she would grow big, juicy red tomatoes and give me a handful. One year I used the tomatoes she gave me to make homemade tomato sauce and hand delivered her a plate of spaghetti for dinner. She loved it. She gave me a big hug and thanked me when she returned the plate. Her gratitude had a dramatic impact on me and was appreciated more than I could ever explain. My own mother had never even made me feel that way.

Carole's hospitality was too good to be true. She told Gina and me that that if we ever had a problem with the rent to let her know and she would help us out. She probably made this helpful offer because she knew I was a student dealing with the financial burden of school while working full time. She also knew that Gina had only recently graduated and was new to her job. Fortunately, we were able to pay our rent on time every month and never had to ask for her help. Just like the time the ladies on the seventh-grade bus offered to buy me a coat, I sure appreciated the gesture. We are so glad that we met this very special lady. Her niceness always made our days a little brighter.

Living in Boston reduced the personal time that Haven and I could spend with each other, so instead we talked on the phone when we had time. Our conversations were always deep, knowledge-enriched discussions about various topics. Every one of our phone conversations would inevitably transition into an analysis of our lives. It was like our objective was to understand and solve why our very existence followed the path it had. We tried to answer questions like: Who was to blame? What was that person thinking when they did this? How successful could we have been in life if we had grown up with people who believed in us and supported our futures? How could we have avoided certain situations? We would talk for hours (we still do today), giving our opinions and speculating on the answers. At some point it became clear to me that the goal of our discussions was to use each other for therapeutic benefits. Haven and I had interacted with the same people, lived in the same household, and suffered from the same dysfunctional training. It was liberating to have someone who had been through similar experiences on the phone with an open ear.

Some of our discussions were focused around Haven and what he was doing to signify his "rebirth." It was clear to me that he was extremely focused and had planned to do well in his return to society. Every time we spoke, he would update me on his aspirations and progress in school. I found it uncanny that even though Haven had been through so much, he was still the same brother I had known fifteen years ago; he hadn't changed at all. I never rationalized how this was possible, but many people who have spent time in prison return to civilization and maintain the prison mentality. This was not true for Haven, as his accomplishments indicated. Haven had struggled through college and acquired a bachelor's degree in business administration from American International College. I was extremely proud of him. He had persevered and accomplished this task with no car, minimal funds, and with the word "convict" written across the back of his shirt—absolutely amazing! Unfortunately, I was unable to attend his graduation ceremony.

There was more. The next time we talked, he told me he was about to take a lovely bride and that they would be moving in together; this was another step in the right direction. I finally realized that Haven was unstoppable a few years later when he told me that he only had a few more credits left to get his master's degree in accounting and taxation. I was in awe. This time nothing was going to keep me from missing his graduation. When Haven approached the stage to receive his second college degree from American International College in the Springfield Civic Center, I shouted louder than everyone in the entire arena.

That day, I was especially proud that Haven was my brother. His character aligned with people who never quit, and his very existence represented the point at which survival, dedication, and drive intersect in the game of life. Haven had accomplished everything he had with minimal help and direction from anyone. He made every decision on his own and independently shaped a new future. To this day, I call Haven a *miracle child* for several reasons. It was a miracle that he did not get killed by police during the nation-wide manhunt; it was a miracle that he was granted an appeal; it was a miracle that his prison sentence was reduced from life in prison to manslaughter; and it was now a miracle that he was getting his second master's degree with bare-minimum resources.

Like Haven, I, too, had fought through every barrier and roadblock that I came upon in order to get my degree a few years before he did. I never gave up, and in the end I proved all the folks who said I would not return to continue my education – wrong.

Walking to the stage to get my degree was a very memorable moment, but my last week of school is what I remember most. It was exciting, stressful, and scary all at once. It was the last few seconds of the NBA finals with the score tied, it was waiting for cancer biopsy results, and it was riding in a plane at thirty-two thousand feet with bad turbulence all combined into one scenario.

The *excitement* that I felt during my last week of school was because I was almost done with this monumental accomplishment. For someone with my background, achieving this goal was synonymous to getting a PhD. I was going to be the first one in two generations of my family history to accomplish such a goal.

The *stress* that I felt during my last week of school was from being nervous that I would not pass my last round of finals and that I would not be able to graduate. At one point my brain was so preoccupied trying to remember all the information for my tests that I went into a *finals coma* on the highway and received a speeding ticket.

I was driving on the Mass Pike headed into Boston. My eyes were on the road, and my hands were on the wheel, but my brain was doing complex variable differential equations and linear systems analysis. My car must have been on autopilot because I couldn't remember how I had made it to the tollbooths just outside of Boston. I remember approaching the fast lane toll point. I had a fast lane transponder so I could go right through and didn't need to wait in line to pay at the person-operated tollbooths. Still in a comatose state, I failed to notice the fifteen miles per hour sign and blew through the pass way at forty-five miles per hour. I was going so fast that my car lifted a little off the ground because the grade of the highway quickly dropped on the other side of the pass way. When my car came down, I looked to the right and noticed that there was a patrol car that was not visible when entering the pass way. The officer in the vehicle didn't even turn his lights on as he saw me make eye contact. He just pointed his finger at me and indicated that I needed to pull over. The thoughts that crossed my mind at that point contained many four-letter words. The officer approached the car, and we had the typical speeding driver and officer exchange. "Do you know why I stopped you?" "No." "You were driving forty-five miles per hour through a fifteen-mile-per-hour zone." "Oh." "Where are you headed?" "I'm going to Northeastern University. I go to school there." The officer didn't ask for my license or registration because he noticed that my driver's side passenger window had six Northeastern University parking stickers. This was proof enough for him that I wasn't telling a lie. He said, "I'm going to give you a ticket for driving without your seatbelt on." I looked down and noticed that my seatbelt was indeed engaged and said, "But I *have* my seatbelt on." His condescending reply was, "Look, genius, it's three-fifty for going thirty miles per hour over the speed limit, or it's twenty-five dollars for driving without a seatbelt." I disengaged my seatbelt and said, "Yes, Officer, you are right. I did not have my seatbelt on."

The *fear* that I felt during my last week of school came from the fact that I had been followed by a black cloud all my life; something had to go wrong with my graduation. I tried to reconcile this feeling by visiting the School of Engineering office twice during this final week to make sure I had all the credits I needed to graduate. Just like Santa Claus during Christmas time, I was checking my list and checking it twice. I could tell that the girl at the front desk was tired of rechecking my records, but that was just too bad. I think I also pissed off the people at the bursar's office because I visited them several times to make sure I did not owe the school any money.

I had done it! Graduation day was here. I had picked up my graduation cap and gown. My name was in the ceremony graduation pamphlet. I saw it with my own eyes. It was listed in the bachelor's of science in electrical engineering section. I believed it now and was going to actually graduate. I felt like a warrior who had slayed the mighty dragon with no shield and a butter knife. I was beat up, I was tired, but I had defied the odds and had won.

Unlike my high school and community college graduations, this one was different. My wife, my niece, and my in-laws were there to cheer me on as I walked across the stage to get my diploma. My wife gave me a magnificent graduation party in Carole's yard, and Carole let my friends and guests use her pool. I couldn't have asked for more. Another big difference this time was that my post-graduation opportunities had quadrupled. I had drastically increased my market value and broadened my employment capability.

My transformation was complete. I had overcome my social trauma. I was newly married. I had a new family. I had completed one of the greatest achievements in my life, and I was now a marketable provider. I had gone from despair to happiness.

I realize that I did not make it through the difficult times on my own. Many people influenced me to do positive things and be a better person in their own ways. It is these people that I now must thank for helping me defy the odds and become a productive member of society.

Thank you, Grandma, for your nurturing and wisdom.

You fed me, clothed me, and when I was ready, you filled my head with wisdom. You challenged me to be great and to do things that I did not think I could do. You challenged me to be different. "Forget about what the rest of those kids are doing; you get your work done!" Those words saved my life and guided me through the hard times. Thank you for everything, Grandma. I love you, and I miss you.

Mabel India Morgan
1910–1996

Thank you, Sis, for giving me a reason to stay focused in life. Without your *guidance*, I would not be where I am today.

At one time in my life, I protected you, kept you warm, and made sure you were headed down the right path. Now our roles have changed. When I am in trouble, I feel your presence protecting me; when I get cold, I feel you wrap your arms around me to make me warm; and when I come to a crossroad, you always tell me which way to go. I will never be able to repay you, but I dedicate my achievements and accomplishments to you. Thank you, little sis. I love you, and I miss you.

Miss Serena Monique Triplett
1978–1995

Doug and Tim, I want to thank you for the positive influence that you both had on me. I know without a doubt that it was because of both of you that I ended up living a fruitful, successful life. I'm glad we grew up like brothers. Thanks for everything.

Lifelong friends that you accept as your brother or sister can never be anything less. Unlike most people, I believe that you can choose your family. Being born into a family of losers and delinquents does not make you one. It is your choice to accept this as your destiny or to pursue other options. The men you see in the picture above are my brothers. I accept them as such and appreciate everything they have done for me. Their strength and influence helped me through the early years. Thank you.

**Douglas G. Greer, 1968–2010,
and
Tim Jackson**

Carole, I want to thank you for never judging me and for accepting me as your friend.

In my lifetime, I have only met a few people whom I consider genuine. I can explain what that looks like. It looks like a friend of mine named Carole Hannigan. The reason this lady is so special is because since the day I met her, she has been nothing but friendly, considerate, and always greeted me with a smile. She opened her home and heart to me and always made me feel like family. I am so glad we met that fateful day in Somerville and have stayed friends ever since. Your kindness and positive influence in my life helped me transcend my dark past. Thank you.

Carole Hannigan

Words of encouragement from a few good men will never be forgotten.

"Allan"

"Raiders Football Coach"

"In the Raiders camp, if you need something, you don't take it. Ask for it, and we will help you get it."

"You doin' what you supposed to do? You staying out of trouble?"

Gina, thank you for throwing out a lifeline and rescuing me. Thank you for standing by my side through the good and bad times and so much more.

Within beauty lies strength. The woman with me is my wife, Gina. I knew she was the perfect woman for me the first time we met. My initial attraction was all visual as her beauty swept me from my feet, but a big surprise was waiting for me. As we grew together, I found that her soul ran deep, she was compassionate and caring, and she was able to instill a balance to my life and our relationship. She kept an open ear and a loving heart as I told her about my turbulent past and never judged me. For these things and many more, I am fortunate that I met her.

She is my pillar of strength, and I want to thank her for always being there for me. Thank you, baby. I love you.

The following words were on a memento that Gina gave to me when I graduated with my bachelor's degree.

SUR~VI'VOR;

1. N. One who perseveres through life's challenges, hardships, misfortunes, and tragedies.

2. One who refuses to give up, give in, or quit trying.

3. One who triumphs over insurmountable challenges and becomes a better person because of them, i.e. Maurice Triplett.

Until I put it all in a book, I had no idea of how much I had been through. What startled me even more is how far I've come. I started out eating government cheese and drinking powdered milk; now my wife and I go to places like Ruth's Chris Steakhouse for dinner and drink bottles of Chateau de Something. I started out living in one of the worst ghetto housing projects in New Haven; now I own two houses and live in beautiful, sunny Arizona. I started out working as a computer maintenance technician at a small computer repair company; now I am an engineering manager with a staff of fifteen.

My success does not come without issues. I am constantly plagued by my past. I constantly think about the people who are now living where I once had. My built-in barometer for poverty never lets me forget about them. The only way I get peace of mind is by doing a regular penance by giving back through my personal mentorship program. Sometimes even that does not help. When this is the case, I have to remind myself that I can't save the world, even if I wanted to.

My personal life experience has made me realize how extremely important foundation is in a person's life. To me, foundation is realizing that you *did* have help getting to where you are today—no one achieves success alone. Foundation is knowing that family and life are priorities above all. Foundation is realizing that health and happiness are worth more than money.

In a final word, I would like to tell you how I structure my life by quoting the words of Brian Dyson, CEO of Coca Cola Enterprises.

"Imagine life as a game in which you are juggling five balls in the air. You name them: work, family, health, friends, and spirit—and you are keeping all of these in the air. You will soon understand that work is a rubber ball. If you drop it, it will bounce back. But, the other four balls—family, health, friends, and spirit—are made of glass. If you drop one of these, they will be irrevocably scuffed, marked, nicked, damaged, or even shattered. They will never be the same. You must understand that and strive for balance in your life."

With that, I leave you to devise a recovery plan for your family if you need one. If you have dropped any of the balls you were juggling, there still may be hope because scuffed, marked, and nicked can usually be somewhat repaired. Reflect on my life and what I did to try to save my family then dig deep inside and recover yours. If your family foundation is solid, reach out and help someone else.

Writing the thoughts and details of my life in a book was extremely therapeutic; however, I still had questions and wanted to understand why certain things had happened. I had done lots of speculation and had written things as I saw them. But was this the truth? I wanted another perspective on the details of my mother's life that created her character as a mom. I wanted to know more about my maternal grandfather's life, more about my Uncle Ike, and more about Haven's perspective growing up in the same environment.

Fortunately, my brother Haven had also written down the details of his life in order to reap the therapeutic benefits. Between his writings and our phone conversations about our turbulent past, I was able to answer many questions that I still had. Haven's story made me realize that there were so many things that I didn't know about my family. It made me realize that I had misinterpreted so much. I never realized how different our stories were until I read Haven's writings.

For me, Haven's story was like getting in a time machine and going back six years before I was born to "see" the future environment that I would be born into. I was lucky that I was able to get firsthand details of my family from my brother, the first casualty of our broken home. Here is my brother Haven's story – His words, His writing.

I am the oldest of four children raised in this family. These writings give my eyewitness account of the dire circumstances and detrimental consequences of being raised in a very dysfunctional family setting.

My mother chose not to try to make amends for the harm that she was doing to herself and the harm being done to her children. She was very pragmatic, almost to a fault. Her trial-and-error approach to her relationships served to further solidify our disjointed family structure and allowed her to disregard, with impunity, the emotional wellbeing of her children. It must have been easier to be complicit and outwardly reject and deny the dysfunction that was present. My mother's complicity eventually would lead to life-altering consequences for me and my three younger siblings. We would all suffer from varying degrees of trauma: molestation, incarceration, and death.

My sister, Serena, survived the traumatizing and debilitating effects of our broken family for a time but finally succumbed as well. She was sixteen years old and pregnant when she died in a fiery car crash while returning home from a late-night party. Serena's fall from grace has become an example of how neglect and promiscuity without intervention, love, and a caring mother can contribute to an untimely demise.

My youngest brother, Maurice, survived the traumatizing and debilitating effects of our broken family and has become an example of perseverance. He now uses his experiences to mentor and provide guidance to "at risk" youth. He is my hero.

My younger brother, Ervin, survived the traumatizing and debilitating effects of our broken family for a time but ultimately succumbed and became an example of how abuse and punishment that is not tempered with love, compassion, and understanding can lead to a lifetime of confinement. Ervin will die in prison. He is incarcerated for a horrible and unspeakable crime. Ervin is a fallen soldier, a forgotten prisoner.

For me, the eldest of four, I succumbed to the traumatizing and debilitating effects of our broken family and was separated from my family by a sudden and explosive act of violence. I shot and killed my mother's inebriated boyfriend during an argument that became violent when he pulled a knife and threatened my life. My life was transformed by the debt I would pay to society through a ten-year period of incarceration. I have become an example of how perseverance, wisdom gained through life experiences, and the desire for a better life can help an individual achieve success.

For better or worse, this is my family, this is my life, this is our story.

Bitter Fruits from a Poisonous Tree

"Killing a motherfucker is easy. Living with the consequences is the hard part."

—*Inmate #41046*

INMATE HAVEN TRIPLETT
W-41046

DATE: 8/22/86

OFFICIAL VERSION:

At approximately 8:35 p.m. on April 19, 1984, a 911 call was dispatched for a shooting at 650 Union Street, Springfield, MA. The police responded to the scene. Upon arrival, they found the victim face down on the floor lying in a pool of blood. The victim had apparently suffered gunshot wounds to the head and shoulder. The victim was brought to the Wesson E.R. and pronounced dead. Police investigation, which included witnesses' statements, Haven Triplett was determined to have been the assailant.

CRIMINAL HISTORY:

The subject has no recorded criminal history prior to his present offense.

Being convicted of killing another person is *what* caused me to go to prison; being labeled a murderer, a person not worthy of living among society and whose thoughts and feelings have no merit, is what caused me to ask myself, "*Why* did I go to prison?"

It is one thing for me to say that if I could have foreseen the consequences of my past thoughts and actions, things might have turned out differently. It is another to realize that my past thoughts and actions can still give guidance and direction toward a brighter future, whatever that may be.

It is one thing to be involved in an altercation where I killed someone. It is another thing to have the newspaper and media paint an inaccurate picture of me. Most times in our society it is assumed that whenever someone is killed by someone else, the survivor is a vicious killer and the victim was not the aggressor or initiator of the violence.

It is one thing to be unable to put into words what it feels like to hear the judge sentence you to natural life in prison. It is another to find yourself being escorted by two court officers to a holding cell until you can be transported to a prison cell where you will spend the rest of your natural life.

It is one thing to have a natural life conviction overturned and the feeling of numbness removed. It is another to remain mentally positive and physically strong in order to be released one day after serving an eighteen- to twenty-year manslaughter sentence.

The notoriety of killing someone is now a chapter in the book of my life. I will always remember that I am a person who murdered another. My thoughts did not stop there. Things were more complex. I could not just think that a man was killed and that I was punished for his death. I needed to know *why I had killed in the first place.* I had an internal desire to understand why prison became my destiny. If I simply wrote off my actions as circumstantial, I would be denying how my mother, Finch, and I had created a volatile environment full of hostility and distrust.

Much earlier before the murder, there were warning signs that the emotional and mental stability within my family structure was being undermined from within. The center was not holding. This was evident when my brother Maurice prevented me from shooting Finch and possibly my mother.

It happened during the Thanksgiving holiday, shortly after my grandfather had died. I had already been discharged from the Army and was living with my mother. I invited my six-month-old son, Haven Jr., and his mother, Sherry, to join us for the Thanksgiving weekend. Sherry accepted my invite and made the road trip from New Haven to Springfield. I was ecstatic that she and my son were coming to visit. I was especially excited because I hadn't seen Haven Jr. in a while, so this was going to be an opportunity for me to bond with him. I was hoping that during this visit, my entire family would bond with each other.

Once Sherry and Haven Jr. arrived, we all had a meet and greet, and the holiday celebration began. We had food, music, and each room was full of conversation. Things were going well, and for a second I was naïve. I had forgotten the legacy of my family and that the root of its existence was violence, anger, and hate. This good time could not last—and it didn't. Things started to go south after Finch had been drinking a while. For some reason, he now seemed to think that he had rights to make inappropriate comments about Sherry. He zeroed in on the fact that she was a heavyset woman and began making derogatory remarks about her size. I would like to believe that most respectable moms would have put their boyfriends in their place for openly insulting their sons' guests. Instead, my mother joined in the fun and added her own inappropriate comments. She made sly comments about how unattractive

Sherry was and asked Sherry why my son's last name was not the same as mine.

The insults that had been directed toward Sherry made me feel humiliated. I became very angry. The next thing I knew, I had retrieved a loaded pistol from my bedroom on the second floor and was descending a flight of stairs to return to the living room. What else was I supposed to do? As a child, I was taught that when people don't agree with you or when you want something someone has or when people insult you, you should get your gun and coerce them to comply with you. I had learned that this action will force them to give you what you want, make them apologize or show respect. If the desired result is not achieved, sometimes you may have to kill them.

As I was coming down the stairs with my gun on my way back to the living room, I was face to face with my little brother, Maurice. He blocked my path and in a tone that somehow dissipated my anger told me that he was not going to let me hurt anybody and told me to go back to my room. Imagine that! My little brother sent me back to my room! His actions and words had caused me to stop and think about what I was about to do. I returned to my room, put my gun away, and did not return back to the living room at all that night. Maurice and I were the only two people who knew just how close my family came to another tragic, unfortunate incident that night. A short time later, my son and his mother came to my room, where we all stayed for the night. We left my mother's house the very next morning, and I rode with them back to New Haven. Then I had to swallow my pride and return back to the same house where I was insulted. I had nowhere else to go.

This was just one incident of many where Finch and my mother caused me immense stress and challenged my sanity. I was at a tipping point. The depth of my internal frustration and confusion left me poised to blow like a powder keg. My unstable condition during this time was validated years later. A few months after my release from prison, I ran into Tom, one of my high school friends. During our high school years, we had similar interests. We were both chess fanatics, we liked playing basketball, and we loved to eat ham and cheese grinders. We were always together.

It was now ten years later, and both of our lives had changed so much. It was great to see him and fun catching up with each other and talking about old times. Then Tom said something that confused me. He apologized to me for not being there as a friend in my time of need. I wasn't sure what he meant, so I asked him to elaborate. He told me that a few days before I killed Finch, I told him that if Finch put his hands on my mother again, I would kill him. I couldn't remember making this statement. But it clearly shows how frustrated I was, the dangerous state of mind I was in at the time, and the increasing potential for violence that was developing within me.

The environment that was created in my mother's household caused unresolved issues to be addressed in the worst way possible. The most frequently used dysfunctional tools chosen were passive-aggressive manipulation or violence from frustration. Seeing these tactics used has given me a new perspective for maintaining my own emotional and mental wellbeing. Using sound judgement and critical thinking is the only way I believe someone in this situation will be able to avoid the mistakes I made. It is in this sense and only in this sense that I can appreciate why I went to prison.

Many times there is a silent conspiracy, whether intentional or otherwise, that pervades the justice system in the form of collusion between court-appointed lawyers, district attorneys, trial court judges, and compliant witnesses. Many times the participants in the conspiracy decide a person's guilt often before the facts are reviewed or that person enters the courtroom. This was possibly another reason I received the sentence of natural life in prison.

Two things that happened during my trial fit the definition of conspiracy and collusion. The first was that before the start of the third day of trial, before my mother was scheduled to testify, I was brought into a room to speak with her. I remember talking with my mother and telling her that she had been cut on the arm the night of the incident. My lawyer and the district attorney were both present. I remember her denial and my indecision and moment of hesitation before I pointed to the cut on the upper portion of her right forearm. I will never forget the cold and callous look I received from her when I pointed to this cut. I also will never forget the heated rush in which my defense lawyer and the district attorney left the room. An excerpt of the documented testimony follows.

SUPREME JUDICIAL COURT
COMMONWEALTH OF MASSACHUSETTS
S.J.C. NO. 4009
COMMONWEALTH OF MASSACHUSETTS,
Appellee
vs.
HAVEN TRIPLETT,
Appellant.

...Mr. Triplett's account was of a single quick, intense, explosively violent continuous episode triggered by Finch's brandishing his knife. By his account, Finch had threatened him earlier **and had physically abused Mattie Triplett** and her eight-year-old daughter. He knew Finch carried the Barlow knife and a piece of hand brass. He believed there was a loaded shotgun and a rifle under the bed Finch was sitting on. After pulling the knife, **Finch had hit Mattie Triplett with his hand and cut her arm with the knife**...

The second thing that happened occurred when my mother was on the witness stand. She vehemently denied that she had been cut at all. Disturbingly, my defense lawyer would not question her about the cut, which I had pointed out in front of both him and the prosecutor. The conspiracy would not end there and would play itself out at trial with my lawyer providing an inadequate defense. He did not challenge the prosecutor's inappropriate questioning tactics and had abandoned the theory of self-defense as a plausible option. The trial judge also played a role in this conspiracy by failing to give the jury the proper trial instructions. These purposeful blunders contributed to my demise and almost coerced me into pleading guilty to second-degree murder instead of maintaining my innocence. Perhaps the shortcomings of the prosecutor, defense lawyer, and trial judge were a blessing in disguise. Their actions were the reason my appellate attorney would later be able to successfully get me a new trial.

An observation and conclusion that I had made during my trial proceedings made me think that my life was actually saved by being convicted of first-degree murder. Throughout the trial, Finch's mother and sister had always sat on the opposite side of the courtroom facing me, but for some strange reason, during the sentencing phase, they sat directly behind me. My lawyer noticed this and looked back at both of them with a quizzical look on his face but said nothing. My deduction was that if I had been convicted of anything but first-degree murder, I would have been killed or suffered serious bodily injury at the hands of Finch's mother and sister. My reason for saying this is that when I looked back at them, Finch's sister had both her hands in her coat pockets, and Finch's mother had her left hand on her purse shielding her right hand. Neither would look at me, and both had a stare that can best be described as a look desiring cold, calculated vengeance. They both had the look of someone who would not hesitate to administer her own misguided sense of justice. Being convicted of first-degree murder not only brought to light the violent situation at my mother's home, but I strongly believe it had saved my life in a less obvious but equally disturbing way.

I avoided apprehension from the police for about six weeks with the assistance of friends. To those individuals, I am grateful. My days were filled with anxiety and stress. I was a fugitive from justice and more dangerous than ever. Running from the police was only a temporary solution and unsustainable. At the behest of my children's mother, Sherry, I turned myself into the New Haven Police Department during the seventh week of the manhunt. I was held in the Whalley Avenue Detention Center until I was transported back to Springfield. It was during this three-week period that I worked through the feelings of disbelief. It was difficult for me to accept that I had shot and killed someone. In only a few moments during a violent confrontation, my life was changed forever.

When I was taken back to Springfield, I was held at York Street County Jail in the west block section for seven months. There, I met a black female correctional officer during this seven-month period who gave me further insight into the cruel and violent nature of the individual that I had killed. She told me that she had gone to school with Finch and that at one time he had tried to rape her. It was clear to me that she looked to me as the person who avenged her painful experience when she angrily exclaimed, "I'm glad he is dead. He got what he deserved!"

While at York Street, I was forced to suppress my overwhelming feelings of frustration of not knowing what was going to happen to me. The unsure feelings of what my fate would be were further compounded by a lack of support from my mother. In fact, in the only letter she sent me while I was going through this painful transition, she condemned me. She felt that I should have showed her more gratitude for allowing me to live in her home. Because of this alone, she stated that I was totally in the wrong for defending myself against the threat of violence from her boyfriend. Upon receiving this letter, I knew what my fate was going to be. When my trial had concluded in 1985, I had been sentenced to a term of natural life in prison. My life had instantly been reduced to nothing. I was going to be another waste of human life living behind brick and steel. I was transported down a dark and lonely highway to the Massachusetts Correctional Institution at Walpole and stayed at this state prison for about two years in a one-man cell.

During this period of my incarceration, I received several disciplinary reports for minor infractions of the rules and an anonymous letter that was meant to antagonize and insult me. The author of the letter wrote that I was a "monkey-face nigger" and claimed that my mother was a whore and that Finch was her pimp. In the final paragraph of the letter, the author reminded me that I would have the next ninety-nine years to think about all these things; however, the author was wrong. My case was overturned in 1987.

Springfield Union
Tuesday, July 14, 1987
Man admits reduced charge of manslaughter
By CYNTHIA SIMISON (Union Staff)

A Springfield man whose conviction for first degree murder in the shooting death of his mother's fiancé three years ago was overturned by the State Supreme Judicial Court pleaded guilty yesterday to a reduced charge of manslaughter. Haven Triplett, now 24, was sentenced by Judge William W. Simons in Hampden County Superior Court to an 18- to 20-year state prison term as a result of a plea bargaining agreement...

I was remanded back to York Street County Jail in Springfield and kept in the main block section of this facility to await the proceedings of a new trial. I spent most of my time replaying the incident, my life, and my circumstance in my head. Every day I had to deal with new disturbing information that tested my sanity, like the visit I had from my mother when she asked me about the sexual abuse of my sister, Serena. She did not outwardly accuse me but instead tried to cleverly trick me into an admission of guilt through my reaction to her questions. She failed miserably. This was the first time I had heard about my little sister's abuse.

My mother told me that Child Protection Services was involved and had determined that the abuse had occurred between the time we had lived on Boston Road and Union Street. There were only four people living in the house at the time: me, my brother Maurice, my mother, and Finch. It was hurtful and disturbing that my mother would think that I would ever hurt my little sister in that way. It made me extremely angry to think that she probably felt that Finch was innocent of this indecent act. It was hard for me to fathom that she would first accuse her son, her flesh and blood, over her arrogant, untrustworthy boyfriend. There was no doubt in my mind that Finch was responsible for this heinous act of violence.

My suspicions were confirmed by a woman who was like a second mother to both my brother Maurice and my sister, Serena, when I was released from prison. She told me that she had personally asked Serena if Finch had touched her, and Serena responded by bowing her head and looking away from her. From the charges of sexual abuse that my mother was implying that I had perpetrated, I realized that there was no way I could depend upon her to now tell the truth and change her testimony about the night of April 19. I knew that I would have to take whatever reasonable deal I could get from my appeal because not only was my mother still against me, but equity does not exist within the legal system when you are poor, black, and unversed in the law.

I left York Street County Jail and returned to Walpole in July of 1987 after pleading guilty to manslaughter. My trip back was just as horrible as my first trip there. This time instead of having to sleep on an individual cot in a recreation room with several other inmates, I was locked up in an isolated cell. My cell had a urine-soaked mattress and pillow, which I had to cover with the prison-issued blanket I was given. The cell walls, screens on the windows, sink, and toilet were covered with dried food and feces. The deplorable condition of my cell sent me into a tailspin, and I started thinking about how it reflected my childhood. I was both terrified and angry when I realized that I was in a six-by-eight-by-ten-foot cell, and all my hopes and dreams of a family and future were now just momentary thoughts that would never be reality. Damn! How could I even begin to understand how being abused and being manipulated within my own family circle had brought me to this very low point in my life? More importantly, how could I move beyond the point of self-blame and hate toward those adults who I had relied upon for love and guidance but who had provided neither? Trying to find the answers to these questions would help me to understand one word: acceptance. My thoughts forced me to search for love within myself. My uncertain future compelled me to draw upon internal emotional resources to remain positive and hopeful and not succumb to despair and hopelessness.

External issues beyond my prison cell haunted me daily. In one phone conversation with my children and their mother, Sherry, I found out that Sherry was dating a drug dealer and that she had starting using drugs. The first thing I thought about when I heard this was *who was going to take care of my children.* Sherry on drugs was bad enough, but it was like a stake through my heart when my I spoke to my daughter and she asked me, "Daddy, when are you coming home?"

Somehow, someway, I made it through this trying time and left Walpole in December of 1987. My next stop was The North Central Correctional Institution at Gardner, a medium-security facility.

While at Gardner, I was again reminded of the type of person Finch had been. This time the information came from my cellmate who had grown up with him. As kids, he and Finch loved to pitch quarters to see who could get closer to an agreed-upon wall. He told me that he had been warned by his aunt to stay away from Finch because he was a troublemaker and a bully and someday someone was going to kill him.

In many ways Gardner was a pivotal point for me and defined the serious mindset and attitude that I developed toward doing time. Seriousness of purpose marked my three-year stay at Gardner. This was apparent by a facial expression that I wore, which was one of deep focus and thought; however, it was often mistaken for anger by correctional staff and other inmates who knew me. This institution was a rest stop for a weary, traveling soul. I mentally transformed my personal area within my two-man cell into a space where I could nurture hope and begin to heal. My timing for self-therapy was perfect as more bad news was brought to light in a letter from Sherry. In her letter, she expressed that she had waited for me for five years and had decided to move on with her life. She told me that she had met someone, was pregnant with his child, and that he was going to be a suitable father for our two children. The confined space I was in was not enough room to deal with the intense emotional pain that her letter brought to my heart and mind. It was only through my preparation of self-therapy that I was able to sustain and not self-destruct with the delivery of this news.

I left Gardner in November of 1990, and was sent to the Lancaster Co-ed Minimum and Pre-Release Center. Lancaster was my new residence for almost two years. In this less stringent, more relaxed environment, I was slowly able to work through the bitterness and loneliness that I felt because of the many losses that had occurred up until this point during my incarceration. Lancaster was a bridge over troubled waters. At this co-ed institution, I had an intimate relationship with a white woman who had killed a child in a sudden fit of rage. I learned about her tragic crime through our letter writing, which ended shortly after my release from prison. I eventually had to pay the price for breaking the "no fraternization" rules at Lancaster once we were caught. My penalty was a two-month transfer to the medium-security Institution at Concord. Concord was a shocking reminder that I was still an inmate confined within a prison setting with no control over how infractions of the prison rules were handled. It was there where I learned that the authorities were on a worldwide manhunt for my brother Ervin, who was accused of murdering an elderly woman.

After two months I was reclassified back to Gardner. For a large portion of the time, I attended counseling to understand what was happening inside of me. I wanted clarity on how my thoughts and feelings would manifest once I was released. I eventually made my own assessment of my sanity and determined that I was just as sane, if not more sane, than many of the counselors who were there for superficial purposes. Their interest did not lie in helping inmates understand their own psychology; they were there only to get a check.

With approximately nine months left before my release, I was transferred to the minimum facility of the Shirley Minimum and Medium Correctional Complex. I was a prisoner at Shirley for about six months and was nearly overpowered by the irresistible impulse to escape. I felt that I had been punished long enough for my crime and had a compelling desire to reconnect with the people in my life who had once been my source of strength and encouragement. Using a little rational thinking, I was able to fight my urge to escape and did not attempt it for two reasons. The first was that I did not have any place to go, and the second was that I worried about the consequences that I would have to deal with if I was caught. A few months later I had no regrets about not trying to escape when I heard the fate of a fellow inmate from the Lancaster facility who was unable to resist the temptation. He had reached his breaking point and decided that he did not care about the consequences of his actions. He was able to steal a car and successfully escape from Lancaster. Subsequently, he attempted to kill a state trooper after a routine traffic stop. The only thing that saved the trooper's life was his bullet-proof vest. In a feverish attempt to escape the officer's gunfire and continue fleeing, he killed himself by crashing into a tree. As a result of this escape, the commissioner of correction issued a memorandum that ordered any inmate incarcerated for either a violent crime or for being a potential escape risk to be returned to the next highest level of security. This meant that I had to be transferred from the Shirley minimum security facility to the Shirley medium security facility.

The transfer to the Shirley medium facility affected me psychologically. I started having a recurring nightmare where I would see myself thinking about being a prisoner within a prison cell that had no door or windows. I had this same nightmare on the night prior to Finch being shot and killed. The stress caused by this disturbing dream was further compounded by circumstances that occurred with my cellmate. For a three-month period I was cellmates with a young black gang member from Boston, Massachusetts. He was removed from our two-man cell for having several knife-like weapons hidden in his mattress. Had a correctional officer not spoken on my behalf, I could have been taken to court and given additional time for being in possession of dangerous weapons. I was very tense for a few days as I was expecting to be labeled a snitch and to be confronted with the threat of violence, but the time passed without incident, and I was able to prepare myself mentally for my release.

Being incarcerated turns people who are good into bad people and turns people who are bad into evil people. This primarily happens because of the treatment convicts receive while doing their prison sentences. My assertion comes from many personal experiences that I had witnessed or was involved in while I was incarcerated.

There are two groups of very dangerous people in the prison environment. The inmates who are incarcerated within the prison system are the first group and the correctional officers who willingly incarcerate themselves for eight hours a day, five days a week, for fifty weeks a year are the second group and are by far the deadlier of the two.

During my first year at the maximum-security prison at Walpole, I was housed in a unit named Bristol-two. Here I witnessed an inmate come into the unit and request to speak with another inmate. Suddenly, the officer on duty hit his body alarm then he wrestled the inmate to the floor and handcuffed him. By this time, another officer who was responding to the body alarm arrived on the scene. When the new officer approached the inmate who was lying face down on the floor with his hands cuffed behind his back, he kicked the inmate directly in the face. I was on the first floor of this unit less than thirty feet away when I observed this act of unnecessary violence. Seeing this occur was mentally and emotionally shocking to my conscience. I immediately froze where I stood. To this day, I cannot imagine what that inmate could have said or done to make the officer kick him in the face after he was already restrained.

I would get one possible answer to how this could occur many years later in a letter that I received from my brother Ervin. In his letter he described how he had been "booted" in the face by a correctional officer while he was restrained. It occurred when he was awaiting trial for murdering Alice Kelly. The correctional officer who booted him was a Kelly family member.

I was housed in a unit called Suffolk-two at Walpole, and I was enrolled in an educational program that taught electronics and heating and refrigeration. This class was held in a secure part of the prison Monday through Friday. Several inmates and I had to be let in through a locked door by a correctional officer to get there. This officer was a piece of work. Every morning when he unlocked the gate to let us go to class, he directed verbally abrasive comments at specific individuals, and sometimes his comments were directed at us collectively. The emotional badgering and verbal abuse went on for a few weeks until he finally directed a degrading insult at me. In a calm, monotone voice, I replied, "As a correctional officer, you have no more authority than what I as an inmate choose to respect. It would be wise of you to remember that." My remark caused the smug look of contempt on his face to change to an ugly sneer as he gave me an icy cold stare but said nothing. After our confrontation, the group and I did not see him for a few days, but when we next saw him, something about him had changed. If I had to guess, I would say that he had taken the time to read each of our files, especially my file, and discovered that I had been sentenced to natural life in prison for first degree murder. From that day forward whenever he addressed me or the group, he spoke to us with respect, which was acknowledged and reciprocated.

Much of my time at Gardner was spent meeting with the prison counseling staff. My interest in meeting with the counselors was to make sure my mental health was prepared for what the future held. I had documented approval from the warden to leave my unit a few minutes early in order to eat lunch before meeting with my counselor. My accommodation did not sit well with two housing officers who monitored the electronically controlled door of my housing unit. They knew I had permission to leave early but they still warned me not to do it. I ignored them and left my unit early anyway by walking through the door when they opened it for other inmates. My disobedience caused me to get written up and resulted in fifteen days of lockup in an isolation unit. In an isolation unit, individuals are locked up for twenty-three hours a day and are released for one hour of recreational time at the discretion of the correctional officers on duty. After I served my time in isolation I was able to solve the conspiracy of how I ended up there. Apparently the correctional officers wanted to teach me a lesson to show me just how much power they had. I had given my permission documents to one of them; however, it somehow had conveniently "fallen" behind a desk and wasn't found until I was released from isolation. Without paperwork I was in violation of the rules, so I was written up by a different correctional officer on duty. The alarming thing about this whole incident was that when I spoke with the officer to whom I had initially given my documentation, he made it clear that he was not going to go against his coworker who had written the report. He openly told me that he was going to support his coworker's lie.

Part of why this occurred was due to the esoteric power struggle between correctional officers who guard the inmates and counselors who try to help the inmates. Usually when the smoke settled, the counselor's ended up battered and bruised and the inmates were collateral damage as a result of being in the middle of this tug of war.

I had the unfortunate pleasure of witnessing the havoc brought upon my counselor at the hands of the correctional officers. One day I saw my assigned counselor on his way to his office. I noticed that his clothes were desheveled, his shoes were untied, his shirt was partially tucked in, and his belt was unbuckled. He had a look of utter humiliation and confusion on his face and was dragging his feet as if he was in extreme pain. He was walking as if each leg weighed a ton. When I saw him, I immediately knew he had just been strip searched. He now knew exactly what it felt like for inmates who were subjected to this type of treatment on a regular basis. Shortly after this happened he resigned from his position and left the institution. I was assigned to another counselor.

I had approximately ten months left before my release. I was incarcerated at the Shirley minimum security facility when I had the most unsettling experience during my time in prison. I was in the process of filing a lawsuit to receive earned good time credits that I believe I had been denied. Earned good time credits are a way for inmates to reduce their correctional sentence by attending institutional rehabilitation programs. These programs are offered to help inmates change their counterproductive behavior. When I asked the librarian if I could use one of the law books to draft up my lawsuit, I was told that the book I needed was being held in the superintendent's office under lock and key. I found it disturbing that the only book from the library that was kept in the superintendent's office was a book that could help inmates by showing them step by step how to draft a legal claim. Later that day I went to the superintendent's office to ask permission to use the book, only to find that the superintendent was absent.

The following day I was angrily confronted by the superintendent. It was lunchtime, and I was eating at a table by myself. He approached me in an aggressive manner and directed derogatory remarks at me while pointing his finger in my face. This was his attempt to get me to react in a violent manner. If I had, I would have been restrained and removed from the institution. I was aware of what he was doing and was not baited by his game to measure my emotional stability. I remained under control and kept cool. If I would have touched him in any way or threatened him, I would have been taken to court and given additional time regardless of what he had said or had done. Shortly after this interaction with the superintendent, I spent time reflecting about each of these unpleasant interactions. I asked myself, *How does kicking a restrained inmate in the face help his rehabilitation? How does hurling insults at inmates for no reason help their rehabilitation? How does a conspiracy to punish an inmate in a show of power help his rehabilitation? How does denying an inmate access to legal information help his rehabilitation?* I found that the answer to each of these questions was pretty simple: it doesn't!

I think it is pretty easy to see how this type of treatment may cause inmates to carry the unnecessary burden of anger or blame toward the correctional officers. I was no different. It was easy for me to blame others and be angry because my thoughts and feelings had been disregarded by others while incarcerated. Correctional officers at all levels and in all positions prey upon the anger and blame they initiate, and thrive upon the discomfort within the environment they create. What the correctional officers fail to realize is that the blame and anger that many inmates harbor is the primary reason riots occur inside the prison. They also fail to realize that if this blame and anger is not addressed before an inmate leaves prison, the result is a deadly cycle of recidivism that adversely affects mainstream society. Each time this occurs, the ex-cons carry out violent acts upon the public that get progressively worse each time they are released.

Something as innocuous as a pat search, where an inmate is routinely frisked to determine whether he has any weapons or contraband on his person, can become a lethal weapon of abuse in the hands of a correctional officer. Anyone knowledgeable about Pavlov's dogs and the conditioned reflex experiment he discovered when he manipulated a dog's salivation from the ringing of a bell will be able to relate this to my next experience.

In prison, I witnessed conditioned reflex firsthand. I noticed that as inmates left the prison dining hall, they would suddenly raise up both arms to be pat searched upon noticing a correctional officer tapping his leg with his hand. My awareness of this form of conditioning made me create my own unique way of rejecting it. While I could not outwardly refuse to be pat searched, I led my own resistance campaign by raising my arms very slowly when I was told to prepare to be pat searched. This form of silent insolence put me at odds with one correctional officer who satisfied his frustration by striking me in the sensitive nerve centers under both of my arms. Our exchange was done. I had revolted. He had retaliated. I knew it would be pointless to report the abuse because I was an inmate with no credibility. Even though I had been physically assaulted, I was satisfied that I had not succumbed to their little experimental conditioning game.

It is sad and ironic that the compulsive, deviant, erratic behavior that prison is supposed to help an individual address is only further perpetuated through the correctional officers' antagonism and abuse of power. The only thing that helped me to handle the harsh and unjust treatment I was subjected to during my incarceration was my personal desire to grow as an individual.

Roots of a Dysfunctional Tree

"There is nothing more frightening than ignorance in action."
                                                    —*Johann Von Goethe*

I am not sure if dysfunction is a genetic trait or if it is passed on through patterns of habit, but I am convinced that the dysfunction within my family started with my maternal grandfather. It was manifested through his dislike of my paternal grandmother, Ollie, and her son, my father, Benjamin.

When I lived with my grandfather Isaiah, he would not hesitate to tell me that my grandmother Ollie was a self-righteous, obnoxious bitch who thought her shit didn't stink. Why he felt a fifteen-year-old needed to know this, I am not sure. Perhaps my physical features reminded him of Ollie in some way, so he would just take his dislike for her out on me.

To add insult to injury, my mother reinforced my grandfather's dislike toward my grandmother by stating her own contemptuous character judgments. I felt that their assessment of my grandmother was inaccurate and untrue, but I had enough sense not to voice my opinion. From experience, I knew that the only things that would come from voicing my opinion were either a tongue lashing or butt whippin'. This left me in a constant state of fear. Both my mother and grandfather constantly made me feel like I did not have a right to my opinion. My grandfather enforced this by glaring at me and staring straight into my defenseless soul when he wanted me to agree with his viewpoint. My mother did this by speaking in a harsh tone of voice that struck just as hard as the slap that often followed.

I first met my grandmother Ollie shortly after my grandfather Isaiah died. She was already divorced from my paternal grandfather, whom I didn't have a chance to meet. When they went their separate ways, contact, even for the sake of family continuity, was lost.

In one of my many conversations with my grandmother, I learned that she had witnessed her mother shoot and kill her father. After years of abuse, her mother finally reached her breaking point. She decided that she was not going to allow her husband to beat her any longer. My grandmother remembered hiding under a table when the fighting between her parents started. She watched as her mother, who was being chased by her father, grabbed a loaded shotgun that was over the mantle. She put her head down and her hands over her ears. Then she heard a loud boom and looked up to see her father fall. She watched him lie on the floor and moan in agony until he was dead. Her mother was never charged with a crime as the police determined that it was a case of self-defense.

Years after her mother's domestic abuse, my grandmother told me that she had to deal with her own issues of being abused. There were two underlying reasons why her husband would physically abuse her. The first was jealousy stemming from his own insecurity in his marriage. The second was because he had to account for gambling away money that was made from a business that they owned together. The last time my grandmother's husband abused her, she hit him on the head with a brown glass milk bottle. After this incident she immediately filed for divorce. She had seen her mom go through much of the same abuse and decided long ago that she would not.

Her decision to divorce left her with minimal financial support from her ex-husband and the difficult burden of raising her children alone. Conversations with my grandmother helped me to realize that she had been misunderstood by my grandfather and mother. They had both misinterpreted her desire to have a better quality of life for herself and her children.

It made sense to me now why she had not gotten remarried and had remained alone for many years. From my conversations with her, I came to understand why she had zero tolerance for physical violence and why she later became an advocate against domestic violence.

Today, I can understand why my father left behind an unfulfilled legacy. He was raised in a home with a struggling mom and no father. Although his mom was physically present, she was burdened with a great deal of overwhelming pain from her divorce and could not be emotionally available to him. As a result, my dad grew into manhood without the mentorship from his father, which would have prepared him to become a man. This parental void led to him being shot and killed during an argument over money in a game of craps.

The New Haven Register
Monday, July 12, 1971

Man Is Slain in City Fight; Suspect Held
By BOB GOUDSWAARD

A city man shot during an argument on the street early Sunday night died several hours later in Yale-New Haven Hospital. Police said Benjamin Lewis, 30 of 49 Henry St., was shot in the abdomen and right leg about 7 p.m. at Congress Avenue near Arch Street. He died around midnight. A man, identified as Willie Everson, 30 of 438 Columbus Ave., was arrested a short time later at Derby Avenue in connection with the shooting. He was charged with murder. A police official said Lewis and Everson became embroiled in an argument over money. Everson claimed he was threatened by Lewis with a long pocket knife before the shooting. As Everson fled, he dropped the small caliber gun believed used in the shooting, but police so far have been unable to find the weapon.

⌘　⌘　⌘

Words Written on My Father Benjamin Lewis's Tombstone: "He Is Just Away..."

Many times we walk within the light of our parents' shadows without even knowing it. My father had died during an altercation. Over a decade later, I would kill someone during an altercation. My father had gotten shot during an argument that had turned violent after pulling out a knife. A decade later, I would shoot someone during an argument that would turn violent after the victim pulled out a knife.

> *Springfield Union*
> Friday, April 20, 1984
> Police seek gunman in slaying
> By RICHARD NADOLSKI (Union Staff)
>
> On April 19, 1984 Mr. Triplett shot and killed Finch in the Triplett apartment. The killing followed hot on the heels of an argument started by Finch, which became violent when Finch pulled a knife and threatened Mr. Triplett with it. Mr. Triplett left his mother's bedroom, went to his room, and confronted Finch with a loaded pistol. He fired once...

Devastated by my father's death, my grandmother vowed to pursue a better quality of life. This led her to go to college in order to further her education. When she graduated, she was finally able put down the mop bucket, broom, and cleaning supplies to become an elementary school teacher.

My grandmother Leola's death was very traumatic for me. She died of heart failure when I was eight years old. While my biological mother had claimed the rights of my birth, it was my grandmother Leola who had truly taken care of me. She was the only mother that I had ever known during the early years of my life. At her wake I remember screaming at her, crying uncontrollably, and trying to wake her up when she would not speak to me as I viewed her body.

My mother's weakness as a parent began to emerge following my grandmother's death. It became clear that she was not ready to be a full-time mom. She had been dependent on my grandparents for everything. But she now had to bear the full responsibility of taking care of me and my brother Ervin. Her mom was gone, and her disabled father could not handle two grandchildren on his own. Up to this point she had not developed the patience and understanding required to properly rear two children.

In a step toward her independence, my mother moved us out of my grandfather's house and into an apartment on Ashmun Street with Ervin's father. She quickly found that she was now required to wear several hats that each required a different level of responsibility. She needed to be a full-time mother for two children, a full-time wife to Ervin's father, and she needed to maintain her home on a full-time basis. In trying to fill so many roles at once, my mother lost sight of what needed to be done to keep her household in order. The load was too much. She could not handle all of the responsibility and failed horribly at being a caring mother and wife. The frustration from her failures turned her into an angry, hateful person. She was out of control, and Ervin and I felt her wrath.

It was at this point that I realized that my grandmother had left me alone and unable to defend myself from the emotional instability of my mother *as well as my grandfather.* When my grandmother was alive, she was the peacekeeper and had a calming effect that somehow put my mother and grandfather at ease. I could see that my mother was already showing signs of self-destructive behavior; it was only a matter of time before my grandfather did the same. With my grandmother gone, I no longer had my protective shepherd.

My grandfather, Isaiah, was raised in a family of thirteen siblings in the sharecropping state of Georgia. He grew into adulthood during the Great Depression, in the Jim Crow South. These early years helped shape his mindset, which placed a very high priority on obtaining money. Money was more valuable than the relationships he established, and he had no problem obtaining it through questionable means.

On one occasion, when I was fifteen, I was playing poker for money with my grandfather and several other people. There was fifty in the pot, and I won the hand with four kings. My grandfather had the second highest hand with four jacks. Not to be outdone by me, he snatched all the money off the table while simultaneously reaching for his gun. I didn't say anything as he took all the money, but my relationship with him was never the same after that. I realized that he was not going to let anyone come between him and his money.

I believe one incident in my grandfather's life more than any other put into motion the sense of deprivation that would eventually define the quality of life that he chose to pursue. My grandfather was a handsome, dark-skinned man and was quite popular with the ladies. For personal protection, he always carried a gun. However, on one occasion, his girlfriend Leola hid his gun from him. Leola's action would prove to be a defining moment in his life before he lost the use of his legs.

My grandfather's philandering had finally caught up to him and he did not have the benefit of his gun for protection. The incident occurred when he was confronted by another man over the affections of a woman who was walking him to work. This woman was currently in a relationship with the man who confronted my grandfather. A heated verbal exchange ensued, and my grandfather began to shout vulgarities at the man. He convinced the man's girlfriend to do the same.

Unable to restrain himself, the man became enraged and wrestled my grandfather to the ground. My grandfather easily overpowered the man and began pummeling him. Unfortunately, my grandfather was not aware that the man's brother was in the crowd that had gathered, and he had no one there watching his back. As he was getting the best of the man, the man's brother emerged from the crowd and stabbed my grandfather in the back. As the knife blade went into his back, a small piece of it broke off next to his spine. By the time he felt the sharp pain from being stabbed, the man he was pummeling and his brother both made a quick escape through the crowd. Unable to give chase, my grandfather lay on the ground until he was taken to the hospital by a few bystanders. Medical technology was not that advanced at the time, so my grandfather received an inadequate medical assessment. As a result, the broken portion of the knife blade was undiscovered.

My grandfather carried the metal shard in his back for several years. During this time he experienced intermittent impulses of intense back pain that would manifest into unpredictable outbursts of violent anger that he directed toward others. Over the years internal movement of the shard caused irreparable nerve damage and left him confined to a wheelchair. He was now disabled and could not work; however, he was resilient and found a new livelihood. With an entrepreneurial spirit, he became a bootlegger. He started selling alcohol after the liquor stores closed in order to supplement his disability benefits.

It is my belief that conviction—defined as unquestioned assumptions that are confirmed by one's life experiences—and the subsequent denial of evidence that disproves these assumptions are the root cause of dysfunction. I've witnessed every one of my adult relatives prove this assertion. For example, my uncle Isaiah, through learned dysfunction, thought it was okay to physically and verbally abuse his wife. I actually witnessed his cowardly abuse of my aunt Geraldine. Seeing him do this gave me a great deal of insight into the type of home life that my grandfather shaped and the type of family values he passed on to his son. It also gave me some insight into the cold and callous nature of Gregory Finch; he is the man that I would one day kill.

I had recently been released from the Army and had moved into my grandfather's apartment in order to keep his bootleg business operational while he was recovering from surgery at my uncle Isaiah's home. My grandfather had moved there while I was away to recover from an operation he had to remove an ulcer. The ulcer formed because of his limited mobility and because of inadequate home medical care. His plan was to stay at my uncle's temporarily and return home once he was healthy enough.

Now that I had returned I could have moved him back home but I decided to leave him at my uncle's until he regained his strength. I visited him every other day to make sure he was doing well. On one visit, he asked me to go to the neighborhood convenience store to get him a pack of Camel cigarettes. When I returned to the house, I found my aunt Geraldine lying in the prone position on the floor next to the back door of the first floor apartment. She was holding her eye and crying inconsolably. I could see that her right eye was swollen shut. I asked my grandfather who was sitting in his wheelchair, what had happened. All he could do was point his finger at his daughter-in-law and with tears in his eyes say, "My son hit his wife." I yelled for someone to call an ambulance. I looked toward Finch and his friend Al to assist me, but they did not offer to help. They were there because they had made the trip from Springfield to see my uncle on a spur-of-the-moment visit. My mother was not with them. They had both witnessed the abuse when it occurred, and neither of them moved a muscle to help. My uncle, who was also in the room, was standing a few feet from my aunt and had remained motionless and silent. They all watched me panicking to get my aunt some help.

Apparently my gesture to help my aunt made my uncle angry because he stepped in front of me and prepared to throw a punch. I gave him a verbal warning that it would be a bad idea to swing at me as I pointed the barrel of my grandfather's gun toward him. I did not pull the gun out of my coat pocket; I just let the barrel stretch my coat toward my uncle. However, he knew that I was dead serious—no pun intended. In my uncle's mind, I was another punching bag, or so he thought. What right did I have to say anything concerning how he treated his wife in his house?

My uncle Isaiah was over six feet tall, weighed over 250 pounds, and was solid muscle. Standing six feet three inches tall and weighing in at only 175 pounds, I had no way to defend myself without the deterrence of a high-powered handgun at my disposal. My uncle knew that I would not hesitate to protect myself and wisely decided not to throw his punch. Instead, he began to verbally assault me. With hate and anger in his eyes, he told me to get the hell out of his house. As I backed up in the direction of the front door, he shouted every profanity he could think of at me.

As I reached the front porch, I noticed that my cousin Rodney, my uncle Isaiah's third-eldest son, was walking downstairs from the second floor to the room that I had just left. Rodney observed his mother on the floor but did not say a word to anyone in the room as he continued walking toward the back door to go upstairs. I was sure Rodney remained silent when he saw his mom because he was in a no-win situation. If he would have let his anger get the best of him and had confronted his dad he would have probably ended up on the floor next to his mom. Instead, he made the more sensible choice to go back upstairs to call the police.

A few minutes later, a police cruiser arrived and parked a few houses away from where my uncle lived. My uncle came outside to meet with a police officer who was walking toward the house. I am not sure what was said, but my uncle must have convinced the officer that there was no problem at his home because he and the officer walked back toward the police cruiser and talked for several minutes then the officer left. I had just witnessed my uncle get away with a crime. I could not fathom how he could be so heartless, to assault his wife, prevent her from getting medical attention, and attack anyone who tried to help her.

Being a witness to this tragedy left me to ponder several questions. How was my uncle able to do what he had done without being accountable? What type of person brutally assaults his wife in front of his handicapped father? What values had my grandfather passed on to his son? What type of person was Finch to idly stand by with a smirk on his face and observe this act of violence without intervening? What type of person was Finch's friend Al? He had observed this entire incident with a look of shock on his face, yet he, too, had remained silent and did nothing. Both Finch and Al would one day physically assault my mother just as my uncle had done to his wife. Had my uncle's actions just given Finch and Al a license to abuse my mother?

That day, I was fortunate that I had my grandfather's gun for protection. The close call I had with almost shooting my uncle made me think about the very interesting history of the gun I had in my possession. My grandfather had purchased the gun from his friend, a Connecticut state trooper who was on the verge of retiring. I was fifteen years old when I first saw it. I was lying in my grandfather's bed dozing off to sleep when the trooper removed the gun from its holster and fired a shot into the ceiling of my grandfather's apartment. The trooper's thoughtless action was meant to show the functionality of the gun. Still half asleep, I slowly sat up after hearing the gunshot, and through groggy eyes I looked at the trooper then at my grandfather then I lay back down.

Any other fifteen-year-old would have probably been startled by the sound of the gun, but I wasn't. My grandfather was sitting in the bed next to me, so I had no fear and was not concerned about being harmed. Today, I also believe that the gunshot had not scared me because, to some degree, I was oblivious to the ever-present danger around me.

After the gun hammer twang and firecracker sound dissipated, there was a moment of silence; then my grandfather and the trooper began negotiating a price for the gun. The next day our upstairs neighbor named Kenny informed my grandfather about the hole in the floor of his bedroom closet. It is fortunate that Kenny was not in the path of the bullet as he could have been shot or killed by the reckless gunfire.

The dysfunctional behavior that my uncle had learned from my grandfather was contagious. He passed this disease on to his wife, as her overt sexual escapades dwarfed his despicable domestic abuse.

I had actually witnessed them both step outside of their marriage with other people; however, my uncle tried to be discrete about his philandering. Not that this made it any better. My aunt, however, did not understand what the word "cheating" meant. Not only did she have extramarital affairs, but she would boast about them. This may have been what pushed my uncle over the edge and led to his explosive acts of violence and physical abuse against her.

I was at my grandfather's apartment once when a man named James arrived there with my aunt. I can still picture how relaxed and shameless my aunt looked. She sat on the couch while James asked my grandfather if he could use the back room to have sex with her. While my grandfather did not run a brothel, on more than one occasion, for a small "rental" fee, he let friends and strangers use the back room to consummate an intimate transaction.

My grandfather refused James's request and told him in no uncertain terms that the woman he was with was his son's wife. As my aunt and James left the apartment, my grandfather picked up the telephone and started to call his son but changed his mind and angrily slammed the telephone receiver down.

The very open and public humiliation that both my aunt and uncle caused each other continued. There was a time when my grandfather tried to be generous by giving my aunt some money because he had won a windfall from playing the illegal street numbers. As she and my uncle were leaving his apartment, my grandfather gave my aunt fifty dollars and told her to go buy a nice skirt. When my aunt took the money, my uncle turned to her and snapped, "Oh, you are fucking my father now!"

A few days later, my grandfather, with a troubled look on his face, told me that my aunt had returned a few hours later. She told my grandfather that his son had been badgering her and was accusing her of having sex with him. She told my grandfather that she was so upset about it that she wanted to have sex with him to make it true. My grandfather ignored this profane idea and instead tried to console his daughter-in-law. After that, my memory of this incident fades...

Being raised by a mother who was a single parent and having disposable "uncles" and exchangeable "dads" hindered my growth in many ways. My emotional sensitivity toward others was numbed, my sense of intellectual creativity was stagnated, and my sense of what it meant to be a teenager was distorted.

I was oblivious to the presence of the dysfunction I was exposed to, and I was suffering through the growing pains of immaturity. My mentality was crippled and trapped within the bounds of my environment.

That which I experienced at home was not discussed in school, and that which I learned in school could not solve the real-life issues that I encountered at home. There were many days that I suffered silently due to the absence of a mentor. I had no one to help me with problems that I encountered during my adolescence.

With my circumstances, it probably would not have mattered anyway because nothing could have prepared me for the physical and mental challenges that I would experience while spending ten years in prison. Unable to sleep, on many nights I found myself looking out of a barred prison window into the reflection of all that I had ever been: a son, a brother, a father, a friend, and a lover. Sometimes the reflection would turn into all the things that I thought I could never be: a murderer, a criminal, a convict, a prisoner, and an inmate. Now that my existence was defined by the iron bars, sliding doors, concrete walls, and an identification number—Walpole 41046—the many moments of silence helped me find peace within myself about what had happened.

I now found myself accountable for all the things I did not know and totally responsible for all the things that I did not understand. I had been deprived and abandoned as a child and had grown into an immature adult. I had been chastised for inconsequential things when a few words of caution would have been sufficient. I had been deprived and abandoned emotionally because my childhood dreams and aspirations were not given the chance of an adult reality. The pain of my past had still not healed, and I still had not confronted my past fears. I had been led to believe that my thoughts and feelings did not count. I had been constantly degraded by my mother's words: "If you had a brain, you would be dangerous!"

I was not given the tools that were necessary to make intelligent decisions as an industrious husband and as a loving father. I was deprived and abandoned spiritually because the adults in my life had not given me a basic moral foundation, a foundation that I could use to understand how to treat others, a foundation that I could use to understand why rules and laws were necessary to govern behavior in society. Once I was able to understand how I had been deprived and abandoned as a child, I was able to take a step toward individual growth.

My childhood and teenage years were riddled with violence and abuse. The madness I witnessed or was directly involved with began to desensitize me to violence. Initially these events were traumatic, but eventually they became the way things were. I became so insulated to violence that even when I was the recipient of the abuse, I began to think it was okay.

I vividly remember a time when my brother Ervin and I were traumatically abused by my stepfather. It was early evening on a warm summer day at our apartment in the Ashmun Street projects in New Haven. My mother and her first husband, Ervin Triplett Sr., were arguing. As the arguing escalated, my brother Ervin Jr. and I were told to go into our bedroom. The reason we were told to do this was not because they were concerned for our safety; it was so that we would not get in the way of the fighting when it started. The catalyst for this argument was the child abuse that occurred a week earlier to me and Ervin. We had had been left alone in the apartment, and in our careless horseplay, we tripped over cords that were connected to a stereo amplifier that was perched on an open closet shelf. The amplifier crashed down off the shelf, hit the floor, and broke. Not knowing what to do, we put the amplifier back on the shelf and continued playing. A short time later,

Ervin Sr. came home intoxicated and discovered the broken amplifier. In his state of inebriation, he beat me and my brother Ervin with his fists. With full force, he punched Ervin in the eye and then threw him into a wall. For me there were two hits. He backhanded me, and then I hit the floor head first. The pain I experienced felt as if someone was sticking pins and needles into the left side of my head and face. We were beaten up by a grown man and were left hurt in a corner next to the front door like two crumpled-up pieces of paper. This is how our mother later found us.

Knowing that he would have to answer to her for how my brother and I were bruised and battered, Ervin Sr. took refuge in my uncle Isaiah's basement. Ervin Sr. knew that my uncle Isaiah would provide him sanctuary so that my mother could not find him to "discuss" what had happened.

When I was old enough to understand the details of this story, it was not surprising to me that my uncle had shielded my stepfather from a just reprisal. It occurred to me that my stepfather and uncle were one in the same. My uncle physically abused his children just as badly, if not worse, than Ervin Sr. and neither felt shame for doing it.

One day I witnessed my uncle Isaiah beat the life out of his youngest son, Wesley. I'm not sure what Wesley had done, but nothing could justify the beat down he received. My uncle used the bottom piece of a wooden crutch, in a fit of rage, to administer his discipline. I remember sitting at the kitchen table with Wesley's older brother Rodney and watching Wesley follow my uncle into the living room. We both knew what was coming next once the door closed.

My uncle Isaiah let the corporal punishment commence. Rodney and I heard Wesley's cry for mercy begin with a high-pitched scream. Several blows later, his cry turned to a low, weak moan of agony. After a few more hits from the bottom of the crutch we no longer heard Wesley moaning; however, the beating continued. The only thing we could now hear was the sickening sound of wood striking a limp body. Finally the living room door opened, and my uncle came out with beads of sweat on his forehead and went into his bedroom. Wesley slowly staggered out of the living room a few minutes later. He looked hurt and exhausted. He sat next to me and his brother at the kitchen table, and with tears in his eyes, he whispered in a low voice, "I hate him."

Stupid is the only appropriate descriptive for parents who send a young child to the store alone to cash a check. Ignorant is the appropriate descriptive for these parents when the store is in an impoverished, dangerous neighborhood. This example of poor parenting happened when we were still living in the Ashmun Street projects in New Haven.

I was seven years old and foolishly put in harm's way when Ervin Sr. made me go to the local drug store to cash his check. The store was about half a mile from our home and was located between Winchester Avenue and Canal Street. To get there I had to cross a parking lot, a set of railroad tracks, and walk up a steep hill. It was early in the evening and was starting to get dark outside.

When I entered the drug store, it was full of kids. Some of them were running around, some were looking at the toys on the shelves, and others were sitting on stools at the dining counter. There was one teenage hoodlum who I did not notice at first standing next to the drug store entrance. When I reached the counter, I asked the pharmacist to cash my stepfather's check. At first he refused and asked me for my phone number so he could call my parents. I am not sure which of my parents answered the call, but he told whoever he was talking to that cashing the check and having me walk home with a pocket full of cash was not a good idea. His words fell upon deaf ears, and he was instructed to cash the check anyway. After giving me the cash, the pharmacist grabbed his coat and prepared to walk me home. He changed his mind at the last minute because he was not comfortable leaving his female assistant in the store alone. He suggested that I hold the money very tightly in my hand and walk straight home.

After seeing the pharmacist give me the money, the teenage hoodlum who had been observing from the door suddenly disappeared. As I reached the bottom of the hill and crossed the train tracks, the teenage hoodlum snuck up behind me and snatched the money out of my hand. As he snatched it, his fingernail cut the top of my thumb. I grabbed my injured thumb and said "ouch" as I watched the young hoodlum run across the railroad tracks and quickly disappear into the darkness.

I continued home to tell my parents what had happened. Both of them now decided to get dressed to walk to the drug store with me. They spoke with the pharmacist about what happened, and they subsequently spoke with the mother of the alleged assailant. The mom vehemently denied her son's involvement in the crime, and the conversation with this parent led nowhere.

While returning home with my parents, I had my head down and found myself thinking about one of the funny cartoons that I had watched earlier that day. The image in my head made me laugh out loud. My mother must have thought I was laughing about the fact that I was robbed and in a sharp, angry tone said, "It's not funny!" After that, the memory fades...

The perpetual lessons in violence continued. This time I was used as a pawn to assist my mother as she tried to hurt my stepfather Ervin Sr. during a fight. I was sitting on my bed and my brother Ervin was standing in the bedroom doorway watching them fight. I remember hearing scuffling, shouting, and things falling. My mother had overpowered Ervin Sr. and had pinned him down on our living room couch. Once she had him locked into a position where he could not move, she called me out of the bedroom and directed me to go into the kitchen and bring her a knife. As I moved toward the kitchen, Ervin Sr. yelled "Haven..Stop!". With both adults simultaneously yelling at me and demanding me to take the exact opposite action, I remained motionless in the open space that divided the kitchen and living room. Out of breath from my mother wrestling him down, Ervin Sr. became silent. My mother took advantage of this moment and ordered me to immediately get a knife from the kitchen sink. I didn't move. I was paralyzed because I anticipated a response from Ervin Sr., but this time he did not say anything. When I didn't hear him respond, I went into the kitchen to get a knife.

In plain view of both adults, I reached into a sink full of dirty dishes and grabbed a six-inch serrated steak knife. The handle was made of plastic, and it had a daisy flower design on one side of the handle. Not knowing what my mother was going to do with this knife, I began rinsing it off. She impatiently yelled for me to bring her the knife and then laughed at my effort to clean it off. She was still struggling to keep Ervin Sr. pinned down, but he was fighting and reaching for the knife as I got closer. I held the knife above his grasp and gave it to my mother, and then I was told to go back into my room. Sitting on my bed, I could hear grunts as the struggle continued. Then I heard someone running and a door slam. My brother Ervin was still standing in the doorway of our bedroom, watching. He had seen everything. I later found out that the person who ran out of the apartment was my mother. She was gone now, and Ervin Sr. once again took his anger and frustration out on Ervin Jr. and me. Without compassion, he told us both to get out of the apartment. I was seven; Ervin was four. As we left the apartment, I remember seeing an ugly gash on the top of Ervin Sr.'s forehead. My mother had tried to scalp him!

After being kicked out of the apartment, Ervin Jr. and I had no choice but to play out in front of the apartment building until our mother came back home. We had been playing for ten minutes when I noticed an ambulance and police cruiser pull up in front of the building. The flashing white and red lights drew my attention to my stepfather, who was dressed in a black hat, black coat, black slacks, and black shoes as he was being escorted into the ambulance. Once the ambulance drove away, Ervin and I were on our own. Neither of us had a key to the apartment, so we were forced to wander around the project complex for several hours until our mother came back that evening.

Once my mother and Ervin Sr. separated, my mother let Maurice's father move in. His name was Lynwood, but we called him Butchy. Making a change to her new boyfriend did not make things any better for my mother. As a matter of fact, things got worse. Unlike Ervin Sr., who was a small man that my mother could easily overpower, Butchy stood six feet, two inches and weighed over two hundred pounds. There was no way she was going to win a physical match against him. Unfortunately I witnessed this firsthand as I experienced the first taste of violence that traumatized me.

I had just come home from school and had started washing dishes. This was a daily chore that my mother had assigned to me. I heard a loud commotion outside the kitchen window of our fifth-floor apartment. When I looked outside down into the parking lot of our high-rise housing complex, I saw my mother and Butchy fighting. Butchy was on top of my mother, and he was punching her in the head and in the face. The sight of my mother getting beaten was traumatic and frightening. In a state of panic, I jumped back from the window. I was confused and unsure of what to do, so I just resumed washing dishes and did not look out the window again.

A few minutes later my mother came upstairs, and she had brown pieces of grass in her hair and on her dress. When I looked at her face I noticed that her glasses were lopsided. I was still in shock and speechless, so I didn't say a word. My mother looked at me and said, "If Butchy comes up to the apartment and knocks on the door, do not to let him in." Hearing those words gave me a sense of relief but the next day I found that my mother's words amounted to a false sense of security. When I returned from school the next day, Butchy was sitting on the couch talking to my mother. When I entered the house and saw him, I jumped backward and froze.

From that day, I remember all the changes that occurred within me; I no longer did well in school. It became very difficult for me to concentrate in class. I stopped asking the teacher questions, and my love of reading suddenly diminished. Before this incident I was reading two grade levels ahead of other children who were my same age. I started getting sent to the principal's office frequently for reasons that I could not explain. I became absent-minded. I started leaving my house key in the door, and my perception of time was thrown out of synch. I'm not sure if my mother noticed all of my behavioral changes, but if she didn't, I would categorize this as neglect. If she did notice, I will never understand why she stayed with Butchy and why she moved to Springfield with him a few months later. This was one of the worst decisions that she could have made; not only because of how their relationship was affecting me, but also because Butchy had been cruel to every one of us. As a matter of fact, there was a time when he almost killed me, Ervin, and my mother.

We were still living in New Haven on Ashmun Street at the time. I had just come down the stairs from our fifth-floor apartment to the first floor when a young girl who was running into the hallway of our apartment building ran into me. I grabbed her to keep her from falling and asked her why she was running. She told me that there was a man chasing a woman around the parking lot and that I should not go out there. I thought to myself – *yeah right* and ignored her concern for my safety. After all, the people outside had nothing to do with me but that could not have been further from the truth. As I reached the sidewalk adjacent to our apartment building, I saw my mother, who was visibly shaken. She was holding Ervin's hand with her right hand. When she saw me, she took my hand in her left hand and started quickly walking down the sidewalk in the direction of my grandfather's house. We all looked in horror when we saw Butchy appear thirty feet in front of us. He was standing on the top of a concrete embankment with a tire iron raised above his head. He started running down the embankment toward us. I will never forget the wide-eyed, crazy look on his face. I had no doubt in my mind that this was the end. The only thing that prevented him from delivering a death blow from the tire iron was Maurice's Aunt Elaine. She had looked out the window from her fifth floor apartment window just in time to yell, "Butchy, don't do it!" Miraculously, he stopped running and froze where he stood. I was confident that if Maurice's Aunt Elaine had not been there to stop him, Butchy would have killed us all.

This was the man my mother chose to be with. He had beaten her during several arguments and humiliated me and Ervin countless times. I recall a time when Ervin and I were left alone and ended up roaming the streets of New Haven. Ervin was four; I was seven. No one was watching us, so we just left the house and began walking the streets and exploring the city. On a stroke of luck we were spotted by my grandfather, who picked us up and took us to a department store to buy us new clothes. When we were done, he dropped us off at home but did not stay to speak with my mother. He probably was too upset with her for neglecting me and my brother.

As we left my grandfather's car, I remember the smile on Ervin's face as he admired his brand-new coat. He was so thrilled to have it that he had left the price tag hanging from the sleeve. Along with the new coat, my grandfather had purchased Ervin a shirt, a pair of slacks, and a pair of shoes. I received the same.

We paraded our new clothing all throughout the project complex until we ran into Butchy. When he saw us, he took us upstairs to our apartment and made us take the clothes off and change back into our Goodwill seconds. Instantly, my brother and I were transformed from being stately dressed young gentlemen back to street urchins. Then Butchy made us tell him where the clothes had been purchased and took us with him as he went to return them for a cash refund. With no receipt, I remember Butchy becoming irate and arguing with the store owner for several minutes to get a refund. After that, my memory of the incident fades.

This story became a painful memory for me and clearly indicates how abusive, irresponsible adults can emotionally damage children. The actions of my mother, Ervin Sr., my Uncle Isaiah, and Butchy had started a slow metamorphosis within me. They had all exposed me to violence and trauma so much that I was becoming used to them both. They were becoming foundational building blocks of my character.

As I grew into a teenager, this foundation manifested itself, and my propensity for violence escalated. I had my mother in one ear telling me to pick up the first thing that I could put my hands on to protect myself, and I had no one in the other ear to contest her message. There would be no one to tell me that when the stick that I once used as a weapon becomes a two-by-four with eight-penny nails in it and a fifteen-year-old boy's skull is fractured over a comic book, that I could be charged with assault and battery. There would be no one there to tell me that when fear turns to panic and the board that I once used as a weapon becomes a gun, that I could go to prison for killing someone in self-defense.

When we relocated to Springfield, we were evicted constantly—almost every ten months. We moved from Massachusetts Avenue to James Street, from James Street to Magazine Street, from Magazine Street to Fernbank Road, from Fernbank Road to Eastern Avenue, from Eastern Avenue we moved to Florence Street, from Florence Street we moved to Chester Street, from Chester Street we moved to a different location on Eastern Avenue, from the new location on Eastern Avenue we moved to Boston Road, from Boston Road we moved to Union Street, from Union Street we moved to Draper Street, from Draper Street we moved to

Quincy Street, and from Quincy Street we moved to Granada Terrace. At one time we were moving so much that we had four different addresses in less than three years. This continuous upheaval only reinforced the uncertainty, instability, deprivation, tension, and volatility that defined our dysfunctional family.

In our household the velvet glove of neglect and the iron fist of abuse would leave no member of our family unscathed. The neglect was like a choke chain that slowly tightened around the throat, while the abuse slowly strangled the life out of each of us. My mother and Butchy could always find money for a gallon jug of white port wine, or an ill-advised automobile purchase, or a weekend joyride to New Haven, or a fishing trip to whereabouts unknown. Yet for some strange reason, they could never seem to find money for basic necessities such as oil for heat, food beyond the government handouts, quality clothing beyond the Goodwill seconds, a basic haircut for their children, or money to pay the rent so we would not get evicted.

The neglect and abuse extended to all those beautiful and majestic animals that had been called King, Bruno, and Mrs. Pepper. These were the pets that had once been a part of our household. In the end, their unquestioned loyalty and companionship were rewarded with abandonment. They, too, like me and my brothers had become forgotten silent victims within our depraved dysfunctional family; they were collateral damage.

I witnessed violence at almost every location where we lived.

Eastern Avenue—Guns and Pedophiles

Butchy's brother named Ezra, nicknamed Chick, came along for the ride when we moved from Connecticut to Massachusetts. His presence put me and my siblings at risk for further abuse. There was a time when he tried to molest me in front of my brothers, but I was fortunate and was able to escape his perverted sickness. I later found out that he had been successful in molesting my little brother Ervin. I believe that this act of pedophilia single-handedly destroyed any chances that Ervin had of living a normal life as an adult.

Three years later, Chick was killed in a particularly violent act of murder. His body was found mutilated in his Worcester, Massachusetts, apartment. His killer or killers stabbed him over fifty times. They have yet to be caught, and I hope they never are. His murder was a twisted act of justice that was proper retribution for what he had done to my little brother and for what he had tried to do to me.

⌘ ⌘ ⌘

During our stay at Eastern Avenue, I found a small twenty-two-caliber handgun behind a kitchen radiator while sweeping the floor. It was ironic that *I* was the one who found the gun—or had the gun sought me out as an ominous prophecy I would one day fulfill? Not knowing what to do with the gun, I gave it to Chick. He in turn gave the gun to Butchy. A few days later, Butchy and my mom were in our living room arguing. Butchy pulled the gun and fired a shot at my mother that just missed her. In fear for her life, my mother ran out of the house. Butchy ran upstairs, grabbed my little brother Maurice, and fled.

This type of craziness was a typical occurrence in their relationship. One day they would be hugged up and in love, and the next day one of them was trying to shoot or stab the other. The shooting incident marked the time when my mother interchanged Butchy for James Jackson; we called him J.C. He was the future father of my little sister, Serena. It also marked the time for us to move to our next temporary address on Florence Street.

Florence Street—La Familia

The dysfunction continued on Florence Street. This time my brothers and I were put right in the middle of a life-threatening altercation between my mother and J.C. With a common enemy, our allegiance as brothers would rise to meet the threat of violence. The argument between J.C. and my mother became violent when J.C. hit my mother in the face with a two-by-six piece of wood. My mother retaliated by trying to stab J.C. with a butcher's knife. He avoided getting stabbed by using the bed mattress as a shield. While he was protecting himself, my brother Ervin punched him in the throat, and I tried to push him through a window. Somehow he was able to recover, catch his balance, and avoid falling through the window. As he stood there after being attacked by all of us, he threatened to kill everyone! A short time later, cooler heads prevailed, everyone's anger deescalated, and we all went to bed.

This would not be the last time that a common foe would cause us as brothers to band together. Right or wrong, we had come to our mother's defense against J.C. She, however, would abandon us when it came time to validate her child's right to voice his individual thoughts and feelings to J.C.

The incident in question occurred when Ervin, Maurice, J.C., and I were walking to our mother's job to meet her during her lunch break. When we were close to my mother's job, we stopped at a store to purchase sandwiches. J.C. said something in a bossy tone to Maurice. Maurice replied, "You are not my father." J.C. responded with, "Okay, then let your father get you a sandwich," as he ordered sandwiches for everyone except Maurice. Once we were outside the store and continued walking, Ervin and I each offered Maurice half of our sandwiches. J.C. noticed our gesture and would not let us share with Maurice. I remember not enjoying my sandwich very much since Maurice was left hungry. As we walked behind J.C., Maurice in a very low voice said the following words, "Tongue of frog, eyes of a snake, always catching flies." I am not sure what he meant by these words, but I do remember the look of intense contempt and hate that radiated from his eyes.

When we finally reached our mother's job and met with her, we told her what had happened. Tragically, but not surprisingly, my mother said nothing to J.C., did nothing to right the wrong, and only smiled. After that, my memory of this incident fades. This was one example that set a precedent that forced me, Ervin, and Maurice to choose whether it was better to remain silent and eat or speak up and go hungry.

Chester Street—The Rifle Man

Chester Street was where my sister, Serena, was born. Unfortunately, her splendid arrival to our household was unable to curb the problems between my mother and J.C. In fact, their problems escalated.

One evening they got into a quarrel, and J.C. grabbed a twenty-two-caliber rifle that they kept under their bed for protection and threatened to shoot my mother. I remember grabbing the rifle from J.C. as my mother started struggling with him. With no weapon for protection, J.C. ran into the bathroom and closed the door. As I prepared to fire a shot through the bathroom door, my mother jumped in front of it to protect J.C.

Chester Street was the last place where I would claim residency with my family for any length of time. Upon graduating from high school, I immediately joined the Army. While I was in the Army, my family moved from Chester Street to another location on Eastern Avenue. My home base, Fort Devens, was only two hours away from Springfield, so I was able to visit almost every weekend.

Eastern Avenue (New Location)—Six to Ten

Tragedy would strike again at our new apartment on Eastern Avenue. During one of my weekend visits, we decided to go visit my grandfather in New Haven. During this trip, J.C. was involved in the accidental shooting death of one of his friends. His sentence was six to ten years for manslaughter. J.C.'s misfortune opened the relationship door for Gregory Finch, who my mother had met through J.C.

⌘ ⌘ ⌘

Once I was discharged from the Army I moved to New Haven to live in my grandfather's apartment. I was there alone because he was ill and was moving between the hospital, nursing care centers, and my uncle Isaiah's apartment. I stayed as long as I could, which was until my uncle Isaiah forced me to move out. He didn't like the fact that I had access to my grandfather's bank book and was afraid that I was going to frivolously use up all the money. Before I was forced out, my mother had invited me to return home to live with her and Finch. They were now living on Boston Road. I accepted her offer as I felt that this option might give me the opportunity to put things in place so that I could go to college.

Boston Road—Deceit and Manipulation

I later found that my mother's invite for me to return home to live with her and Finch had strings attached. It was not done out of any great love for me or because they shared my college aspirations. The offer was made because I was a means to an end. They were going to use me in order to live out their dream of owning a home. Their plan was to have me use my veteran status and the Veterans' administration to purchase their home. But just like everything else, they did not plan it well. I did not even have a full-time job or any marketable skills to find employment. It was going to be next to impossible for me to get a loan, VA or not! I think they must have forgotten why I was moving back in with them in the first place.

In hindsight, I should have expected something like this from both of them because neither of them was trustworthy. My mother proved this to me when I was six years old. She made me close my savings account to withdraw the $6.38 I had saved so that she could go play bingo. She promised to replace the money but never did. Finch proved this to me every day. He was an untrustworthy, selfish bastard who would use *any* person to his advantage. Through force or manipulation, he would take things that were not his. He tried to do this to me when he attempted to claim a pair of gloves that I had left at my mother's home when I moved to my grandfather's apartment in Connecticut. They were black leather military-issued gloves with green wool-fiber inserts. When I saw him wearing them, in the nicest way possible I let him know that the gloves he was wearing were mine. He immediately became belligerent and sneered, "How do you know *these* are your gloves?" I calmly asked him to expose the tag on the inside cuff of one of the leather outer shells. In plain view was my name and social security number neatly printed on the inside tag. With a look of disgust, he reluctantly returned my gloves. How petty!

I had put both of these interactions out of my mind when I should have been on guard from the moment my mother made the seemingly kind gesture of inviting me to return home. You live and you learn.

⌘   ⌘   ⌘

After my grandfather's abscess had healed, he, my mother, and Finch decided that he should come live with us. The choice was made after my grandfather's lengthy stay with my uncle Isaiah where he received substandard care and inadequate sustenance. The main reason my grandfather received substandard care was because my uncle had a deep-seeded resentment toward his father. I didn't know the exact reason he resented his dad, but I knew it to be true for sure. I once overheard him say that he should put his father in a room and let him rot…and he did exactly that until my mother got wind of the situation and convinced my grandfather to move to Springfield with us.

After living with us for only a few months, my grandfather died from a massive heart attack. We took his body back to Connecticut so that he could be buried in the same cemetery as his wife.

Bad decisions, both financial and otherwise, contributed to our next move from Boston Road to Union Street.

Union Street—My Destiny

Union Street was a turning point in my life where one explosive act of violence sent me to prison for ten years.

> *Springfield Union*
> Friday, April 20, 1984
> Police seek gunman in slaying
> By RICHARD NADOLSKI (Union Staff)
>
> Springfield detectives were searching early today for a gunman who killed a 26-year old man by shooting him in the face with a .44 caliber revolver during an altercation in his second-floor apartment on Union Street late Thursday. Gregory Finch was shot in the living room of his apartment, part of a two family-frame house at 650 Union St. shortly before 8:35 p.m., police said. Finch was rushed to Baystate Medical Center, Wesson Unit by Baystate Ambulance Service. Doctors spent an hour attempting to revive him and Finch was pronounced dead in the emergency room at 9:35 p.m., according to a nursing supervisor. Police said Finch's girlfriend, Mattie Triplett, of the same address, was in the apartment at the time of the shooting and they were questioning her at police headquarters late Thursday. Police broadcast a lookout for Ms. Triplett's brother, Haven Triplett, for questioning in the shooting. The high-powered handgun was not recovered and it was believed that it was still in the possession of Finch's assailant.

While I was in prison, my mother received a financial windfall as Finch's sole life insurance beneficiary. The life insurance policy of the man I had shot and killed allowed my mother to purchase a home in the Forest Park area of Springfield on Draper Street.

Draper Street—April 19 Again

The drama and dysfunction continued on Draper Street. One night I called home from prison and while speaking with my mother, I caught the tail end of an altercation between my brother Maurice and her current paramour, Finch's friend Alphonso. I heard Maurice tell Alphonso not to put his hands on my mother just as the telephone disconnected.

I frantically tried to call back but was unable to get through. I was paralyzed as I stood at the telephone in disbelief. In my mind, I was reliving the night of April 19 all over again. But this time instead of seeing me killing Finch, I saw Maurice killing Al.

> ...Triplett was the final witness during his three-day trial in Hampden Superior court on a charge of first-degree murder. Jurors are scheduled to begin deliberations today. Triplett, 21, is accused of killing Finch, his mother's fiancé, during a dispute in his mother's apartment at 650 Union St. on April 19...

Living above her means and poor money management caused my mother to lose her house on Draper Street. My brother Maurice explained to me that they were all homeless for a short period until my mother found an apartment on Quincy Street. Soon after this time, my mother received another financial windfall, a twenty-four-thousand-dollar golden handshake from her employer, Digital Inc. Relatively speaking, this temporarily put my mother on Easy Street.

Quincy Street—Divorce and Disown

My mother married her second husband, Richard Murchison, when she moved to Quincy Street. She married him while he was still in prison doing time for being a pimp and for selling drugs. They were married on the prison grounds in a prison wedding ceremony. I met him while we were both serving time at Gardner a few months before he was released.

Upon his release, he returned to his old girlfriend and resumed selling and using drugs behind my mother's back. A short time later my mother filed for a divorce.

⌘   ⌘   ⌘

Upon my release from prison, I had a brief stay with my brother Maurice, and then I moved in with my mother. Again, she found herself the recipient of another large sum of money. This time her financial gain was a result of my sister's death. Serena had been killed in a car accident. It was later found that she might have survived had it not been for an automobile malfunction. My brother Maurice filed a successful lawsuit against the auto maker and was subsequently denied any rights to how the settlement was handled.

By law, all the money had to go to my mother, and she squandered every dime. She spent every penny on buying her alcoholic boyfriend an automobile. Her careless misuse of the money she received from my sister's death was her final act of neglect and betrayal toward her family that made my brother Maurice disown her for life.

My mother's home had not changed, and much of the drama and violence that had preceded my incarceration replayed itself. Like a dog that returns to its own vomit, my mother was still aligning herself with the dregs of society and quickly replaced her divorced husband with another drug-addicted fiend named Mason. Two months into her new relationship, my mother received a busted lip and was bitten on her chest by Mason. Again things were out of control. Mason, who had been living with us for two months, one night took the liberty to rob me. He waited until I had left for the day to visit a friend before sneaking into my room to steal one hundred dollars out of my dresser drawer. I had earned this money from doing odd jobs and had not yet opened a saving account. Once his theft was exposed, Mason apologized to me profusely and even promised to return the money but never did.

⌘　⌘　⌘

With funds dwindling again and another eviction imminent, it was time to move. This time we moved to Grenada Terrace. This would be the last residence where I would live with my mother.

Grenada Terrace—The Final Chapter

The last attempt that my brother Maurice and I made to help our mother get control of her finances was when she was living on Grenada Terrace. At the time, Maurice was living in Boston. I reached out to him and explained that our mom was in financial trouble and needed help. He agreed to help me pay her delinquent bills. We both knew better than to give her cash, so I told her to give me all of her bills and I would pay them off. She responded with a sense of self-righteous entitlement and told me that she wanted the cash and she would pay the bills herself. She followed up by saying that if we did not give her cash, she did not want our help. That was the last time we offered to help her with anything.

⌘　⌘　⌘

My mother had finally exhausted all of her options. Her life of supporting her many boyfriends and neglecting her responsibilities had come to an end. The coup de grace came from the last and final eviction from Grenada Terrace. Her next move was to New Haven, Connecticut, to live with her brother Isaiah Jr. She stayed there until he, too, lost his home.

It has often been said that "some children are born old" and see the world through adult eyes at a very young age. Much of my advanced maturity came from witnessing or participating in arguments that became violent, from being in situations that involved guns, and from hearing phrases like "shoot first and ask questions later." It was circumstantial that I was exposed to these things at such an impressionable age.

The only benefit of this exposure was that as an adult it gives me a great deal of insight into the lives and mindsets of my family members.

These circumstances help to explain all the craziness of my childhood and early adulthood.

It is mind-boggling to think about all the inappropriate lessons I learned and the trauma I endured while living with my grandfather and mother. The drama continues...

The Sapling—A Young, Naïve Tree

"I hate and I love. Perhaps you ask why I do so. I do not know, but I feel it and I am in agony."

—*Gaius Valerius Catullus*

For the longest time, I always felt that I could share my discoveries of the world with my mother. This all changed one day when my eight-year-old ears overheard a conversation that she was having with one of her friends. She was telling her friend about the day she had gotten raped. Suddenly the ugliness of my mother's past was thrust upon me.

One night she had gone to a party against her parents' warnings, and someone at the party put something in her drink that made her pass out. When she woke up, the mother of the youth who had hosted this party was holding her legs, and the woman's son was on top of her. He was inside of her!

I cannot begin to fathom the emotional turmoil that this despicable act of violence created within my mom. Over the years, I watched the trauma manifest through relationships she had with men. She became extremely volatile and quick to resort to brute force and violence with weapons when her husbands or boyfriends verbally or physically challenged her.

She even told me about a time when she took a stand against her own father. She boasted that in a test of wills with him that she had grabbed a hatchet and threatened to cut his head off if he ever harmed her mother again. It didn't stop there. Her inclination to violence was even directed at me during a misunderstanding that occurred while I was home on military leave.

In a conversation among my grandfather, my mother, and me, my grandfather alluded that I had spent the night in my room with my girlfriend Juanita. My mother chose to parent my act of disrespect by smacking me in the face. The truth of the matter was that I had taken Juanita home that night. Being a proficient student of her teachings, I reflexively slapped her back. To address my retaliation, she grabbed my grandfather's rifle that he kept under his mattress and threatened to shoot me. Positive that she would do it, I quickly snatched the rifle away from her. From his wheelchair, my grandfather observed the dispute and attempted to grab the rifle from me. After a brief struggle, I surrendered the rifle to him then I immediately left his apartment and returned to my military base.

After some time passed, I wrote my mother a letter in an attempt to make amends for the physical altercation that occurred. It was obvious to me that my apology was half-heartedly accepted because since that day our relationship as mother and son had never been the same.

One rule that I live and die by is: *"Never do to a child that which you would not do to an adult."* This simple statement issues a challenge that many inappropriate adults cannot meet. Through personal observation, I have seen that many adults are afraid of mistreating another adult because of the consequences they will have to pay, yet they don't think twice when it comes to mistreating a child.

During a time when I was taking a special education course while in school, I was reminded of my own personal experience with this simple statement. I needed to watch a video entitled "Beyond F.A.T. City" by Rick Lavoie as part of a class assignment. The video documented how teachers (who lack the understanding of how learning disabilities affect the way students interpret and process information) badger special-needs students. Before the narrator presented case studies of these inappropriate teachers, he made the aforementioned statement: *Never do to a child that which you would not do to an adult.* When I heard him speak these words, I was instantly struck with waves of emotion as my mind was flooded with memories of my past. I found myself fighting to hold back tears because I knew for that one moment, if I had given into those tears, I would never be able to stop crying. Instead, I sat in silence for a long time. His statement had reminded me of several ugly personal childhood experiences.

One of these experiences occurred during my temporary stay in foster care. Another occurred during the many unpleasant visits with Maurice's cousins and his paternal grandmother.

Foster Care

My brother Ervin and I were placed in foster care for six months when our mother went to jail for identity theft and check fraud. She had come across a woman who had her same name, figured out a way to steal her checks, and then she started cashing them. When she was finally apprehended, she received six months in jail. Butchy took Maurice and moved back to his mother's house. Ervin and I became wards of the state because Ervin's Sr. refused to take responsibility for us. My grandfather would have taken us, but he was handicapped and would not be able to handle two young children, so the state put Ervin and me in foster care. We were placed with the Saddler family. I was eight, Ervin was five.

There were several traumatic things that happened to me and Ervin during our temporary stay in foster care. As part of some bizarre game, Mrs. Saddler divided one thousand dollars between me and my brother Ervin. I was given ten fifty-dollar bills, and my brother Ervin was given ten fifty-dollar bills. She had given us this money to play with. Then she had her two sons, Bruce and Martin, block the front door so that we could not leave the apartment. Ervin and I wandered around the apartment with this money in our possession for about five minutes until we were told to give the money back. When Mrs. Saddler recounted the money, she told us that one of the fifty-dollar bills was missing. Then she threatened to call the police and said they would take us to jail if the money was not returned. Ervin and I looked at each other and remained silent. After a thorough search of the apartment, the missing fifty-dollar bill was found near a sofa-bed couch that was located in a dimly lit front room. Mrs. Saddler's cruelty was thoughtless and irresponsible, but it was nothing compared to what she did next.

In a horrendous act of brutality, Mrs. Saddler physically abused Ervin to teach him a lesson. Perhaps her twisted mind thought Ervin had intentionally hidden the fifty-dollar bill and was going to retrieve it later. She had to let him know that stealing money was wrong.

I was in the kitchen talking with Mrs. Saddler as she heated a penny over the open flame of her gas stove using a metal spatula. Unsure of her plans, I watched as she called Ervin into the kitchen and told him to hold out his hand. When he did, she dumped the penny from the spatula into his hand. Ervin yelled in pain as the penny made contact with his hand. He grabbed his burned hand with his other hand and looked up at Mrs. Saddler to see the expression of amusement on her face. What a heartless bitch!

While not as heinous as Ervin's experience, I can recall my own experience that had long-term ramifications that were just as severe. My grandfather, who was unable to prevent Ervin and me from going into foster care because he was handicapped, lived in the same eight-story building as Mrs. Saddler. He lived on the first floor, and Mrs. Saddler lived on the second floor. One day I witnessed the neighbor's son Charles reach into my grandfather's first-floor apartment window and steal his black and white television set. I was eight; Charles was seventeen.

I was sitting in the front room of my grandfather's apartment when I saw Charles's head and arm come through an open window where the television was. My grandfather had gone to the kitchen.

When Charles saw me, he put his finger up to his lips to tell me to stay quiet as he stole the television. Then he disappeared. I was afraid to tell my grandfather what had happened when he returned from the kitchen and noticed that his television was missing. It didn't matter though because he immediately knew that Charles, who had a reputation for thievery in the projects, was the culprit. At some point he must have confronted Charles about the TV because I heard through the grapevine that Charles was planning to beat me up when he saw me. I hadn't told anyone that he had stolen my grandfather's television, and he still was going to beat me up. Apparently my allegiance to Charles meant nothing; I should have told my grandfather what he had done.

When Charles finally caught up with me, he wrestled me to the ground and punched me in the nose. He would have kept pounding me if not for the fact that his mother broke up the fight. She quickly came down stairs from her apartment and pulled him off me. Mrs. Saddler, who had also witnessed me get attacked by the older, bigger boy, followed close behind Charles's mother to help get him off of me. Mrs. Saddler stood me up and began laughing as she was wiping the blood off my nose. At the time, I did not know if she was laughing at me in an attempt to alleviate my pain or to add to it. Knowing the kind of person she was and how she abused Ervin and me, today I'm sure she was laughing to make me feel bad—and I did.

While in foster care with Mrs. Saddler, I spent most of my time visiting my grandfather since he lived just a few floors away and treated me much better than she did. This all stopped one day when Mrs. Saddler told me that I could no longer visit him. She was my legal guardian, and it was her right to tell me what I could and could not do. It didn't matter that my grandfather was family. The only reason Mrs. Saddler took this privilege from me was because her son Martin was jealous that I had found sanctuary and notified her that I was always visiting my grandfather. From that day forward I was not allowed to visit my grandfather while in the custody and care of the Saddler family.

Never do to a child that which you would not do to an adult—what a powerful, thought-provoking statement. It forced me to ask myself: What type of adult threatens to call the police on a child? What type of adult laughs at a child in pain? What type of adult does not allow a child to visit his own grandfather? I can only wonder how these terrible experiences helped to define my character as an adult.

Family Feud

From time to time my mother would leave me and my brother Ervin at Maurice's paternal grandmother's house. This allowed her the freedom to go "joyriding" with Butchy. I dreaded any day or night we had the misfortune of visiting or spending the night there. Maurice's grandmother always had a houseful of Maurice's Aunt Pinky's children. Ervin and I did not get along with them. There were six of them, three boys and three girls. Individually they were each trouble; together, they were a conniving band of misfits who would lie, cheat, and steal with no conscience. They took great pleasure in seeing me and my brother Ervin get into trouble.

Douglas, who was the oldest of Maurice's cousins, was eleven years old. He was the same age as I was, and he was the worst of the bunch. He once stole a bag full of over one hundred marbles from me when he and his brother George visited my family in Springfield. To cover his theft, he lied to his mother and told her that I had given the marbles to him. His lies and swindling ways made it so I was never able to get any of my marbles back. I never liked him after that.

When my brother Ervin and I were at Maurice's grandmother's house, we were looked upon as outsiders. We were not really considered family because Butchy was not our father. We quickly learned that we had to be very careful of what we said around Maurice's cousins because they would take our words, twist the meaning, and tell a blatant lie to the adult who was left to watch the eight of us. Every time one of them told a lie on us, we were not given a chance to plead our case and would get disciplined whether or not it was justified. Their lies usually resulted in Ervin and me receiving several blows from a leather belt to our backsides.

There were many times when Ervin and I were left alone with Maurice's cousins without adult supervision. *Anytime this* happened, Maurice's cousins would take the gloves off and *literally* begin swinging. Our worst fight happened when my brother Ervin and Maurice's cousin named Claire got into a fight. I don't recall how the fight started, but, in anger, Claire scratched Ervin's face, and in return Ervin bit her to defend himself. His retaliation fueled the fight. When I tried to break them up, Douglas grabbed me from behind. He wanted to prevent me from pulling them apart because he wanted them to keep fighting. Douglas and I began to scuffle. I wriggled out of his grasp and when I saw an opening, I punched him in the stomach. While he was kneeling on the kitchen floor clutching his stomach, he tried to grab my leg to throw me off balance to make me fall. His attempt did not work. It just made me realize I had to take more action to put him out of commission, so I kicked him in the face. With him out of the way, I was finally able to break up the fighting between Claire and Ervin.

When Maurice's Aunt Pinky returned later that day with Butchy and my mother, she was first to enter the house. As expected, her children ran to her and started telling lies about how bad Ervin and I had been. Maurice's Aunt Pinky followed suit just like the other adults and disciplined Ervin and me without giving us a chance to plead our case. First she grabbed a belt and hit Ervin in the mouth—this was for biting her daughter—then she came after me and beat my feet with the belt—this was for kicking her son. She did not even give a thought to discipline her own children who had started the entire fracas. Again, Ervin and I were left battered and bruised like two crumpled-up pieces of paper, and we were innocent. When my mother and Butchy entered the house a few minutes later, Maurice's Aunt Pinky explained that Ervin and I had started trouble and had been bad children while they were gone. She also explained that she had disciplined us.

Maurice's cousins had lied, Maurice's Aunt Pinky unjustly disciplined me and Ervin, and our mother had done nothing to protect us. This is what had stirred up my emotions when I heard the words "*never do to a child that which you would not do to an adult.*" This time it forced me to ask myself: What type of adult administers discipline to children without trying to get the truth? What type of adult hits a child in the mouth with a belt? What type of adult beats a child on his feet?

It is no wonder I became a confused teen and a misguided young adult. It would be my life's struggle to undo the damage that had been done to me as a child. My soul had been tortured, strangled, and left for dead, but like the phoenix, time would help me to find a way to rise from the destructive ashes of my past.

When I turned fifteen, my mother persuaded me to live with my grandfather. This arrangement was not made for my benefit or any great love for her father. Her motivation to do this was strictly financial. It was a self-serving plan that allowed her to receive welfare benefits on my behalf, which she could use as she pleased.

When I moved in with my grandfather, he was using crutches in order to get around. With me living with him, his reduced mobility was no longer an issue. I helped him with everything. I would prepare his breakfast, lunch, and dinner. I would also assist him with his insulin shots that he needed for his diabetes. I was a phlebotomist in training in the morning and a bootlegger in training at night. I was my grandfather's legs; I washed his clothes, did his shopping, purchased his cigarettes, and played his numbers. I did not think much about the danger I was in. In fact, I thought it was pretty cool having this responsibility.

It seemed like I was the only fifteen-year-old in the neighborhood with money in his pocket all the time. I had my own room, I was allowed to have sex, and I was free to go wherever I wanted. I thought I was living the good life, but in hindsight this was not the place for a fifteen-year-old.

Once the liquor stores closed, I assisted my grandfather with the illegal sale of alcohol. Customers had a scent that smelled like the dangers of night life. I served gamblers, prostitutes, and thieves. There was always someone with something to sell or something they wanted to buy on credit, and everyone tried to run a scam.

Allowing me to live in this type of environment with the ever-present threat of a robbery was clearly a bad choice made by my mother. I remember one night where nothing but fate kept me from being right in the middle of a deadly shootout between my grandfather and two armed crooks.

My grandfather had sent me to play his street numbers and to purchase a pack of cigarettes for him. When I returned I found out that my grandfather had defended himself against two armed robbers. He shot and injured one of the would-be thieves while the other one who was armed with a shotgun, escaped, but was later apprehended. To help the district attorney who was prosecuting the case, my grandfather testified in court and both criminals went to jail. Two out of three isn't bad. When both criminals were sentenced, my mother should have been sentenced as well for encouraging me to live in such a dangerous environment. My grandfather was not totally blameless either. He needed my help, but he also knew that by living with him, my life was threatened every single day.

The debilitation of my fifteen-year-old conscience continued while living with my grandfather. I started getting conflicting messages from him. One such message was that it was alright to steal as long as you did not get caught. This helped me to conclude that breaking the law had nothing to do with crime at all. What was important was escaping from the authorities.

I remember stealing my first bike from the Yale University campus. It was extremely easy to do. I used a mini hack saw to quickly cut through the chain that the owner had used to secure the bike to a pole then I rode the bike back to my grandfather's as quickly as I could. In support of my thievery, my grandfather suggested that I buy a can of red spray paint to change the color of the bike and cover up my crime!

This bike I had stolen was a racing bike. It was a beautiful piece of machinery that sparked my love and enjoyment of bicycle riding to this day. I was able to keep my theft of the bike concealed until the day I needed to take it to the repair shop. When I did, the bike shop owner checked the serial number and informed me that the bike was stolen property. He also told me that he was going to call the police so they could pick it up and return it to the rightful owner. The only reason I escaped prosecution of my crime was because I had not left the store owner with any information about where I lived. I was lucky this time; however, this close call was not enough of a deterrent to change my behavior. I took my chances and stole three more bikes from Yale! It started to feel like perhaps my grandfather's philosophy on stealing might be correct, but in reality this was only strike one.

My stealing escapades continued. This time I targeted a place that was nice enough to give me a job. The place was called The Carmel Corn. I started out visiting this location frequently because it had several pinball machines that I loved to play. To support my love of playing pinball, I asked the manager named Claire if she could use someone to do odd jobs. She had seen me at the place so much that she had taken a liking to me and decided to hire me to do odd jobs in return for pay.

Things went well for a while until my grandfather's influence kicked in, and I decided to steal a roll of quarters out of the store's change bag. I was eventually caught and had to deal with the fallout, which was seeing Claire's look of disbelief followed by the tears she shed. She had taken an interest in helping someone who she thought was a good kid, and I had let her down. My actions had deeply hurt her, but she did not give up on me. I assumed that I would be barred from the store, but I wasn't. Claire gave me a second chance—a second chance to disappoint her further.

This time I recruited a childhood friend named Robert, and instead of stealing a roll of quarters we devised a plan to steal the entire change bag. Our plan was executed flawlessly, and we had gotten away with the crime scot-free. While we did not get caught stealing the bag, Claire and the owner concluded that we were the culprits of the crime, and they were planning to press charges. In order for me and Robert to avoid prosecution, my grandfather had to pay back every cent of the money. This was strike two.

Now that my thievery had a financial impact on my grandfather, he gave me a speech about trying to work my way up the "corporate ladder" rather than stealing. His speech was meaningless and contradicted everything that I saw while living with him, so I continued stealing.

This time my target was a department store called King's. This was not going to be the first time I perpetrated a crime in a department store. The first time was when Butchy and my mother had taken me, Ervin, and Maurice with them on a family stealing spree from a department store named Topps. The plan was to go into the store and steal shoes for each of us.

We started by browsing in the shoe department inconspicuously. We did this until my mother told us all to start trying on shoes. As we found the right sizes, my mother quickly put the shoes in a large handbag that she was carrying. Once she had several pairs of shoes, she told us to walk quickly with her toward the store exit. As we exited the store, I remember a store employee chasing after us. He was too slow. Butchy was waiting in front of the store in the getaway car. We all ran to the car, jumped in, and Butchy sped out of the parking lot. As we made our exit, our car was spotted by the West Haven police. This is where things got crazy. With a wild, determined look in his eye, Butchy drove through several back streets with the police in hot pursuit. Initially he was unable to lose the police. I remember tires screeching, gravel flying, and dust clouds whirling. Butchy weaved frantically down the dusty back roads for about ten miles before he was able to shake the police.

As far as I was concerned we had gotten away with the crime at Topps, so I was confident that I could do the same thing at King's. I was wrong. This time I had finally gotten caught stealing and was driven home by the New Haven police. This was the final straw that made my grandfather realize that he had given me the wrong message and was steering me in the wrong direction. My grandfather had made me into an amateur shoplifter who was soon to become a professional thief. Understanding the error of his ways, he threatened to call my mother if I continued to steal. From then on he changed his entire philosophy on stealing and told me that it was wrong, regardless of whether I was able to get away with it. This was strike three. My stealing days were over for now.

Although my mother did not take exception with the dangerous environment I was living in, my school counselors did.

However, they were very tactful about how they approached the subject. They praised me for taking care of my grandfather but explained that, as a fifteen-year-old, my time and energy should be devoted to my education. This sounded like good advice, but I wasn't able to comprehend their concern because this was the first time anyone had spoken to me about the benefits of education. I think they were truly trying to help me, but I wasn't sure that my counselors understood that by living with my grandfather I was receiving an education in life that could not be taught in school. To me, my street education seemed much more valuable than any book knowledge. My life was all about money and how I could help my grandfather make as much as possible on a daily basis.

Ironically, I was a very good student who, aside from being habitually late, stayed out of trouble. I was constantly tardy because every morning

I had to take care of my grandfather and tend to my bootlegger-in-training duties before I left for school.

Not being much of a fighter, I tried to get along with everybody but was constantly bullied and ridiculed. If my antagonists had known that I had access to all types of guns and weapons at my grandfather's house, I'm sure they would have not been instigating trouble for fear of my retaliation. Being ridiculed and bullied unfortunately contributed to a change in my passive and easygoing nature. My metamorphosis from being *an easy target for bullies* to being the *kid not to mess with* had begun.

For weeks a neighborhood bully who happened to be a distant relative began to unjustly terrorize me. His name was Jerome. The harassment started over a comic book. Jerome's best friend had stolen his comic book and had blamed me for the theft. It didn't matter that I was innocent of the charges. On a daily basis Jerome chased me with the threat of harm any time he saw me. Fortunately, I always managed to evade capture.

It wasn't until the day that I was chased by Jerome and his friend and trapped like a cornered rat that I was forced to defend myself. Jerome had a metal pipe, and his friend had a baseball bat. In fear of my life, my self-preservation instinct kicked in. I grabbed the first thing I could find to protect myself, just like my mother had told me to do. Unfortunately for Jerome, it happened to be a two-by-six piece of wood that had several eight-penny nails in it. Without thinking, I hit Jerome in the head with this piece of wood. I noticed a glazed look in his eyes then he fell to the ground. He tried to get up then I hit him two more times, and then he fell back to the ground and didn't move. After seeing this, his friend who had the baseball bat ran away. Now that I was able to escape I ran back to my grandfather's apartment.

The injuries Jerome received from my assault required him to spend several weeks in the hospital's intensive care unit. This was the first time I critically hurt someone. I didn't plan to hurt him that badly; it just happened. After this incident, I gained a reputation as being "crazy," and the neighborhood punks and bullies finally left me alone.

I learned several things from the fight between me and Jerome. The first was that sometimes there is no choice but to fight back. The second was that people will fear and respect you if they know you are not afraid to hurt others. The third was that violence begets violence. I learned this third and final lesson as a result of my uncle Isaiah's thoughtless actions.

A few months after Jerome was released from the hospital, I was contacted by my uncle Isaiah. He explained to me that Jerome wanted to meet so we could resolve our differences. I figured if there was a chance to put this behind me that I was all in, so I agreed to the meet up. My uncle drove me about a block from my grandfather's apartment to the location where Jerome asked to meet. When we arrived, he was there standing up against a fence with his friends. As I was getting out of the car, one of his friends passed him an opened pocketknife, and in an instant I was being chased around my uncles' car by a maniac with a knife. As I was being chased, I remember both the intense fear and anger I felt. I was afraid because I was sure that I would be gravely hurt or killed if Jerome was to catch me. I was angry because my uncle had assured me that I was only going to meet with Jerome to talk! What the hell was my uncle thinking? My narrow escape from grave injury or possibly death that day woke me up. I realized that I could never trust my uncle Isaiah again.

Strangely, I was never bothered by Jerome again. Perhaps he believed that he had gotten his revenge by chasing me with the intent to kill me. Perhaps it was because he knew that I would not be naïve enough to walk into another one of his traps and be caught off guard. Next time I would be ready to defend myself.

While staying with my grandfather and prior to attending high school, I lost my virginity to an older woman named Betty. For young boys like me to lose their virginity to an older woman was common in my neighborhood. And shockingly sad but true, it was almost a rite of passage for a young girl to lose her virginity to a much older man. I had no male role model, no mentor or confidant that could explain the responsibility of having sex. I had no one to tell me that the way my neighborhood viewed the initiation into the world of sex was extremely dysfunctional and potentially life-damaging. Neither my grandfather nor my mother would offer me any protection from the emotional turmoil and grief that came with being exposed to sex at the age of fifteen. Shortly after I lost my virginity, I met my first girlfriend. Her name was Juanita. I was overwhelmed by my own naivety, and without being aware of it I had developed an emotional attachment to her from our first sexual experience. I was in love.

Juanita lived just around the corner from my grandfather's house. We would walk to and from Hill House High School together while holding hands. We would go to the Stetson Branch Library every day after school to study and kiss in the hallway next to the bathrooms. We went to the movies, and we visited the Yale University Art Gallery. We did everything together. Being with Juanita was crazy, fun, and exciting all at once. But I was so naïve that she was able to take advantage of me. She was much better equipped to deal with the emotions that followed from our sexual activity. Through her deception and lies, she was able to keep me fooled with her false portrayal of love. During the time when I thought we were in an exclusive relationship, she was having sex with everybody, including grown men! When I finally came to know about this I consider myself lucky that I did not catch a venereal disease.

One of the men Juanita was having sex with was like a second grandfather to me. His name was Otis, and he was a morally depraved individual who at one time lived in the same apartment with me and my grandfather. A few months after his tryst with Juanita, Otis was killed by a man who was the boyfriend of his estranged girlfriend Maggie. As karma would have it, this man was also Juanita's uncle. This man killed Otis by delivering a series of hammer blows to the back of his head. When I heard what happened, I shed no tears for Otis. All along my grandfather knew about Juanita's deception and lies but did not intervene out of fear that I might grab one of his loaded guns and shoot her.

Otis was not the only older man that I knew who had a relationship with a younger girl. My grandfather had done it too. He was having sex with a seventeen-year-old girl named Marie. By being in this relationship he unknowingly put my life in danger. I never told my grandfather but Marie's mother threatened me at gunpoint because she thought I was having sex with her daughter. But I wasn't. My grandfather was having the sexual relationship with Marie. It became apparent that the main reason Marie's mother threatened me was to make sure that I didn't get in the way of the sexual relationship between Marie and my grandfather. While my grandfather was having sex with Marie, she became pregnant. Fortunately, my grandfather was not the father; a guy named Sherman was. This annoyed Marie's mom because she wanted my grandfather to be the father. So badly, that she would adoringly comment on the child's skin as being smooth and dark, just like my grandfather's skin. I concluded that Marie's mother was a crazy nutcase, unfit to be a parent.

I had stayed with Juanita much longer than I should have because I was in love, and I did not know how to remove myself from our destructive relationship. Even going into the Army did not help me break away from the feelings I had for Juanita. In fact, I ended up feeling worse because now she and I were many miles apart. My mother was no help as I was trying to escape the love spell Juanita had cast on me. In fact, she made things worse because she did everything she could to keep us together. She never took the time to try and really understand the pain, deceit, and manipulation Juanita had subjected me to, yet she intervened anyway. It was a classic case of the blind leading the blind. Perhaps letting my mother get involved was a dumb idea on my part. After all, she could not even manage her own relationships. It took an altercation with Juanita's new boyfriend to remove the love-struck sunglasses I was wearing. Only then was I finally able to come to grips with the mess and madness that I had gotten myself into.

Even though our relationship was built on a pile of lies that Juanita had convinced me to believe, I still considered us a couple when I left New Haven for military duty in the Army. Thinking that we were still a couple was a big mistake and exactly what was about to make my life a living hell.

My military base was four hours from Connecticut so I called Juanita every chance I could, in order to keep in touch. Most of the time I was unable to reach her, and she never called back. I found this strange and confusing. It contradicted how she always seemed happy to see me when I returned to my grandfather's house during my furloughs.

On the last visit that I made to Connecticut before I was restricted to living quarters, Juanita told me that she was pregnant! Naturally I assumed I was the father and I was ready to take responsibility for our child. At the same time I was perplexed and confused about the poor communication between us when I was fulfilling my military duty. Something just did not add up, so I proceeded with caution. Three months after Juanita told me she was pregnant I lost contact with her all-together. I tried calling her without success. On one of my attempts to contact her, I spoke with her sister Christine who said something to the affect that Juanita had moved out and was now involved with someone else! I was confused. How was this possible? She was carrying my child and now I was being told that she had a new boyfriend. My world was spiraling out of control.

As the year passed I slowly recovered from the torture Juanita was putting me through, however, I now began to have problems with my Army first sergeant. The problems between us became so bad that he eventually had me discharged. After this unfortunate turn of events, I returned to my grandfather's and resumed my life as his bootlegger's assistant.

By this time I had pretty much recovered from the games Juanita was playing with my head, however, I still questioned my paternity to the child. I tried to get an answer to my question by going through her aunt, but it ended up being a waste of time. What I did get was Juanita's aunt trying to persuade me to blindly accept paternity of the child. I was naïve but not stupid. Without knowing for certain if the child was mine, I made a decision to permanently distance myself from Juanita. I couldn't get away too far though, because she lived just around the corner.

Close to a year after Juanita told me that she was pregnant, I ran into her when I was returning from a restaurant with my grandfather's breakfast. She was walking with a man who I assumed was the real father of her child. This guy was confirmation that all along Juanita had been stringing me along like a love-struck puppy dog. She was an untrustworthy, manipulative bitch! When she saw me, she whispered something to her boyfriend, and in an instant we were exchanging hostile words. I attempted to walk away, but he picked up a metal bar from a nearby car shop and began chasing me. Once he was close enough, he hit me in the back with the weapon. The excruciating pain I felt from the impact of the bar caused me to fall down and drop my grandfather's breakfast. After seeing me fall, my assailant fled. Once my pain subsided and I was able to get up, I ran a short distance to my grandfather's home and explained what had happened. He didn't say a word. He just pulled his gun from his side (between him and his wheelchair) and passed it to me. I took the gun and ran back to Juanita's apartment. I spotted her boyfriend pushing a cart of children's clothes from the laundry mat. When he saw me, he ran inside their apartment building hallway labyrinth and disappeared. I knew I was not going to be able to catch him, so I took the laundry cart of children's clothes and hid it on my grandfather's back porch. Then I gave my grandfather his gun back.

A short while later, the police arrived at my grandfather's apartment and questioned me about threatening someone with a gun. However, no gun was ever found. Juanita and her boyfriend even produced a witness who claimed to have seen me with the gun, but this mysterious gun was never produced. As a precaution, the police still arrested me, and I had to spend two hours in lockup. When I was arraigned, I received six months' accelerated probation. A few days later Juanita and her boy-friend contacted me and asked if I would return the laundry cart of children's clothes. I agreed to return them if we could work out a fair arrangement. We met in front of my grandfather's apartment and discussed equitable compensation for everyone. I received ten dollars from Juanita's boyfriend as payment for my grandfather's breakfast that I had dropped. In turn, I gave back the laundry cart of children's clothes. Unfortunately, some of the clothing was missing. Marie, the seventeen-year-old girl who was involved with my grandfather, had found the cart on the back porch and had taken some of the clothing for her child. There was nothing I could do about this and as far as I was concerned Juanita got what she deserved.

My past with Juanita had come full circle with this last meeting. I had to endure my resentment for her one final time in order to put closure on the lies and deception that I had once tried to ignore. Through dealing with Juanita, I had been insulted, I had been injured, and now I had clarity of the situation. This helped me to finally put the insanity of Juanita behind me.

Evergreen—The Learning Tree

"When you learn, teach. When you get, give."

—*Maya Angelou*

As I look back, I would describe my school years as a tale of two cities. I attended elementary school in New Haven, Connecticut, and middle school in Springfield, Massachusetts. I started high school in New Haven, and I finished high school in Springfield. My educational experience can be defined by four different phases.

Phase one occurred while I was in the fourth grade attending the Winchester School located in New Haven. The school still exists, and is now called Drexler/Grant Community School. While at this school, I was labeled as gifted and talented because of my love for reading. My favorite book was entitled *Kaleidoscope*, which contained a collection of short stories. Although I was fascinated with all the stories in this book, my favorite story was about a magical car, *Chitty, Chitty, Bang, Bang*.

Many of the children in my class viewed reading as an arduous task; but for me, reading was entertaining and fun. I liked reading so much that if I didn't know what a word meant, I had no problem grabbing a dictionary to research the meaning.

I can honestly say that my love for reading made the Stetson Public Library my favorite place to visit. It was located directly across the street from my school. Many times I would find myself there looking through an encyclopedia, discovering new things.

I enjoyed the sophistication of words and was reading two grade levels ahead of everyone in my class. My teacher, Mrs. Byrd, was more excited with my God-given talent than my own mother. My relationship with Mrs. Byrd was more like a mentor-mentee relationship rather than student and teacher. She worked very closely with me on an assignment for which I researched and documented the life of bees. Through my research, I learned just how amazing bees are. I discovered that they have a language of their own and work together to survive. I remember being very proud of my project once it was completed. I was even more proud when it was selected and put on display in the school gymnasium.

To challenge our class, Mrs. Byrd assigned a project over the Christmas holiday. Our goal was to identify and classify the origin and families of different animals. She knew that we would all lose focus because of the impending visit from Santa Claus, but she gave the assignment anyway. Her goal was to foster self-motivation. It was this project that really made me stand out from the rest of the class because I was the only one to complete it.

Another notable accomplishment that I had made in the fourth grade was writing an essay entitled "Love, Peace, Truth and Understanding." I remember sitting at my desk with a dictionary and thoughtfully composing my essay. Once again, the teacher honored me by displaying my essay, along with a few others, inside an enclosed glass case just outside our classroom.

Phase two occurred when my mother and Butchy decided to move from New Haven to Springfield. This move severely impacted my adolescence. The continuity that I started to establish in New Haven between school and environment was abruptly broken. During this phase of my life I attended the following middle schools: Elias Brookings,

Warner, Armory Street, Forest Park, and Duggan. I was now in a different state, I was shuffled around to different schools, and I was unable to establish solid friendships due to our continuous evictions. This was a period of uncertainty and confusion for me. My confidence in my ability was severely undermined. At one time school was my sanctuary, but now it was a place that was dangerous to my emotional and intellectual development.

Racism was rampant at my new school, Forest Park Jr. High. For me, this was a new thing and new idea. It had a severe impact on my intellectual development and growth. I noticed that white students and black students were pitted against each other. The social underbelly of the school was at war.

One day when I was in between classes, I got into a heated confrontation with a white student. We were arguing because he pushed the door against me and jammed my arm as I was walking through a hallway door. Once the other white students saw the commotion, they joined in with the other student and forced me into a corner. This is when I was introduced to the word "nigger" by the student who had instigated the trouble. I was saved from further humiliation by a teacher who had become aware of the situation. As he approached the crowd of students who had surrounded me, they immediately dispersed to class. From that day forward I became less receptive to my teachers. I became argumentative in class. I became an unruly student who was acting out. Finally, one of my teachers would no longer tolerate my insolence. She told the principal that she did not want me back in her class until my mother came in for a parent-teacher conference. When my mother finally came in for the conference, she and the teacher talked for almost an hour. I don't remember the fine details of the discussion, but what I do remember was that once the discussion concluded, I was left crying in my mother's arms. As I was crying, I remember my mother saying that the teacher had not helped at all and that she suspected that my teacher was prejudiced just like the children who called me a *nigger*. I didn't know if my mother's claim was true or not; all I know is that I wanted to have my class changed. But this did not happen. I was kept in this same class for the rest of the school year.

Public schools in Springfield were divided into school districts. We had to move again and our new apartment was within The Warner School district. My black cloud of bad luck followed me to this school.

At The Warner School, I was unjustly punished and ridiculed by my teacher because a few of my classmates told him a lie about me. The lie was that I had come back to class late because I had ventured off and taken a different path from the cafeteria back to our classroom. The truth was that I was the last student to finish lunch and had not kept up with rest of the class. I pleaded my case to the teacher and explained what had really happened, but he did not believe me. The small lie that my classmates told avalanched into a major issue. My punishment was to sit in the hall at a desk just outside of the principal's office and write the same sentence one hundred times. I complied with the punishment but did not agree with it at all. I could not rationalize why the teacher would believe the other students and not me. I was subjected to more mistreatment when the teacher and the entire class walked by me on their way outside to recess. When the teacher saw me, he started poking fun at me. His ridicule resulted in laughter from my entire class. I began crying. The last thing I remember about this experience was the look of shock on the principal's face as she entered the hallway to see me crying and all of my classmates laughing at me. After that, my memory of the incident fades.

These types of experiences always left me emotionally battered and scarred. The adults in my family had not equipped me with the tools needed to handle inappropriate actions from a teacher or student. During this phase of my education, I no longer had a personal connection with my teachers. They no longer motivated or encouraged me to take an interest in my education, as Mrs. Byrd had done.

I was exposed to a new ideology on how the teachers viewed the books we used in class. An emphasis was placed upon keeping the books in good condition. The focus was no longer the knowledge that the books could provide. Students like me who received books were informed that if the books were not returned in acceptable condition, we would have to pay for them. Now I was worried about having to pay for books that I could not afford. There were clues that I wasn't the only one that felt this way. I noticed that many of the books I received had no wear at all. It was almost like the previous students who had the book had not opened it at all.

The indirect message that I was getting from my teachers was that if it wasn't important enough to go over in class, it wasn't important enough to read or study on my own. I started to view homework as just an exercise in repetition. My inquisitive nature, which once motivated me to do independent research, and was cultivated by Mrs. Byrd, seemed to be a thing of the past. However, I still made a final attempt to reclaim my natural love of learning by using supplemental reference material to complete an assignment. The end result was disaster.

I had to write a paper for my social studies class about the farming and agricultural production of apples. While researching this topic, I came across some information about a machine called an apple picker. When I brought this machine to the attention of the teacher during a class discussion, the teacher remarked that he had never heard of such a machine. He said that he would do some research on it and follow up with me. The next day in front of the class he made a definitive statement indicating that there was no such machine known as an apple picker. I remember trying to explain what I had read but was cut off mid-sentence by the teacher, who adamantly restated that the machine did not exist. I remember wanting to say that I was certain about what I had read but instead sat in silence doubting myself. I did not do well in this class from that day forward.

Instances like what occurred with the apple picker reinforced why I now felt that school was no longer a safe haven, a place to learn and grow. It was a place that represented oppression and instilled within me a sense of resentment that I expressed by being argumentative and refusing to take an active role in my learning. The worse thing teachers did to influence my rebellion from my love of learning during this stage of my adolescence was to ignore my questions or, worse, respond by telling me to read the book when I had asked a question. I viewed such a response as a withholding of knowledge and a road block to understanding. If any of my teachers other than Mrs. Byrd had taken the time to understand that my desire to read was fueled by my natural love of learning, I would have grown to be a much better student.

I left Forest Park Jr. High and The Warner School with completely the wrong idea of what I should be giving and receiving from an educational perspective. I no longer expected any guidance and motivation from my teachers. I no longer expected questions that I asked in class to be answered, and I had no male role model or mentor to whom I could turn for basic life skills. This put me at a monumental disadvantage as I entered my high school years.

An agreement between my mother and grandfather put me back in familiar territory. This was the previously mentioned agreement where my mother persuaded me to live with my grandfather so that she could receive welfare benefits on my behalf and use them as she pleased.

I moved back to New Haven for phase three of my educational experience. For me, this move came at a very high cost. I was an eighth-grade student and budding teenager who was transforming into an anachronism. I was now required to assist my grandfather, who had lost the use of his legs and was confined to a wheelchair. I was responsible for helping to cook breakfast and dinner, and I was responsible for assisting with my grandfather's bootleg business. It wasn't all bad, though. There were some benefits that accompanied this burden. I had my own room, I went wherever I wanted, and I did not have a curfew. While living with my grandfather, I attended Troup Middle School for the eighth grade and Hill House High School for the beginning of the ninth grade.

Bullying, which was something that I was subjected to in the lower grades, now reared its ugly head again while I was at Troup Middle School. In between class periods I was constantly being bullied by a student who kept threatening to beat me up. One time he threatened me as I was going into the boys' bathroom. I tried to ignore him and did my best to get away from him, but he followed me and continued his taunting. Once inside the bathroom, he began pushing me. Before he had a chance to beat me up, a teacher who had seen the trouble developing entered the boys' room and intervened. As the teacher restrained the bully, he tried to wrestle free but couldn't. Now he was really mad. As he was thrashing, he managed to get close enough to me kick me in the leg. It took the teacher a minute to get him under control. Once he did, we both were taken to the principal's office. It was at this moment that I learned a new term–*corporal punishment.* Each of us was given the unpleasant choice of either being suspended from school or being hit with a paddle and returning to class. The bully chose to be hit with the paddle, and he was sent back to class. I, on the other hand, chose to be suspended. I had been hit by bullies, I had been hit by my mother, I had been threatened by my grandfather—I had had enough! I was not going to let a stranger hit me too. As a result of my decision, I was driven home by a teacher who worked in the principal's office.

Upon my return from school suspension, I found that all of my class notes and assignments that I had kept in my desk had been ripped up. Some of my notebooks had even been thrown away. My guess was that one of the bullies who intimidated me chose this as another way to continue making my school experience a nightmare. Being a good student and not much of fighter had not been beneficial at all. Fortunately or unfortunately, my address and school were about to change again.

This time it was an ultimatum that my mother received from the welfare office that initiated my address change. The State of Massachusetts threatened to discontinue welfare supplements, on my behalf, to my mother. The state informed my mother that a whistle-blower had given them information that I was living in New Haven with my grandfather, and that if this continued, welfare benefits would be reduced. The whistle-blower was Maurice's father, Butchy. He and my mom had separated. Butchy was living in New Haven, and my mother was living in Springfield and had just started a relationship with a new man. For this and many other reasons, Butchy resented my mother and would do anything he could to make her life miserable. One day as I was walking from my grandfather's apartment to school, I saw Butchy sitting in a car with several of his family members. I said hello to him—this was a mistake. He knew that my mother was committing welfare fraud—he probably was the one who taught her how to do it. To get back at her for having a new boyfriend, he informed the welfare office that I was not living with her. A few days later my grandfather received a phone call from my mother. She told him I had to move back to live with her in Springfield in order to keep receiving benefits. My grandfather told me to pack my things then he drove me back to Springfield.

I spent the fourth phase of my educational experience at the High School of Commerce. I drifted through high school in a haze and was out of synch with where I was and what I should have been trying to achieve during this period. I still had no positive male role model who could give me guidance. I worked part time without a goal in mind.

I had an afterschool part-time job working as a dishwasher at the Marriott Hotel in Springfield. I was proud and grateful that I was employed, but the reality was that this was a dead-end job. On top of this, I almost had an altercation with a busboy that could have put me in serious trouble with the law. I worked in the kitchen and washed the dirty pots in a big stainless steel sink, and I loaded the dirty dishes into the dishwasher. My problem started when a new busboy was hired. Not only did he do a poor job of breaking down the tray of dirty dishes, but he was sloppy about it and would splash me every time he did. I would either get splashed when he threw the silverware into a gray plastic container or I would get splashed with water or god knows what from the overhead glass racks when he did not empty out the cups and glasses. I spoke to him about this several times, and every time he just chuckled and did not take caution to make sure that I did not get splashed. Enough was enough. I decided that I would set him up to get splashed in the same way I was. I rigged the draining slot that was full of gunk so that when he put the glasses in the overhead glass racks, the liquid from the glasses would shoot out onto him. The very next time he sloppily placed half-full cups and glasses in the glass rack, he literally got a taste of his own medicine. The liquid shot out from the clogged draining slot onto his clothes, and some went directly into his mouth. He knew it was me who clogged the draining slot and immediately began walking in my direction with balled-up fists. As he approached me, I quickly grabbed a brown-handled steak knife with a serrated edge, similar to the one I handed my mother when I was seven. When he saw the knife, he stopped dead in his tracks. With the knife in hand, I smiled as I said, "I'm sorry." With an angry look, he replied, "You better be!" I retorted with a taunting smirk on my face, "I am...believe me, I am." I had no more trouble after that, and he quit his job a few days later. I did not know it at the time but he was reportedly a boxer—a Golden Gloves champ. Not that it made any difference to me because the knife I was holding made all things equal.

Setting a trap to teach the busboy a lesson worked, but in hindsight I should have brought this matter to the attention of the supervising manager. At the time, this thought never crossed my mind. In my world, conflict resolution equated to violence. I look back now, and I am just glad that I didn't do something stupid and hurt the busboy. I could have very easily hurt or killed him that day.

Instead of wasting time with a dead-end job and jeopardizing my future, I should have been more focused on graduating from high school as an honor roll student. What I chose to do instead was spend every dime that I earned on the most popular clothes and trips to New Haven.

My poorly planned approach to my education landed me at the very bottom of my class. I graduated number 392 out of 400 students.

While in high school, I met people along the way who helped to provide me with tidbits of knowledge and advice. There were two teachers who I will never forget. They were positive influences throughout my high school years. The first teacher was Mr. Black. He was my math teacher and the head of the chess club. From him I developed a complete understanding of the "foil" method when factoring binomials. His influence helped me to develop an appreciation for finding simplicity within the complexity of life. Mr. Black was the person who opened my eyes to the world of chess. I discovered that, like chess, life has rules; some are absolute and unchanging, while others are time-sensitive and vary with the circumstance.

The second teacher was my gym teacher, Mrs. Williams. Her sense of enthusiasm was contagious, and she made me feel like I could accomplish just about anything. The things I learned from Mrs. Williams helped to offset the negative effects of my adolescent years. Her influence helped me to re-establish my self-confidence. Her motivation awakened dormant talent that was lying deep within me. This helped me to accomplish my most memorable high school achievement that allowed me to have my fifteen minutes of fame while at the High School of Commerce.

With Mrs. Williams' influence and the help of my twelfth-grade English teacher, Mrs. Karr, I authored an award-winning essay that took first place in a city-wide competition between all the high schools in Springfield. My accomplishment surprised everyone, including my tenth- and eleventh-grade English teachers, who both knew I was taking a remedial eleventh-grade English class while I was in the twelfth grade.

EVERGREEN—THE LEARNING TREE

My essay was entitled:

"America As Great As Its Citizens"

America is great—as great as its people, for America has within its ranks the seven people who combine to make it great as they go about their daily tasks.

There is the Monday person. Marked by motivation and the ability to organize, he uses his day to revitalize America's hope in molding a destination for all to be proud of. He is the foundation of the week.

The Tuesday person follows. He is marked by the ability to take command and make decisions. He puts his plans in action and broadens their scope so that everyone benefits.

Then comes the Wednesday person. Characterized by a strong sense of responsibility and the ability to carry the burden for others, he uses his strength to push ahead. He works at a steady pace until the job is complete.

The Thursday person. He uses his keen insight to look ahead. He takes time to dream, to do research, and then to put his dreams of a better life into action.

The Friday person. He is persistent and rises to any challenge no matter what the odds. He carries out his orders with top efficiency. He overcomes all obstacles by continuing to shoulder his responsibilities.

The Saturday person uses the day to express the lighter side of our culture through the arts and entertainment. He provides the diversion and the pleasure that make the efforts of the other days seem easier and less of a burden.

The Sunday person takes a day to rest and express himself through religion. He reflects on and reviews the week's accomplishments and puts them into perspective so that new strength from God will be used to inspire everyone to be able to start fresh again.

America's people, its greatest resource, unite in their daily work so that as each week flows into the next, there is a never-ending source of strength and industry—the secret of America's greatness.

My hard work and desire to do well in this competition was applauded in a ceremony held at Lido's restaurant, where I was crowned as first-place winner. This ceremony also celebrated the second-place winner who was a girl that attended the High School of Classical. Her school was only a mile away from my high school.

Since we were the first- and second-place contest winners, it was clear to me that we had a love for writing in common. Ironically we also had similar taste in clothing. This was evident when we both arrived at Lido's dressed in almost the exact same outfit. We both wore brown suede jackets. She had on a twill skirt, and I had on twill pants. This coincidence alone started the ceremony off with a vibe that told me it was going to be something special.

The second-place winner had written about the Vietnam War. She was the first to go to the podium to read her essay. When she concluded, she received a short and polite round of applause. Then it was my turn. I was now a master magician and no longer an essay apprentice. The Great Havini was about to make his grand entrance. By reciting an ancient incantation; "America – as great as its citizens", I hypnotized the audience. Like marionettes I brought them to their feet and they were clapping for me. My first act had been executed flawlessly.

My second act, one of legerdemain, had me rolling up my sleeves and exposing my forearms. I held my hands up and let them shimmy. Magically a twenty-five dollar check for being the contest winner appeared. It was a seamless display of prestidigitation. I was on a roll.

My third act required the help of my still enraptured audience. I had everyone close their eyes and think of their favorite meal. I asked everyone to concentrate as they held hands with the person who sat next to them. After a few moments of speaking in the tongues of the ancient mystics, I had everyone open their eyes to the five course meal they had mentally summoned. My meal was veal parmesan and it was simply scrumptious.

I was elated with my third act but I wasn't done yet. My grand finale had to leave them speechless. I thanked the audience for allowing me to perform for them and with top hat in hand, I slowly bowed as I effortlessly levitated through the exit doors.

Photosynthesis—The Tree of Change

*"Continuity gives us roots; change gives us branches,
letting us stretch and grow and reach new heights."*

—*Pauline R. Kezer*

While incarcerated, I struggled with the idea of God and morality and found myself constantly reflecting on my life. I had been exposed to religion through Christianity and Jesus but realized that there were issues with what I had learned.

It wasn't until after I had read two books that analyzed religion on a deeper level that I would have an epiphany: I had been misled. Living my life has never been about following the spiritual teachings of Jesus or Christianity; it has always been about how *I* as an individual treated other individuals and in turn how they treated me. I didn't need to read a Bible to understand that. This thought provided a sobering moment of clarity. My understanding of what life meant finally started to make sense.

I realized that there were many events in my life that had caused me to question the worth and benefit of believing in the biblical prophet Jesus, who is all powerful, all knowing, and all present. I finally realized that logically there was nothing that I could do for Jesus as a human being, so what was the point in wasting time and energy in believing in His existence? I rationalized that everything that I do either has the potential to benefit or hurt another human being. This is when I decided that humanity was going to be my focus in life.

As I reflected on experiences from my past, I recalled many situations that caused me to question the idea of Jesus and Christianity. I thought about a time when I was living with my grandfather in New Haven. His apartment was surrounded by churches. He had a church on each side, and directly in the back of his apartment was an abandoned lot. This was the temporary summer home of a traveling revival tent. Next to this abandoned lot was another church called the United House of Prayer for all People. A short walk out of the front door of my grandfather's apartment would put you in the vicinity of two more churches. I was surrounded by Jesus on all sides, and yet my grandfather remained a bootlegger. With this, I questioned if good always prevailed, why was my grandfather's illegal bootleg business so successful?

In one of my grandfather-to-grandson talks, I received a ticket to a philosophical boxing match between the power of believing in Jesus and the power of believing in a dollar. The first round of this three-round match put Jesus on the ropes early as I listened to my grandfather's story.

In round one, the story he shared with me was about a woman who had just come from a church service at the United House of Prayer. She had stopped by my grandfather's and asked him to prepare a plate for her. My grandfather wasn't only a bootlegger; he was also a fantastic cook. Part of his supplemental income was made by selling dinner plates. These plates contained chopped barbecue or spare ribs along with collard greens and potato salad, and a slice of corn bread and sweet potato pie.

When it came time to pay for the three-dollar meal, the woman told my grandfather that she had given all her money to Daddy Grace, the minister of the United House of Prayer. My grandfather was motioning with his hands as he told me the next part of the story. He made a gesture like he was quickly snatching a plate back from the woman as he told her that she should go let Daddy Grace feed her! The mighty dollar had won round one convincingly.

In round two, Jesus was in the corner reeling from a gut shot and clinching to make it to the bell, and the mighty dollar was looking for an opening to land an uppercut.

I happened to run into a childhood friend who was crossing the abandoned lot behind my grandfather's apartment. The revival tent that was set up in the lot during the summer happened to be in town at the time. When I saw my friend, he looked like he was mad about something. I asked him why he was upset. He turned and looked at the revival tent, and with a tone of anger mixed with a search for empathy he said, "I'm hungry, and my mother gave away all the food stamps to those people, and we have no food in our house. I hate those fucking people!"

Before I knew it, my friend and I began throwing rocks, pieces of asphalt, chunks of brick, and pieces of pavement on top of the moldy canvas tent. For about fifteen minutes we threw anything we could pick up at the tent and made several holes in the canvas. Every time a new hole appeared, we both laughed.

When we tired from throwing rocks, we parted ways. My friend was still hungry when we left, but at least he wasn't angry anymore. Jesus had survived the second round. On wobbly legs, he staggered back to his corner.

In round three where I took a deeper look at religion, Jesus was floored by a right hook!

During my incarceration, I found myself doing a great deal of reading to combat the enforced idleness within such an intellectually deprived environment. Constant reading was one way I kept my mind active. One book I read was an old dusty book written by Arthur Lyons entitled *The Second Coming: Satanism in America*. Of all the pages I read, one sentence stood out among the rest. I remember this sentence as if I had just read this book a few moments ago. The sentence read, "Gods live and die as ideas in the minds of men." Reading something like this was catastrophic to my exposure to Christianity. It made me realize that only *I* was responsible for my life. It made me realize that *I* was responsible for my successes and failures. Me alone—not Jesus or anyone else!

These words liberated me to the point that I would never be afraid to question anything that I had been told or had read concerning religion—or anything else, for that matter. As I continued to read this book, I found myself constantly returning back to the same page to re-read that sentence.

My view of religion was changed further by another book that I read while incarcerated. It was *The Narrative of the Life of Frederick Douglass.* I found myself drawn back to the page where Frederick Douglass wrote how he loathed and despised Christianity. He commented that Christianity had the power to enslave individuals so that other people can dictate their lives. I had seen this firsthand when my friend's mother gave all of her food stamps to the revival tent, and he was left hungry.

I was relieved when I read Frederick Douglass's assertion. It let me know that I was not the only person who felt this way about Christianity. Once I finished reading these books, my view of everything concerning religion and Christianity had changed forever. This was a technical knockout, and Jesus Christ could not be saved by the bell.

Reading two forgotten books that had sat upon a dusty shelf had given me a great deal of insight into so many things. Not only did they give me insight into who I was and who I could become, but, more importantly, these books had helped me to appreciate the importance of taking credit for my own accomplishments, no matter how small or insignificant they might appear to be.

Although I began to take an agnostic view of religion, I did not hide my thoughts and feelings about it. I was always up for a healthy debate with anyone who wished to discuss and compare ideologies. One discussion that I had wasn't so much a debate; it was more of a moment of levity between prison inmates. It occurred when I was at Gardner, and I was speaking with my brother Ervin (he was in the same facility as I was at the time) and his cellmate. We began to talk about the religion of Islam and Christianity. During this conversation, Ervin's cellmate asked me if I believed in Jesus Christ. Before I realized it, I said with raised arms and trembling hands, "I believe in Jesus. The first words out of my mouth when the judge sentenced me to natural life in prison were, 'Jeeesussss Christ!'" There was a moment of silence then we all laughed.

Although I have a secular view of the world, I believe that all things that occur have a degree of interconnectedness. I believe that the connectivity in events is real. It is something that I have learned to appreciate as I have grown older. The most convincing experience of this that I can recall began during the time when I was a prisoner in York Street Jail awaiting a new trial. As coincidence would have it, my brother Ervin was a prisoner in this same jail for some petty breaking and entering crimes.

There somehow was a mix-up in communication, and both Ervin and I were called out of our cells to see a visitor. This must have occurred because we had the same last name. When I exited my cell, I was standing on the second-floor landing in front of a large metal door that separated the prison from the waiting area and visiting room. Suddenly, I was confronted by a correctional officer who had walked up the stairs from the first floor. The officer asked me why I was out of my cell and then rudely interrupted me before I could offer an explanation. In a show of force and in an effort to abuse his power, he told me to return to my cell before he knocked me over the railing. With calculated certainty, I replied, "You might very well knock me over the railing, but a day from now, a year from now, I will kill you! The dog! The cat! And any little babies that you might have running around when I am released!"

Before our confrontation escalated any further, a higher-ranking correctional officer quickly ran up the stairs to the second-floor landing and intervened. In a curt but nonthreatening manner, the ranking officer told me to go back to my cell. Then he began speaking with the other officer. The next day another inmate told me that he had heard the high-ranking officer explain to the other officer that the reason I was a guest in York Street was because I had shot my mother's boyfriend in the head. The inmate told me that upon hearing this, the officer who had threatened me was visibly shaken.

My brother Ervin had been watching the entire confrontation from the first floor of the prison block. At the time I did not know it but Ervin's witness of my confrontation with the officer would have far-reaching consequences that would extend beyond the prison walls. The officer's last name was Kelly. He was related to Alice Kelly, the seventy-nine-year-old elderly woman who my brother Ervin would murder *five years later.*

One could conclude that my confrontation with the guard, the fact that he was related to Alice Kelly, the fact that my brother Ervin witnessed the deadly clash of wills, and the future murder of Alice Kelly could all have been a twisted coincidence; however, it is my belief that there is a degree of interconnectedness between all things.

When I had finally put together all the pieces of how the seemingly random events were interconnected, I would say it was an unfortunate surprise. However, it was no surprise to me that Ervin would end up killing someone based on his childhood experiences. Our mother had neglected him. His father had disowned him. He had suffered the same physical abuse that I had, and he had been molested. The signs could not have been any clearer, but there was no one there to help him.

For all but 10 months during the past 10 years, Triplett has been locked up in one jail after another—either serving time for his 1983 conviction for breaking into a home in the Forest Park section or for parole violations he committed after his release from prison, Triplett's first arrest as an adult came less than a month after he turned 17, the threshold for the adult correctional system. He was charged with breaking into two homes in Forest Park section, including one where a prayer meeting was underway. After Triplett pled guilty to one count, Judge Porada—citing Triplett's lengthy juvenile record sentenced him to a fifteen-year term at Concord State Prison, leaving him eligible for parole in 18 months. "If you don't change your ways and stop this nonsense," Porada said, "then you are going to end up in jail a good part of your life. ...I just see your life going down the drain," the judge said. Triplett's first parole, issued on Jan. 3, 1985, came after two years and lasted exactly one month. Triplett's next parole came in August 1986; he lasted three months before being arrested twice in one week—first, on an illegal firearms charge after a fight outside the

After Five Lounge; and then again after allegedly stealing a car and leading six police cruisers on a chase through downtown Springfield before ramming an unmarked cruiser. ... he had compiled a juvenile record that one court official described as "horrendous" during a sentencing hearing. While records of Triplett's juvenile offenses are not public, Lauro recalls that he was one of the youngest defendants ever held at the state's detention center in Westfield.

"He was a troubled kid"

"He was a troubled kid, to put it mildly," said Springfield attorney Phillip Lauro, who encouraged Triplett to pursue a boxing career during his teen-age years. "He had some talent, but he never really developed it." How Triplett found the freedom to commit his alleged crime spree, particularly given his lengthy adult and juvenile record, is a question that has disturbed Springfield residents and law enforcement officials. ... Despite Triplett's extensive criminal history, despite his arrest in June on the Westfield housebreak charges and despite an appeal by a Hampden County prosecutor, Superior Court Judge Richard Cannon released him without bail... The population cap at the overcrowded Hampden County Jail had been reached that day, meaning Triplett could have been locked up only if jail officials released another inmate. ...Triplett's case demonstrates how the criminal justice system fails to hold dangerous offenders, other view it as an example of how prison can turn young men into hardened, habitual criminals. "Obviously, it doesn't look as if the system has worked in this case," said Springfield defense attorney David Hoose, who represented Triplett during the early 1980s. "What you seem to have here is a pattern of escalating violence, the longer he was in the system. The adult system just breeds violence." The portrait of Triplett that emerges from interviews and court documents suggests a man whose entire young adult life had been shaped by crime and its consequences.

My brother Ervin was constantly in trouble and was going to one day get into real trouble and have to answer to the court. My day in court was now. At this moment I was trying to understand how I had been railroaded into a first degree murder conviction. I had time to think about the facts of the case and do my own analysis of what had happened during the trial. I played it over and over in my mind. I discovered several issues that I categorize as prosecutorial misconduct that, even today, leave a bitter taste in my mouth. Every time I replayed my trial in my mind I became angry with my trial lawyer, the judge, and prosecution. The only thing that was able to diminish my anger was the expert handling of my case by my appellate attorney. To him I am indebted. His expert handling of my appeal helped me to understand just how badly our justice system is in need of an overhaul. His effort helped me to appreciate the individuals like him who work behind the scenes to uphold the good and honest virtues of our flawed justice system. He explained that many times the truth gets lost in a one-sided presentation of manipulated facts.

I remember the first time we met. I was a prisoner at Walpole. During his visit he had me answer several questions about what had happened on the night of April 19. We discussed two primary aspects of my case that highlighted my individual candor and the ultimate truth about what really occurred on that night. After being apprised of all the facts, he determined that I was only serving a life sentence in prison due to ineffective assistance of counsel. Using his knowledge of the law and attention to detail, he was able to successfully argue his claim to get me a new trial.

My appellate attorney argued the following in his brief: he claimed that the defense counsel failed to cross-examine my mother on her grand jury testimony, which described the events of April 19, in a fashion similar to my account of that night's events. He also claimed that the defense counsel failed to cross-examine my mother on medical evidence that contradicted her account of the angle of the second gunshot the victim received. He also relied upon the following legal principle: the incident leading up to a killing and the actual killing itself are not necessarily two separate and distinct incidents.

According to my mother's trial testimony, Finch pulled a knife out of his back pocket but did not lunge at me. I calmly walked out of their bedroom and went into my room. This left her alone with Finch for several minutes as she tried to calm him down. She then came to my room and found me loading a gun. I declared my intent to kill Finch. She grabbed me, but I pulled away, knocking her off balance. I ran back toward the bedroom where Finch was waiting. She followed me and saw me point the gun toward the foot of the bed and fire one gunshot. I then backed out of the room all the way to my bedroom door. She and I scuffled for control of the gun, and then there was a thud. She turned around to see Finch lying face down on the floor. I turned around, pointed the gun downward, and shot him two more times.

While it may appear that my mother's version of what happened is undisputable, my lawyer noted that her version before the trial jury is not in accord with her Grand Jury testimony, which painted a rapidly developing scenario:

> The next thing I knew was Haven was in his bedroom loading a pistol. He was standing in front of his dresser and putting shells into the pistol. The pistol is a handgun, with a cylinder that opens, black looking, and about an eight shot. I said, "Haven, don't do this." As I said this, he put three shells into the gun. Haven then said, "I'm going to kill the motherfucker." Haven came towards me and I grabbed him. He tussled and pushed past me and went back into my bedroom and Finch was still in the bedroom.

There is no mention of my walking to my room at a normal pace or of her calming Finch for two minutes. The encounter she describes with me outside of my room is a fleeting one. Equally disturbing is her testimony given at trial where she testified that I had shot Finch twice as he lay face down.

> As I reached the bedroom door, Haven was backing out and Finch was coming towards Haven. Haven backed all the way out into the living room and reached his bedroom door. Finch had taken a few steps out of the bedroom and he tripped and fell on the floor face first and he didn't move. After Finch fell, I grabbed Haven by both arms; he wrestled out of my grip. Haven then pointed the pistol at Finch lying on the floor and fired twice more.

This testimony given at trial by my mother contradicts the physical evidence as outlined by the medical examiner. The medical examiner testified that Finch had suffered four wounds inflicted by three shots. One bullet entered Finch's right cheek and exited in front of his right ear. Another entered his right shoulder, and another entered the back of his skull. The medical examiner further stated that the shoulder wound was caused by a bullet that had entered the top of the shoulder and traveled down the back in a downward angle. How something so obvious could be disregarded by my defense attorney is almost beyond belief. My appellate attorney highlighted this point about the shoulder wound in his brief. He concluded that the medical examiner's testimony made it clear that Finch could not have been lying face down on the floor when he was shot in the shoulder or cheek. He noted that the medical examiner's statement is consistent with my testimony where I stated that Finch came out of the bedroom, lunged at me, and was shot while in a crouching posture. The medical examiner's testimony also made it clear that I could not have shot Finch twice while he was lying face down, as my mother stated.

I believe I understand why our testimonies of what happened that night contradict. I believe that my mother identified with her abusive relationship and abuser so much that she unconsciously modified her story to protect and preserve her distorted view of their relationship. Also, as I would find out later, my mother was the sole beneficiary of Finch's life insurance policy. This gave her seventeen thousand reasons to lie about what had happened on that night.

It is very difficult to describe my frame of mind during this tragedy. Had I acted in the heat of passion based upon sudden provocation? Had I reacted to a threatening gesture made with a deadly weapon? Was I protecting my mother, who had been cut on her arm by Finch during the heated altercation? The only thing that I can say with any certainty is that in my mind, the confrontation between Finch and me was one continuous altercation in which I felt compelled to defend both myself and my mother.

Before killing Finch, I never gave much thought to resolving confrontation without the use of violence. I wasn't really aware that there were any other options because I had been a victim or perpetrator of violence all my life. The circumstances of my environment did not give me the time to second guess whether I should shoot first and ask questions later. I did not have the benefit of meaningful self-reflection or the wisdom of mature responsible adults to teach me alternative ways to resolve conflict. Ten years in a prison cell was more than enough time for me to realize that I needed to implement self-reflection and critical thinking into my decision-making process—especially as it applied to violence. My awareness that I needed to change helped me to understand that being traumatized by violence bonds us to violence in a very deceptive and dangerous way.

I had initially been scheduled for release from prison in June of 1994, but due to a "clerical error" my release was conveniently delayed for two weeks. My minor inconvenience was going to help the prison inflate its budget that quarter. The longer I was held, the more money the state needed to fork over to the prison. The residual funds from the proceeds could be kept and dispersed at the warden's discretion. This was a nice, inconspicuous way to put money in someone's pocket.

The flawed process essentially supports the notion of a neglected society. I say this because it only takes a little common sense to know that inmates who return back to mainstream society without money, education, or options are apt to recommit crimes to take care of themselves. To help prevent this, I believe that any extra money the prison receives should be allocated to help prisoners reintegrate back into society.

After ten years and three months of incarceration, I was released from prison with less than two hundred dollars cash in my pocket, no marketable skills, few job prospects, and an associate's degree and small business certificate that were not worth the paper they were written on. Ironically, my release from prison mirrored my release from active military duty, which had occurred ten years before.

After only one year, eleven months, and sixteen days in the Army, I was discharged for *failing to maintain acceptable standards*. I left the Army with less than five hundred dollars cash in my pocket, no marketable skills, few job prospects—and the documented military training that I had received would prove useless to me as a civilian.

Being released from incarceration and being discharged from active duty unknowingly bound me to additional servitude to both establishments. The details behind my release from both prison and the Army also had a significant impact on why I was not able to find meaningful employment.

I was physically out of prison, but my arms were still behind my back in a pair of CORI handcuffs. Under the Criminal Offender Record Information law (CORI), I was required to disclose that I was an ex-convict on any application that I submitted for employment for the next fifteen years. My new ex-convict label meant that I wasn't even qualified to sweep or mop floors or clean toilets. The only way I survived was by receiving welfare benefits from the Massachusetts Rehabilitation Commission and from picking up returnable bottles and cans to earn extra money.

My discharge from the Army came with a stipulation that I could be called back to active duty for two additional years after fulfilling my initial obligation. I was not told about this obligation upfront when I enlisted. I guess this was something that my recruiter had conveniently forgotten to mention. At the time when I joined the Army, recruiters commonly left out information during their sales pitch in order to entice potential recruits to enlist. Deceptive enlistment tactics like this still occur today. In my case, my recruiter's misdirection and sleight of hand didn't matter because when I was recalled to active duty, I was incarcerated and serving a natural life sentence.

The terms of my discharge made it difficult for me to find gainful employment. It was just like when I was released from prison. There were two main reasons I ran into problems finding a job: my discharge papers contained character-damaging stipulations and my military record had been sealed where the truth could be found. Both of these things were done by my first sergeant, who was a racist and did not want me in the Army. His first show of racism occurred on one instance when he commented that I might make an excellent chauffeur for a military officer. I guess in his mind the job of a chauffeur was the height and extent of my aspirations. There was also a time when another black soldier in our unit requested a transfer to Kentucky. He had also had a problem with my first sergeant. Before he left, he personally spoke with me and told me that the first sergeant was a racist and that it would be in my best interest to get out of the unit as well. My last evidence of the first sergeant's racist views occurred a week before I was discharged. I was in his office, and he began taunting me to try to provoke me into a fight. While he was doing this, I noticed that he had a folded knife on his desk and he never made eye contact. I believe that he wanted me to go for the knife on his desk so that he would have a reason to defend himself. I was sure that he was holding an open knife, which was being concealed by his desk, and I was sure he was ready to use it. I didn't fall into his trap and kept my mouth shut the entire time he was degrading me. As I was leaving, he made a really nasty comment, and he said that he would have taken me out if I had tried anything.

My desire to learn while I was incarcerated and while I was in the military seemed to be the only constant that kept me motivated. However, I was still fighting an uphill battle, and I was still losing. Determination alone was not enough. The prison correctional staff and Army personnel both undermined my desire and ability to further my education.

In prison, my educational aspirations were undermined in many ways; however, two main reasons stand out. The first is that the correctional staff had independent discretion in regard to helping inmates with educational options in prison. They control the financial budget that can help inmates pay for their education, and they control an inmate's ability to get to class. The second is that, at the time, the state of Massachusetts did not offer an educational assistance package to correctional officers. This made them despise inmates even more than they already did. One officer personally told me that he hated the fact that inmates could get money for college when he could not. It was no wonder that my effort to educate myself in prison was met with resistance from all directions.

I began taking correspondence courses along with college classes in order to achieve a sense of purpose and direction. Things were going well until I made the decision to take a calculus correspondence course. I started the course while at Walpole and attempted to continue it after I was transferred to Gardner. This is where my troubles started. I was told by the institutional school principal at Gardner that this was going to be the last correspondence course that I could take at Gardner. He also told me that if I wanted to finish the calculus course, the institution would not pay for the mailing expenses of the correspondence.

I was an indigent inmate with minimal funds and resources. All of my previous educational correspondence had been paid for by the institutional school program. I quickly realized that the pay that I received for sweeping and mopping floors would not allow me to complete this course. In anger, I remember throwing all my course materials in the trash because the cards were stacked against me. Between the new rules at Gardner and my inability to pay the correspondence fees, I was forced to quit the course.

My head was bloodied but not bowed. I wasn't defeated yet. I now set my sights on earning an associate's degree in general studies. My previous college courses were all accepted by the community college that was offering courses at Gardner. Everything was going well until I transferred all my general studies courses into the small business program. I was assured by the principal of the college program and the small business instructor that I would receive college credit for successfully completing each course. I was misled and only received a certificate that was not worth the paper it was written on. I contacted the federal government and reported an abuse of federal Pell grant funds. An audit was done and still nothing was done to right the wrong. This was another devastating blow toward my education. At this point I was thoroughly frustrated. To add to the list of issues I had to deal with, I was getting moved to Lancaster. I was disgusted because I made absolutely no progress in my education, but I still did not give up. I re-enrolled into a community college general studies program at Lancaster and eventually earned an associate's degree in general studies.

In the Army, my educational aspirations were undermined the day I enlisted; This continued throughout my military career. My recruiter convinced me that my aspirations to become a physician would be fully supported. He painted the picture that I could serve my time as a soldier and could begin my education to become a physician in parallel. He indicated that there was an educational fund that was set aside specifically for recruits who sought to further their education. This was a line of bullshit! The education fund existed, but it was a savings account, not an account for recruits to withdraw funds for college. He knew this but embellished the facts so that he would be able to sell this pipedream to a poor teenager who wanted to get an education.

At the time I was eighteen years old. I had no idea that my recruiter was not going to give me the information I needed in order to make an informed decision. Unfortunately, my mother, who was there during the enlistment interview, was no help. She just sat in silence the entire time. My recruiter picked up on this and used innuendo and deception to keep my interest. When he was finished with his pitch, I signed the enlistment papers. It wasn't until later that I realized that enlisted military personnel are first and foremost a soldier. Education and goals are an afterthought. The trickery used to get me to enlist never sat well with me once I realized what had happened. This is a big reason my military career only lasted one year, eleven months, and sixteen days. The sad thing is that these deceptive practices still occur today.

I was stationed at Fort Devens and was working as an assistant to a medical doctor. I worked in the Cutler Army Hospital as an ear, nose, and throat (ENT) specialist. I was also assisting an audiologist and occasionally gave hearing tests. The ENT clinic had a visiting practitioner, so appointments for this clinic were only scheduled three days out of a five-day work week. This left me at the clinic with nothing to do for two full days. On these days I would spend several hours listening to music in the booth where hearing tests would normally be administered.

The optometry clinic was in the same building as the ENT clinic. They were connected by a short hallway. The supervising optometry clinic officer asked me to get on-the-job cross training so that I would be qualified to work in the optometry clinic. His thinking was that I could assist the optometry clinic when there were no appointments at the ENT clinic.

This wasn't a bad idea; however, I had some reservations about being unofficially cross-trained. I was already feeling that I was being pigeonholed into becoming an assistant at the optometry clinic with no clear plan toward my ultimate goal of becoming a physician. I declined being cross-trained on the job and instead asked to be transferred to Fort Sam Houston, where the official optometry training was held. I felt that being officially trained would be more valuable to my future.

My resistance to the cross-training put me at odds with the supervising optometry clinic officer and made my first sergeant hate me just a little bit more. For my first sergeant, my refusal to cross-train was the final straw that put me in his crosshairs. From that point he closely scrutinized everything that I did, and when I finally slipped up, he was there to make me pay.

My last and final mistake that ended my military career was getting back to Fort Devens late after a weekend furlough. I had missed the only bus that would get me back to the base in time for work, so I called the clinic to let them know that I would be late, and then I took the very next bus back to the base. When my first sergeant heard about my slip-up, he viewed this as an opportunity to get me kicked out of the service.

He requested to have me discharged through the expeditious discharge program because of a *failure to maintain acceptable standards,* and his request was granted. Although I was targeted and essentially forced out of the Army by my first sergeant, I still received an honorable discharge.

Autumn Leaves from a Pruned Tree

The hardest thing in life to learn is which
bridge to cross and which to burn."

—*David Russell*

There were three bridges that I had to cross and burn and there were two bridges that I had to preserve once I was released from prison. It was time to destroy relationships, restructure thoughts, and embrace new ideas to begin rebuilding a stable mentality for self-preservation. It was also time to reach out and preserve precious relationships that were more important than my survival itself.

The First Bridge

To burn this bridge I would have to travel to New Haven, Connecticut, and meet with Sherry, the mother of my two children. The bridge that existed between Sherry and me had been built upon the frailty of a teenage kiss. Ten years had passed, and this bridge had grown old and damaged. The price my soul was paying to keep this bridge standing was too much. For me to know this was a sign of my own progress in the right direction. Now I just needed strength—a filled gas can—and the words—a match—in order to burn this bridge.

When I was incarcerated, Sherry had sent me three letters. Her first letter took away all my hopes and dreams of a better tomorrow. I had been in prison for five years, and she could no longer wait for me. She had met someone new and had gotten pregnant. She decided that at this point it was best for us to end our relationship. She needed to move on. When I read her words, I hated my existence and wished that I could encapsulate the intense emotional pain I was feeling and "throw" it away. I had deceived myself into believing that time would not make a difference.

Sherry's second letter arrived two weeks later. Her letter gave me a false sense of hope. She told me that her pregnancy resulted in a miscarriage and that this loss had once again given her the strength to want us to be a family again. This restored my hope. I remember scrambling to piece together my heart and what was left of our relationship and asking for a second chance to make things right. I asked her to bring the children to visit me. Seeing them was going to renew my hope that I would one day have my family again. They never came.

Sherry's third and final letter arrived a few weeks later. In this letter she told me that she had become pregnant a second time. She told me that the man she was with would make a wonderful father for my children and that she intended on staying with him. The knife blade of April 19 had silently reappeared and was violently thrust into my heart. Suddenly I couldn't breathe; I couldn't catch my breath. I was going to be incarcerated for another five years, and I was dying in every sense of the word. Through teary eyes I remember writing back to her and suggesting that she ask her boyfriend to adopt our children. I had sincerely believed that she had found someone who would take care of her and the children. I was a condemned man—this was my final request. Our letter writing to each other would end at this point.

When I was released from prison five years later, I began making attempts to establish a relationship with my children. I first reached out to the maternal grandmother of my children to find out how to get in touch with them. Once I was able to find them, it was an extremely difficult time trying to get back in their lives. Their mother, Sherry, had filled their heads with very damaging information about me. She labeled me as a murderer and told the children I was a bad man. Yes, I had killed someone, but it was in self-defense, and I was not looking for trouble that day. I didn't think the label fit. However, the damage was done, and I had to fight an uphill battle to change the image my children had of me. The more I tried to communicate with them to change the image they had of me, the more Sherry did to sabotage my effort.

During the time I was trying to re-establish a relationship with my children, I found out that Sherry was dating a crack dealer nicknamed Sport Coat. This man already had several children of his own from his past relationships. Through her association with Sport Coat, Sherry became addicted to crack and almost lost our children to Child Protection Services. My children had almost become wards of the State of Connecticut. To make sure this didn't happen again I tried to work things out with her and rebuild the family that we once had. I tried for months to establish a new future with Sherry to no avail and finally realized that I was only wasting my time and energy. Two things finally made me give up trying to reunite with Sherry: her new dependency on drugs and the fact that she was unsure whether she was ready to leave Sport Coat. I did not accomplish my goal, but at least now I had the clarity to know that things between Sherry and me could never be as they once were. I had tried and failed. Now it was time to focus on getting back into my children's lives.

I tried everything I could to make up for the years that I had not been there. I took them shopping with the little money I was able to save from doing odd jobs. I made sure that they had clothes for school. I tried everything I could, but I was unable to undo the damage that Sherry had done. In their minds I was a deadbeat dad. On top of that, Sherry was still driving a wedge between me and the children. I wanted to be involved with their education. I knew I could help them with school because I was already a tutor, but for some reason Sherry went out of her way to try to keep me out of their lives. She even blocked my attempts to get a copy of their report cards from their schools.

At some point Sherry decided to move from Connecticut to Georgia. Her unilateral decision to do this was going to make it almost impossible for me to be in my children's lives. I think she did this because, in her eyes, I was still a murderer and did not deserve to have contact with my children. Sherry was wrong and really did not know me at all.

It was painful to accept, but I soon realized that the mother of my children and I were two very different people who had grown apart. We no longer wanted the same things from life, from each other, or for our children. I made sure my children were a safe distance away then I poured gasoline on the bridge that connected Sherry and me, lit the match, and set it on fire. It was time to say goodbye, have a good cry, and move on with my love and my life.

The Second Bridge

To burn this bridge I simply had to move out of my mother's apartment and realize that the bridge between mother and son was beyond repair. The bonds of love were weathered and frayed and unable to support the load of indifference that had grown exponentially heavier by the weight of lies and deception. The price my soul was paying to keep this bridge standing was too much. For me to know this was a sign of my own progress in the right direction. Now I just needed strength in the form of a letter and the words in the form of a stamp in order to burn this bridge that was holding my mental growth captive.

My mother and I had been through too much. I tried to hold on to our relationship as mother and son and put the neglect I endured as a child and the lies I uncovered as an adult behind me. But it was too much weight to bear. Even when I was incarcerated, my mother's practice of lies and deception continued. I can recall the time that Sherry allowed my mother to pick up the children in New Haven so she could bring them to see me. When my mother picked them up, Sherry gave my mother fifty dollars and asked her to purchase my daughter a coat once they returned to Massachusetts. Retail was cheaper there, so my daughter would be able to get a better quality coat. After bringing my children to visit me, my mother gave my daughter one of my sister Serena's lightly used coats and kept the fifty dollars. When she took my kids back to Connecticut, my daughter told Sherry exactly what happened. Sherry held me responsible for my mother's deception and would not allow my children to come see me again. The next time I would see them was when I was released from prison.

Once I was released and met the woman that I was going to marry, I explained my life story to her. As we planned for the day of our wedding, we both agreed that it was best if we did not invite my mother to the ceremony because of the company she kept. She was sure to bring one of her alcoholic boyfriends, and on this day, neither of us needed or wanted to see this. We had taken the privilege of being invited to our wedding away from my mother. In her mind she felt that it was her inalienable right to be invited and that she could not be denied. She was wrong.

I explained to her in a one-page letter that my wife and I would be willing to spend time with her and her companion after our wedding but not before or during it because of her past indiscretions. This was unacceptable to her. She sent me a handwritten letter stating that she was deeply hurt by my actions and did not want to have anything more to do with me.

I had outgrown being manipulated by my mother. She could no longer tug on my heart strings. It was time to burn this bridge and move on with my life. I purchased a postage stamp and drafted a return letter stating that I was fine with her decision. I have not spoken with or seen my mother in over three years. She has two grandchildren and several great-grandchildren that she will never know. With her past track record, that is a good thing.

The Third Bridge

To burn this bridge was more difficult. I had to confront the person responsible for everything that had gotten me to this point in my life. I had to confront the person within. I had to confront myself. This bridge was built from being a victim of child abuse and neglect. It was built from learning dysfunctional ways, and it was built from a rudimentary thought process for problem resolution: shoot or kill first! The price my soul was paying to keep this bridge standing was too much. For me to know this was a sign of my own progress in the right direction. Now I just needed strength in the form of a mirror and the words in the form of self-therapy in order to burn this bridge that was suppressing my ability to grow and become a better person.

The abuse I was subjected to as a child was rampant. I had been physically abused by my stepfather. I was constantly bullied—at home and in school. I was taught that it was acceptable to coerce and manipulate others if you were physically stronger, older, or more experienced in deception, and I was taught that respect is deserved, not earned.

For many days, months, and years I sat in my prison cell trying to understand how I could turn the mistreatment that I received as a child into something positive. I finally realized that knowing exactly how *not* to treat a child was a benefit. I planned to embrace and address the abuse and neglect that I endured as a child in order to keep from doing the same to my children and other individuals.

At one time I reflected in my cell about my transformation from a child to a teenager and how it was coupled with baggage from an abusive childhood. I had learned that hurting people was the first approach to take in response to an act of aggression. I realized that I had learned to react first and think later. My transformation from a teenager to a mature adult came with the consequence of being sentenced to natural life in prison. When my metamorphosis was complete, I had been completely desensitized to my own feelings and the feelings of others. It meant nothing for me to take someone's life.

Even though I had survived the child abuse I had received from Ervin Sr. and recovered from the inadequate legal defense by my trial lawyer I struggled constantly with giving in to the urge of systematically killing both individuals. I imagined different ways of killing Ervin Sr. and my trial lawyer with each scenario more violent and vicious than the last.

The trial attorney would have been the easier of the two to murder because since the day I was released from prison I had crossed paths with him several times in Springfield. The first time was during the early morning hours at the intersection of Maple and Union Streets. He was putting on a tie while walking from the parking lot to his office and he did not recognize me. In my *mind*, it would have been all too easy to stab him in the throat so he could not scream and watch him choke on his own blood as he lay dying on the sidewalk.

There was another time that I observed him getting out of his car on Wilcox and Main Streets. In my *mind*, it would have only taken a few seconds to run up behind him with a barbed wire garrote, choke the life out of him, and leave him slumped over in the seat of his own car.

Ervin's father would have been just as easy. It would not have been too difficult to find his current address in Connecticut. By now he has probably forgotten about what he had done to me and Ervin Jr., so I'm sure he would not have considered me a threat. In my *mind*, it would have been very easy to walk up to him, shoot him in the face, and after he had fallen to the ground put two more bullets in his head for good measure.

To address the revenge that my *mind* wanted to exact, I began asking myself questions. *Why* did I want to kill my lawyer and stepfather without any concern for the consequences? *Why* did I want to commit a crime without any concern for my own future? *Why* did my anger make me feel that I had to hold them accountable for what they had done to me? I thought deep and hard, but I could not find answers within.

The answers did not start coming until I had read a book entitled *Letting Go of Anger: The Eleven Most Common Anger Styles and What to Do about Them.* This book helped me to put my anger into perspective. I began to view all the wrongdoing that I had been subjected to differently. It started to become clear that these things had destroyed my sense of empathy. I had stopped caring about others, and in a sense I had stopped caring about myself. I had stopped believing in the goodness within me. My emotional growth had been hindered. I was still harboring unresolved anger within me. It was time to unload the baggage. It was time for that little boy who had been afraid to challenge and question his mother and grandfather to finally find his voice. In my *mind* the little boy stood on a pedestal and started speaking about the difference between right and wrong. He spoke about good and bad. He spoke about the difference between depravity and morality. Then he looked directly at me and as his eyes pierced my soul, he told me to confront my deep-seated anger and lack of empathy.

At that moment, the fear of asking myself, "Why am I so angry?" could not be ignored anymore. Then and there, I found the conviction needed to put my anger to rest.

The Fourth Bridge

This was a bridge I had to preserve. To re-establish my relationship with my children, Haven Jr. and Natoya, I would have to embrace past memories and follow up with visits to New Haven and Georgia. Some of the memories I had about them were good, and some were bad. This was something I could not change and refused to dwell upon. I instead focused on what I needed to do to effect a change. As far as I was concerned, our bridge was built by hardened steel—my love for them—and was reinforced by concrete—my desire to earn their love back. Because of the void I left in their lives so long ago, I am not sure that my children ever believed that I loved them. I have always loved them; nothing will change that. My goal now was to get them to forgive me for being absent from their lives.

It was a challenge to get my sixteen-year-old daughter, Natoya, to understand my position and to respect me as her father. I guess I couldn't have expected any other reaction from her. I had left her alone at one time and had not been the father she needed me to be. None of this stopped me from giving my all .

In one attempt to re-establish a bond with my daughter, I arranged to have her visit me in Springfield. Her visit put me on an emotional roller coaster. There were moments when I was happy, and there were moments when I was sad. I felt a flood of happiness when Natoya let me cook her pancakes for breakfast. My joy continued when I took her to a late-night Christmas light display called Bright Nights.

Sadness came during the times when Natoya was angry and unruly toward me. She constantly told me that she did not have to listen to me and that I was not her father. It really hit home when she claimed that the only reason she was visiting was because her mother had made her. Her words and disposition toward me were so fierce that I began to doubt my paternity. I had been in this position before with Juanita. My daughter's words were a shocking realization that I needed a paternity test. For now, I just kept hoping that she and my son were in fact my children. Natoya's visit helped me realize two things: the first was that there was still hope to rebuild our relationship, and the second was that it was going to be very, very difficult to do.

Natoya's allusion that I was not her father had traumatized me so much that I did not dare arrange a visit with my seventeen-year-old son, Haven Jr. Hearing this from him as well would have broken me. Instead of asking him to visit, I traveled and visited him in New Haven. Our conversations always left me feeling like an inadequate father. Like his sister, he, too, was angry with me. On several occasions he would say the phrase "my biological didn't bother." This was slang from a rap song that simply meant that one's father did not bother to take care of his child. It was a lot to take, but I could not dispute his charges against me. Every time I heard him make this statement, all I could think of was what I would have done if I had been there. I would have tried to impress upon him the importance of furthering his education, and I would have walked with him through life, just as I had done when he had taken his first steps as a baby.

As he vented his anger, I thought about the time when I was incarcerated and received a picture that he was in. I remember looking at my son in this picture and struggling with the thought that I might never see him again. At that moment, I wished that my mother had not restrained Finch on the night of April 19 and that his knife had found its mark. My death from this attack would not have been as painful as having to look at my son and think that I would never see him again. Despite our contention, I kept trying to stay in touch and called him every chance I could. Over time, our conversations started to became a bit more bearable.

My attempts to rebuild my relationship with my children were cut short when Sherry moved the family to Georgia. This made things more difficult for me to stay in touch with them. I lost contact with them for a short period but was able to reestablish contact through their grand-mother who gave them my phone number. When I received my first call, I was thrilled that they had taken the opportunity to reach out. We were communicating! This was enough for me for now.

I still was very troubled and needed to silence my daughter's words that kept playing over in my head: "You're not my dad!" It was time to put closure on the issue of paternity. Once I had enough money, I arranged a trip to Georgia so that I could have a paternity test done. While I was there, my relationship with both my son and daughter remained strained. I did everything I could to make them understand why I need-ed to have this test done. Sometime later I received the paternity test results, and I was ecstatic to find out that I was indeed Haven Jr. and Natoya's father. Now that I was able to put my paternity doubts to rest, I needed to recover my title as their dad.

In a roundabout way, I learned that my son, Haven Jr., had become a father. I was happy and proud when I heard the news. I was now a grandfather. Soon after my son's child was born, I heard that my daugh-ter, Natoya, had become a mom. Again I was filled with cheer and had my own personal celebration. I wish I could have been there when both of the children were born, but my children and I were still working on our own relationship and needed stability before I could get involved with the grandchildren. Despite our challenges, I was able to keep a dialogue with both of them, up to the point where my daughter asked me to wire her some money via Western Union. I was unable to send her the money because she was unable to provide Western Union with a telephone number. This was something they required. I think my daughter became angry with me for not being able to send her the money. After this, she stopped talking to me and ceased communication altogether. I knew she was still working out her subconscious resentment toward me, so her choice to cut ties did not surprise me. I was prepared to be patient, and I was confident that we would get by this speed bump. When the time is right, I will reach out to her in hopes to make amends. I need to be a part of my daughter's life and will never give up on reclaiming our father-daughter relationship. Our bridge is in bad shape, but it is still standing.

My relationship with my son, on the other hand, had progressed much better. During the next ten years he had three more children. As the children came, our relationship slowly improved. It still is anything but great. However, we are to the point where we speak on holidays, and he sends me pictures of my grandkids. I know we still have a long way to go before I can say that we truly have the relationship I so desire, but I have learned to be a patient man.

The Fifth Bridge

This was the bridge I had to preserve. To do this I would have to travel to the Ohio State Correctional Facility to meet with my brother Ervin. Our bridge was formed through the bonds of a tragic childhood that had been shared by two brothers.

My brother Ervin cried a great deal as a little boy. It would be my turn to cry when I visited him while he was incarcerated in an Ohio state correctional facility. I remembered looking at him as he sat in the glass enclosure that separated us and thinking how much he resembled his father. I was happy to see him, and the conversation was cheerful and pleasant for most of the visit then it turned dark. We began to talk about when he was molested by Maurice's Uncle Chick. I found myself crying as he described his moment of horror. He told me that he was awakened out of a sound sleep to find himself being violated while a hand tightly gripped his throat. As he told me about the dreadful experience, the only thing I could do was picture Maurice's Uncle Chick's face, and I wished that he had felt each and every one of those fifty-plus stab wounds that he had received when he was savagely murdered.

The pain I felt as he told his story made me think about when Butchy taunted and humiliated him when he was a little boy. We were living in Springfield at the time, and my mother and Butchy had taken me, Ervin, and Maurice to get haircuts. We were able to afford haircuts because we had gone to the barber school located on Main Street. This place was the learning ground for up-and-coming barbers, so haircuts were cheap. At the time, you could get a haircut for one dollar.

For me, Ervin, and Maurice, all things were not equal when it came to getting a haircut. Maurice and I were happy to get our heads shaved clean, and Ervin was not. Maurice and I both had coarse and nappy hair; Ervin's hair was of a fine texture, like his father's. Getting my hair cut short was a blessing in disguise and relieved me of the burden and pain of having to comb it. Ervin, on the other hand, had maintained his genetically fine-textured hair with a sense of pride and dignity. He had it styled into an afro that was so nice-looking that I as an older brother even admired it. I guess none of this mattered to Butchy and my mom as they told Ervin's barber to "cut it all off."

We all soon found out that Ervin had more to be upset with besides getting his nicely groomed hair cut off. Ervin's parietal bones on both sides of his head were more pronounced than normal. Without being hidden by his afro, the unusual structure of his head made him look like some kind of an alien. Once Butchy noticed this, he took this opportunity to be the ignorant bastard that he was and began laughing hysterically at Ervin. I remember the look of pain in Ervin's eyes as the tears ran down his face. That day a part of his soul and a sense of who he was died.

I snapped out of my daydream and was back in the visiting room with Ervin. His story and my thoughts made me realize that he and I were bound by a tragic childhood, and we needed each other—if only to remind each other that we had survived.

It was at this point when my life started to radically change. Communicating and interacting with my brother Maurice helped me to begin the process of shedding the trauma of my past. I made a conscious decision to push away everyone who was holding me back: my mother, Sherry, and the man in the mirror. These were the bridges that I had burned. I had made a conscious decision to pull everyone who I needed in my life closer: my children and my brother Ervin. These were the bridges that I had preserved. My metamorphosis had started. I could feel inmate #41046, the little boy who had been abused, and the confused, misguided teenager all dying, and Haven Triplett the man being reborn.

Uprooted—A New Tree is Planted

"If I had to live my life again, I'd make the same mistakes, only sooner."
—Tallullah Bankhead

The year is 2013. The month is April. I am fortunate that I can look back and embrace the positive change and the positive direction that my life has taken. I have a new sense of who I am and what I can accomplish. Opportunities abound.

It has been twenty-nine years since the tragic day Finch was killed. It has been nineteen years since my release from prison. I have experienced a great deal of adversity in my life to only be fifty years old.

When I was fifteen, I was already drowning in despair, and no one was there to throw me a life buoy. I never realized that I was already on the wrong side of the line that would determine my future. I was born and raised on the side that is defined by failure and prison. It has taken me thirty years to get back to the other side, which is defined by success and freedom.

In a few weeks I will be graduating from Lesley University in a ceremony that will be held at the Bank of America pavilion in Boston Massachusetts. My name will be listed among several other students who will be graduating. I will be receiving a master's degree in education with a focus in middle school math. This is my second master's degree. I earned my first master's degree from American International College in accounting and taxation in 2001. It has taken me nineteen long years to complete my education.

My wife of four years uses the word "perseverance" to describe the drive within me that has helped me to rise above the adversity within my life. She said it is what helped me to achieve my educational goals.

> Perseverance: a noun: steady persistence in a course of action, a purpose, a state, etc., especially in spite of difficulties, obstacles, or discouragement.

I am happy that I was able to complete my goals as the odds were stacked against me. But my true happiness lies in the fact that I had the opportunity to accomplish my goals at all. These accomplishments have helped to transform my life. I am now ready to make a positive impact on society. I am ready to educate our future leaders of tomorrow.

"In a completely rational society, the best of us would be teachers and the rest of us would have to settle for something else."

—Lee Iacocca

Going through the process of becoming a teacher was not only a very proud moment for me and my wife, but it has also been an uplifting experience. It has helped me to transcend my past and validate my own abilities. It is no surprise that I became an educator because I was already practicing as one. When I was in school a large part of my time was spent teaching and mentoring the youth in my community at different libraries in the city of Springfield. I taught youth activities that included card games like Yugioh, Magic, Kai-Judo, and Poke'mon, and I provided homework help and tutored math. I also held workshops to teach kids how to play dominoes and chess.

Teaching kids how to play chess helped me to refine a board game named Pschent that I had developed while I was in prison. I created the game with other inmates by combining strategies of several games with tic-tac-toe.

For my volunteer work with the children in the community, I received an award from the Key Players Project when I was nominated by a library supervisor. This award is given to men of color in Springfield for making significant contributions to children. Todd Crossett, a professor from the University of Massachusetts who taught in the Isenberg School of Management, personally brought the award to my apartment. My contribution was further celebrated during an official ceremony at Montenia's restaurant in Springfield, where I was named a Key Players Project ambassador. I did not think much of this award when I first received it, but today I view it as a significant accomplishment. The depth of my accomplishment is just now starting to sink in. I had temporarily forgotten that my life and focus was humanity. I had followed my dream. I had given the youth in my community guidance. I had given them something that was never given to me. I formed a connection and bond with the kids in my community. This is something that is not easy to do. I dedicated time and made a commitment to teach the children the game of chess. These are a few things that I had mistakenly overlooked. Being able to connect with children at this most basic level was a clear indication of the type of person that I had become. I was an entirely different person.

My work with the youth in Springfield continued beyond receiving the award. My continued teaching and mentorship was acknowledged when I received a Mayor's Proclamation and Governor's Citation. Both awards that I received were born through the Key Players Project and their joint effort with the mayor of Springfield and governor of Massachusetts. The Mayor's Proclamation is an award that was given to me during a ceremony in 2007 to acknowledge my continued standing as a Key Players Project ambassador. The Governor's Citation is an award that was given by the governor of Massachusetts to acknowledge individuals who have provided positive contributions through mentoring, teaching, and tutoring youth in specific cities in Massachusetts.

I received both awards in Boston, Massachusetts, at the TD Garden in a halftime ceremony during one of the 2007 – 2008 Boston Celtics championship season games. I received free tickets to the game, heard my name announced over the Garden loudspeaker in front of eighteen thousand fans, and received a legendary green and white Celtics basketball that was autographed by the "Big Three": Kevin Garnett, Ray Allen, and Paul Pierce. Receiving these two awards was an eye-opening, humbling experience. I started to realize that I really had made a positive difference in society.

Although I now realize that teaching children was extremely beneficial, it does not come close to my most prestigious accomplishment while volunteering at the library. Uncontested, my most prestigious accomplishment while volunteering at the library was convincing an unsuspecting librarian named Delphine to go on a date with me. Years later, I would ask this lovely lady's hand in marriage.

During our courting period, I had arranged the delivery of a bouquet of flowers to the Pine Point Library where she was working. Once she received the flowers the phone at the library began to ring constantly. The calls were from the other librarians who were working at different branches in the city. It was amazing how fast the word traveled from library to library. Today, we still laugh about the commotion the flower delivery caused.

Dating Delphine was fun and exciting. On one of our dates, we played pool, watched movies, and had dinner together. On another date, we met during Delphine's lunch break and had pizza for lunch. We enjoyed each other's company so much that we had completely forgot about the time. When we finally looked at a clock, we had extended her one-hour lunch break to two hours. On another date, I made Delphine a spinach and mushroom quiche. She enjoyed it so much that I think she smiled for a week.

We talked on the telephone every day for hours when her work day was done. We both had so much to say and so many questions to ask. She wanted to know everything about me, and I wanted to know how well she kissed. Talking with Delphine has always been easy. When I shared my past with her, it was no different. She accepted me unconditionally. During our conversations, I learned that Delphine had three sons from her previous relationships. The two oldest had children, so, like me, she, too, was a proud grandparent.

Delphine and I have been together for over fourteen years, but surprisingly, of these fourteen years, we made the decision to celebrate the last four as husband and wife. Communication is key to our marriage. We have never forgotten the importance of talking to each other, sharing our feelings about everything, and listening to each other. My wife wishes that we would have found each other sooner; I feel the same way. Thinking about how we met each other and how long we have been together has helped me to realize just how lucky we both are.

Today, my relationships with my son, Haven Jr., and my daughter, Natoya, are works in progress. I truly wish that they will read my book so that they will understand both stories of my life—the side that has all but been forgotten and the side that I am still writing. I know through choppy communication channels that I am the proud grandfather of five children. Antonio, Heaven, Havelyn, and Harmony are my son's four children, and Timyrah is my daughter's child. I have only been blessed to see my son's two oldest children, Antonio and Heaven. My son has helped me to see how much all of his children have grown and changed by sending me pictures. For that I am thankful. Now that I have finished school and have begun the process of looking for work as a teacher, I realize that it is time to plan a visit in the near future. I have not given up on my estranged daughter and hope that in visiting my son, I will be able to see her and my granddaughter, Timyrah, as well.

My relationship with my brother Ervin is one of tolerance and patience. I am tolerant of his misdirected anger and frustration. I am equally patient in defining my limits and explaining my reasons for either doing or not doing something that he has asked of me. I am no longer bound by family ties. I no longer feel guilty that I was unable to protect him from harm that was caused to him by the neglect of our parents and the abuse from our relatives.

When I first started writing this book, it was my way of trying to understand my own life and to reconcile the pain and anger of my past. This book has become *something more*; it has become a diary from which I can reflect on my turbulent past, and it has given me permission to condemn my default personality traits and become my own man.

This book has become *something greater*; it has helped me to appreciate how rising above a dysfunctional family's influences gave my brother Maurice the direction and insight to become a beacon of hope to At-risk youth.

This book has become a *sobering reminder*; it has helped me to put into perspective how a brother's life sentence and the death of a sister can all be attributed to the cruel and unforgiving dynamics of a broken home.

This book has become a *promise of hope;* there is still time to build healthy relationships with my children and grandchildren.

This book has become *something special;* writing it has helped me understand that forgiving myself for my past mistakes will allow me to take responsibility for my own quality of life and my own family values.

Writing this book has also helped me to appreciate and understand something very important about love, life, and respect. Love, life, and respect are things that not only must be earned, but they must also be maintained by something more than a title, name, or predetermined relationship.

My past mistakes have prevented me from doing so many things. My wish and dreams are simple. I wish to grow old with my wife, who is also my soul mate. I wish to one day see a contemporary Jazz concert. I wish to one day walk on the white sand beaches of Tahiti while holding hands with my wife. I wish that my wife and I will one day own our own home. I wish to one day take an air-brushing class. I wish to make a book from the collection of chess games that I have recorded. I wish to see each of my grandchildren graduate from college and go on to live positive and productive lives.

My last wish is that my story will be an example of hope and perseverance for everyone who reads it.

Author contact information

M. Triplett and H. Triplett know that they are not the only people that have, or that will, face the circumstances of a broken home and a life of poverty and neglect; so next to writing Perforated Fiber for their own self-therapy, they wrote it to help others who have similar circumstances.

Perforated Fiber is currently being used in the Behavioral Science / Psychology field of study as supplementary curriculum at Springfield Community College. The professor has integrated the book into his psychology course and requires his students to read the book and write a Human Development paper. This assignment is followed by having the student participate in a Self-Actualization discussion with the author. To view the professor's syllabus and/or work with the authors to set up a supplementary curriculum program, visit: www.perforatedfiber. com

Perforated Fiber is also required reading for a program named Survival Metaphysics which is a workshop that M. Triplett and H. Triplett sponsor for city and community agencies that work with At-Risk teens. To learn more about the program, visit: www.perforatedfiber.com

We hope you enjoyed our story and appeal to you to add your honest book review to Amazon.com. Hopefully it will be a favorable review that will help us sell more books which in turn will give us the financial means to keep helping those that are less fortunate.

Final Thoughts

"A journey of a thousand miles begins with a single step."

— *Lao Tzu*

As two brothers we started our journey from despair to happiness in ignorance. We were surrounded by individuals with misguided beliefs about life, happiness, education, family and health. We understood at an early age that all these things were intertwined, but failed to realize that like a chain a family is only as strong as its weakest link.

As two brothers, our journey from despair to happiness has helped us to understand that the fundamental building blocks of success are those interactions with others that help us persevere through life's challenges, hardships, misfortunes, and tragedies, and not the other way around; We are stronger because of who we interact with and not because of what we endure. We both still believe this.

Even though our journey through life has taken us both down different paths, challenged our beliefs, and exposed us both to some of the harsh realities of life, we both believe that no matter how you chose to measure success, success is not achieved alone or in a vacuum.

For both of us, the meeting of two unselfish hearts has given us an unconditional love that we can share with our wives. We have been successful in love.

For both of us, an open mind to furthering our education has given us the opportunity to compete for a better quality of life. We have been successful in obtaining an education that promotes understanding.

For both of us, communication between two brothers has given us the opportunity to heal from our hurtful past and support each other's aspirations. We have both stumbled and managed to regain our balance. Our journey of life continues upon a path that we now shape by our own thoughts and actions. We have both been successful in reclaiming the family that remains.

-H. Triplett / M. Triplett

Works Cited

Nadolski, Richard. "Police seek gunman in slaying." *Springfield Union* 20 Apr 1984.

Lightstone, Helayne. "Murder suspect panicked." *Springfield Union* 10 Jan 1985.

Lightstone, Helayne. "Murderer sentenced to life in prison." *Springfield Union* 11 Jan 1985.

Simison, Cynthia. "Man admits reduced charge of manslaughter." *Springfield Union* 14 Jul 1987.

Flynn, Jack. "Slaying suspect a symbol of system's failure." *Sunday Republican* 13 Sep 1992.

Melley, Brian. "Triplett pleads guilty to first degree murder." *Springfield Union* 5 Feb 1993.

Made in the USA
Charleston, SC
25 April 2015